中國成語選粹續篇

編 者　司徒談

英譯者　湯博文

插 圖　丁 聰

海峰出版社

中国水质要科学書

BEST CHINESE IDIOMS

(Volume 2)

Compiled by

SituTan

Tr. into English by

Tang Bowen

Illustrated by

Ding Cong

HAI FENG PUBLISHING CO.

© **Hai Feng Publishing Co., Ltd.**
ISBN 962-238-093-X

Published by
Hai Feng Publishing Company Limited
Rm. 1503 Wing On House,
71 Des Voeux Rd., Central
Hong Kong

Printed by
Friendly Printing Company Limited
Flat B1, 3/F., Luen Ming Hing Ind. Bldg.,
36 Muk Cheong St., Tokwawan, Kowloon
Hong Kong

Second Edition May 1989

出版：
海峰出版社有限公司
香港中環德輔道中71號
永安集團大廈1503室

印刷：
友利印刷有限公司
九龍土瓜灣木廠街36號
聯明興工業大廈4樓B1座

一九八九年五月第二版

HF-71-P

前　言

　　漢語有豐富的詞滙和各種形式的固定詞組。成語就是一種經常使用的固定詞組，在漢語詞滙中佔有重要的地位。

　　漢語成語形式簡潔、含義深刻。它們常被用來說明一件事實、一個道理或比喻一種形象，從而構成漢語的獨特風格。

　　漢語成語是在漢語的長期發展過程中形成的。大多數成語由四個字組成，在使用的時候實際上相當於一個詞。在談話、演講或寫作時，如運用得當，將會增強語言的感染力，產生其他方法所不能比擬的表達效果。

　　正確地運用成語，首要之點在於瞭解它的意義。有些成語的意義，從字面上不難瞭解；有些成語則不能按字面望文生義，而必須知道它的來源，才能準確掌握和運用。

　　漢語成語，數量龐大，除來自民間口語者外，相當大的部分來自古代典籍。這些來自古代典籍的成語，有的出自寓言故事，有的出自歷史事件或神話傳說，通常也叫典故。本書所選的大都屬於這一類。

　　中國的古代典籍記載了大量絢麗多彩的寓言故事和神話。這在先秦諸子的著作中尤為顯著，其中許多寓言故事和神話都有成語的概括形式，如“害羣之馬”（參見第 182 頁）、“鵬程萬里”（參見第 292 頁）。歷史上的事件，也常常被概括為一個成語，如“三顧茅廬”（參見第 26 頁）、“投筆從戎”（參見第 99 頁）。這些來自寓言、神話和歷史事件的成語，有不少蘊含着深刻的哲理和寶貴的生活經驗，直到今天還有其現實意義。此外，還有一些成語，來源於古代作品中的名句，因而成了格言。

　　本書為一九八四年出版的《中國成語選粹》的續集，共收錄常用的和有故事性的成語二百零三條。在介紹成語故事時，為使讀者容易瞭解起見，有的地方作了一些刪節和修飾，增加了一點背景材料。許多中國成語並列有意義相近的英語成語。此外，還在成語條目的下面附加漢語拼音，不懂漢語的讀者，可以借助於"漢語拼音發音指南"（見書後），直接讀出漢語成語。

書前成語"目次"按首字筆劃順序排列。書末附有按漢語拼音字母順序排列的"條目索引"。

Foreword

The Chinese language is rich in vocabulary, phrases and idioms. As a form of set phrases, Chinese idioms are in wide use and occupy an important place in the language as a whole. Concise yet meaningful, they illustrate certain specific facts, carry certain moral teachings or suggest certain particular images, thus constituting a unique characteristic of the Chinese language.

Chinese idioms, which emerged and developed in the long years of Chinese history, mostly consist of four characters which go together and virtually function as a set term. When used properly and cleverly in everyday conversation, speeches or writings, they add to the appeal of the language and make it more to the point and achieve what cannot be achieved by other ways of expressing the same thought.

A correct understanding of their meaning is the key to the correct use of Chinese idioms. While some can be taken literally, others cannot be interpreted or used correctly without first delving into their real meaning and origin.

Being numerous and having backgrounds that can be traced back to ancient times, Chinese idioms are partly derived from oral language and partly — perhaps in the case of a greater percentage of them — from ancient historical records, literature and other writings. The latter category, with which this book chiefly deals, embraces those coming from parables or fables, historical stories or anecdotes, and fairy tales or legends.

Chinese historical records of the remote past abound in wise fables, didactic parables and thought-provoking tales. A case in point is the works of the philosophers of the various schools prior to the Qin Dynasty (221-207 B.C.). Many of the fables and tales contained in them are summarized in a few words, such as "The Harmful Horse in the Herd" (see p. 182 of this book) and "A Roc Can Fly Ten Thousand Miles" (see p. 293). Some idioms deal with historical events or anecdotes, such as "Calling Thrice at the Thatched Cottage" (see p. 26) and "Throwing Down the Pen and Joining the Army" (see p. 99). Quite a number of Chinese idioms belonging to the above categories carry a philsosophical note and draw on practical experiences, which make them significant even for contemporary life. There are also some idioms which have been taken from well-known ancient works and have thus become maxims.

The present book, a continuation of *Best Chinese Idioms* published in 1984, contains 203 Chinese idioms which are in common use and behind each of which there is a story or an anecdote. Generally speaking, the stories and anecdotes are based on the original versions in classical Chinese but, where necessary, abridgement and modifications are made and brief descriptions of their backgrounds given. Many of the Chinese idioms are accompanied by English equivalents. Chinese phonetic spelling (*pinyin*) is given to each title, and for readers who are not familiar with this system the appendix "Guide to Chinese Phonetic Alphabet" at the end of the book may prove useful.

The table of contents in this book has been arranged according to the number of strokes of the first Chinese character in each title. There is an index at the end of the book compiled alphabetically, using the *pinyin* system.

目　次
Contents

一字千金

yī zì qiān jīn

一字值一千金；形容詩或文章寫得好，用字精妙恰當。

戰國末年，秦國相國呂不韋召集門客編寫成一部《呂氏春秋》。這部書有二十六卷，一百六十篇文章，二十餘萬言。呂不韋非常得意，把它貼在咸陽城門上，並且宣佈："有誰能在本書上增加一個字或者減少一個字，就賞他一千金。"可是，呂不韋官做得這麼大，誰敢品評他的文章呢？

出自《史記》*

* 《史記》中國第一部紀傳體歷史書籍，作者司馬遷（公元前145年—？），西漢人。全書共五十萬字，記述了從黃帝到西漢武帝三千年間的歷史。

A Word Is Worth a Thousand Pieces of Gold

A Literary Gem

Said of a well-composed poem or essay with ingenious use of words.

IN the closing years of the Warring States Period, Lü Buwei, the Prime Minister of the state of Qin, assembled a group of his followers and compiled the *Lü's Annals,* a book of twenty-six chapters, comprising 160 essays and 200,000 words. Lü was very pleased with it. He had it pasted on the city gate of Xianyang and announced that if anyone could add a word to the book or delete one from it, he would be awarded a thousand pieces of gold. Of course, nobody was audicious enough to critize the writings of so powerful an official as Lü Buwei.

*Written by Sima Qian (145-? B.C.) of the Western Han Dynasty, this is China's first history book written in the form of annals and biographies. It records the events of three thousand years from the Yellow Emperor to Emperor Wu of the Western Han Dynasty in 500,000 words.

一字之師

yī zì zhī shī

改正一個字的老師；比喻用詞嚴謹，詩文稍加改動即可達到完美程度。

　　唐代僧人齊己，喜歡寫詩。有一次，他作了一首名為《早梅》的詩，其中兩句是："前村深雪裏，昨夜數枝開。"有個叫鄭谷的人見到後，經過反覆推敲，認為既然梅花數枝已開，就不能算早梅了。於是將這兩句詩改為："前村深雪裏，昨夜一枝開。"齊己對鄭谷修改的詩句非常佩服。後來，人們稱鄭谷為"一字之師"。

出自《唐詩紀事》*

＊《唐詩紀事》本書採錄唐代詩人的若干詩篇及其有關的本事和品評。南宋計有功（約公元1126年前後在世）撰。

A Teacher of One Word

A metaphor for a carefully worded writing, which can be rendered perfect by only a slight alteration.

QI Ji, a monk of the Tang Dynasty, was fond of composing

poems. Once he wrote a poem entitled *Early Plum Blossoms*. The first two lines read: "In the deep snow before the village, Twigs of plum blossomed last night." When a man named Zheng Gu read it, he gave it a close scrutiny. If there were several twigs, they were surely not early plum blossoms, he thought. He suggested changing a word. The two lines became: "In the deep snow before the village. A twig bloomed last night." Zheng Gu's revision was very much admired by the author. Zheng thus became known as "a teacher of one word".

Notes on Tang Poetry*

*A collection of Tang poems together with notes about their origin and comments. It was compiled by Ji Yougong of the Southern Song Dynasty around the year 1126.

一衣帶水

yī yī dài shuǐ

一條像衣服帶子似的江水；比喻江流狹窄，彼此間距離甚近。

南朝末年，在長江以北，隋文帝楊堅正在進行統一全國的戰爭，他想消滅長江以南的陳國，但浩浩蕩蕩的江水攔住了文帝的兵馬。文帝站在江邊望着霧氣迷茫的江南，對左僕射高熲說："陳後主業已陷陳國百姓於水深火熱之中，我作爲百姓的父母官，難道因爲有一條像衣服帶子似的江水阻隔，就不去解救他們嗎？"於是，文帝下令造船渡江，終於滅掉陳國，統一了全國。

出自《南史》*

*《南史》紀傳體歷史著作，唐李延壽撰。本書記述了南朝宋、齊、梁、陳四代歷史。

A Narrow Strip of Water

Said of close neighbours.

AT the end of the Southern Dynasties, Yang Jian, Emperor Wen of the Sui Dynasty, on the northern side of the Yangtze River, launched a war to unify the whole country. He wanted to destroy the state of Chen on the southern side but his army was stopped by the torrential river. Standing by the river and looking towards the south that was enveloped in mists, he said to his minister Gao Ying. "The emperor of Chen has plunged the people of Chen into the depth of sufferings. As an official of the people, am I to be stopped by a narrow strip of water and not come to their rescue?" He ordered boats to be built and eventually subjugated the state of Chen, unifying the whole country under his leadership.

History of the Southern Dynasties*

*Written by Li Yanshou of the Tang Dynasty, the book records the histories of the four Southern Dynasties of Song, Qi, Liang and Chen.

一身是膽

yī shēn shì dǎn

整個身體到處都是膽；形容極其勇敢，無所畏懼。

三國時，魏國的曹操與蜀國的劉備爭奪漢中。曹操派大將張郃等搬運大批糧草屯於漢水北山脚下。劉備的老將黃忠和趙雲奉命前往燒劫糧草，不幸黃忠被曹兵所困，無法脫身。趙雲前去接應，救出了黃忠。曹操見趙雲英勇無比，便親率大軍前往助戰。這時，趙雲退回到劉備部將張翼所轄的沔陽城。張翼見曹軍來勢兇猛，閉門據守。趙雲不允，反將城門大開，偃旗息鼓。曹軍見此情景，唯恐

中計，便轉身就走。趙雲乘勢擂鼓追擊，大敗曹軍。次日，劉備來
到趙雲營寨視察，感慨地說："子龍（趙雲，字子龍）眞是一身是膽
啊！"

出自《三國志》＊

＊《三國志》紀傳體史書，分魏、蜀、吳三志，西晉陳壽（公元233－297
年）作。

Full of Courage

Describing a fearless man.

DURING the period of the Three Kingdoms, Cao Cao of the kingdom of Wei and Liu Bei of the kingdom of Shu fought with each other for the control of the city of Hanzhong. Cao Cao sent his general Zhang He to stockpile a large quantity of grain and fodder at the foot of the North Mountain by the Hanshui River. The aged general Huang Zhong was dispatched by Liu Bei to seize and burn Cao Cao's grain and fodder. Unfortunately, Huang Zhong was encircled by Cao Cao's men and could not break the cordon. Zhao Yun came to his rescue and saved him. Seeing that Zhao Yun was unrivaled in his courage, Cao Cao led a great army himself to reinforce his men. Zhao Yun had by then withdrawn to the town of Mianyang garrisoned by Liu Bei's general Zhang Yi. When Zhang Yi saw that the Cao army was bearing down on them ferociously, he wanted to close the gates in order to defend the town. Zhao Yun would not hear of it. He had the city gates opened wide, furled the flags and stopped the drums. The Cao army thought this must be a ruse and started to pull back. Taking advantage of the situation, Zhao Yun thumped the drums and gave chase. The Cao army was utterly defeated. The following day, when Liu Bei came to Zhao Yun's camp, he said with feeling, "Zilong (Zhao Yun's familiar name), you're really full of courage!"

*Written by Chen Shou (A.D. 233-297) of the Western Jin Dynasty, it is divided into three parts covering the histories of the kingdoms of Wei, Shu and Wu.

一狐之腋

yī hú zhī yè

一隻狐狸腋下的皮毛；比喻珍貴的物品。

春秋末期，晉國有個貴族名叫趙鞅，他處事為人善於謀略。公元前511年至前475年，晉國國君晉定公大權旁落在趙鞅、范氏和中行氏手中。為了爭權奪利，他們發生了內訌。在內訌中，趙鞅打敗了范氏和中行氏，擴大了自己的封地，為以後建立趙國奠定了基礎。

趙鞅手下有一個叫周舍的大臣，他為人耿直，經常向趙鞅提出建議，因而很得趙鞅的賞識。後來，周舍死了，趙鞅非常難過，每次上朝都表現出很不高興的樣子。大夫們見此情形，都來問是不是自己辦了什麼錯事得罪了他。趙鞅說："你們沒有得罪我。但是，我聽說，一千隻羊的皮也不如一隻狐狸腋下的皮值錢，現在朝廷之上，只是聽到你們唯唯諾諾的順從，聽不到周舍據理直諫的聲音了，所以我才悶悶不樂。"

出自《史記》

The Underfur of a Fox

A metaphor for something very precious.

ZHAO Yang, a noble of the state of Jin at the end of the Spring and Autumn Period, was known for his astuteness. Between 511 and 475 B.C., the powers of Duke Ding of Jin, the sovereign of the state of Jin, fell into the hands of Zhao Yang, Fan and Zhonghang. In the scramble for power and profit, internal strife broke out among them. Zhao Yang defeated Fan and Zhonghang in the struggle and expanded his fiefdom, thus laying the foundations for the later establishment of the state of Zhao.

One of Zhao Yang's ministers was named Zhou She. As an honest and straightforward man, he often gave Zhao Yang advice, which was much appreciated by the latter. Later, when Zhou She died, Zhao Yang was very sad. He looked unhappy at court. The other ministers wondered if they had done anything to displease him. "You haven't done anything to offend me," said Zhao. "But I've heard that the skins of a thousand sheep are not worth as much as the underfur of a single fox. All I hear now at court are your submissive voices. I can never hear Zhou She's reasonable arguments and advice again. That's why I'm unhappy."

Records of the Historian

一敗塗地

yī bài tú dì

一旦失敗，就要肝腦塗在地上；形容失敗到不可收拾的地步。

秦末，各地諸侯起兵抗秦朝暴政，農民領袖陳勝在大澤鄉也發動了起義。這時，沛縣縣令見局勢不穩，心裏恐慌。縣吏蕭何、曹參建議把逃亡在外的劉邦召回來。縣令派人去召請劉邦，可是當劉邦的人馬來到城下時，縣令又怕劉邦回來罷自己的官。因此，他不但下令關閉城門，還打算殺掉蕭河、曹參。蕭何、曹參逃出城外，得到了劉邦的保護。劉邦寫了一封信射進城裏，號召百姓響應起義。城裏百姓果然齊心響應，殺死了縣令，打開城門迎接劉邦進城，並請他做縣令。劉邦推辭說："現在天下大亂，如果當縣令的人推舉不當，一旦失敗，就要肝腦塗在地上。請你們另外推舉更合適的人吧。"雖然劉邦多次謙讓，最後還是擔任了縣令，被尊爲"沛公"。

出自《史記》

A Ruinous Defeat

Meaning once defeated, one's liver and brains will be scattered to the ground.

TOWARDS the end of the Qin Dynasty, the feudal princes in many places revolted against the tyranical Qin court and the peasant leader Chen She staged an uprising at Great Marsh Township. The magistrate of Pei county was greatly alarmed by the perilous political situation. At the suggestion of the county officials Xiao He and Cao Shen, the magistrate sent someone to fetch Liu Bang who had been exiled. But when Liu Bang and his men were outside the city, the magistrate feared that once Liu Bang was in the city, he might remove the magistrate from his post. The magistrate closed the city gates and planned to have Xiao He and Cao Shen killed. Xiao and Cao managed to escape from the city and received Liu Bang's protection.

Liu Bang wrote a letter calling on the people to rise against the magistrate, tied the letter to an arrow and shot it into the city. The people in the city responded to the call with one heart, killed the magistrate and opened the gate to welcome

Liu Bang into the city. They wanted him to be the magistrate, but Liu Bang refused, saying, "The whole country is now in a great turmoil. If you don't choose the right person to be the magistrate, you may suffer defeat with your livers and brains scattered to the ground. I wish you could choose a more suitable person." After declining several times, Liu Bang eventually assumed the post of magistrate and became known respectfully as Lord Pei.

Records of the Historian

一朝一夕

yī zhāo yī xī

一個早晨，一個晚上；形容時間很短。

戰國時，有個叫季梁的人生了病。季梁的兒子見父親病得厲害，便請來了三位醫生。

第一位矯醫生診斷了季梁的病後說："你冷暖沒有節制，虛實失調，中氣不足。病源是飢飽失度，縱慾傷身，可以慢慢治好。"季梁聽後對兒子說："這是個一般的醫生。"

第二位俞醫生對季梁的病經過診斷，他說："你的病不是一個早晨一個晚上形成的，病由來已久，恐怕治不好了。"季梁聽後對兒子說："這是位良醫。"

第三位盧醫生對季梁的病進行了診斷，說："藥物對你已經沒有什麼作用了。"季梁聽後讚許地說："你真是一位神醫啊！"於是，送給盧醫生許多禮物，讓他回去了。

原來，季梁得的是精神方面的病症，不久就好了。

出自《列子》*

In a Morning or Evening

Overnight

Describing a very short period of time.

AT the time of the Warring States, a man named Ji Liang fell
ill. Seeing his father's condition was critical, his son sent for
three doctors.

The first one, Dr. Jiao, after examining Ji Liang, said,
"You've failed to deal with cold and heat properly. Your
functional metabolism is in disorder and your functional
power is weak. The cause of your illness is over-hunger and
over-eating and indulgence in carnal desires. It can be cured
only slowly." Ji Liang told his son afterwards, "He is only a
mediocre doctor."

The second one, Dr. Yu, looked over Ji Liang and said,
"Your illness did not come in a morning or evening. It's been
there for a long time. I'm afraid that it can't be cured." Ji
Liang then said to his son. "He's a good doctor."

The third one, Dr. Lu, also examined Ji Liang's condition.
He said, "You're beyond the cure of medicine." Upon
hearing his words, Ji Liang praised him, saying, "You're
really a wonderful doctor!" He gave Dr. Lu many presents
before sending him back.

Ji Liang was actually suffering from nervous disorder. He
soon recovered.

The Book of Lie Zi*

*Attributed to Lie Yukou (who lived around the time of 314 B.C.),
the book contains a great number of ancient fables.

10

一登龍門，身價十倍

yī dēng lóng mén，shēn jià shí bèi

一旦登上龍門，聲名身價就提高了十倍；指社會地位迅速提高。

黃河中游，有一個名叫"龍門"（即禹門口）的山口，兩岸峭壁對峙，形如闕門，傳說為大禹治水時開鑿。龍門出口處，河床高，水勢急，因此龍門以下的魚類游向黃河上游非常不易。於是就有一個"鯉魚跳龍門"的傳說：凡是能跳過龍門的魚，就可以變成龍。

"龍門"一詞，被古代人比喻為威望極高的名人家門。一般人走進名人家門，就被視為"登龍門"。唐玄宗時，韓朝宗名聲很大，李白想登門結識他，希望得到薦舉，曾寫過一封信給他，信中就有"一登龍門，則身價十倍"這樣的話。

出自《與韓荆州書》＊

＊《與韓荆州書》唐代著名詩人李白（公元701－762年）寫給荆州刺史韓朝宗的一封信。

Once the Dragon Gate Is Crossed, One's Status Rises Ten Times

Describing a meteoric rise in social status.

A gorge in the middle reaches of the Yellow River is called the Dragon Gate (or the Yu Gate). Here the river is flanked by two precipitous rocks facing each other across the river like a gigantic gate. It is said that the gate was hewed out by the legendary Yu the Great during his fight against flood waters. The river bed is high at the Dragon Gate and the current swift. It is very difficult for fish to swim upstream. Hence a legend arose that if a carp can jump over the Dragon Gate, it will become a dragon.

Dragon Gate was used in ancient times as a metaphor for the house of a highly prestigious family. Ordinary people who have entered such a house was described as having entered the Dragon Gate. Han Chaozong was a man of great fame at the time of Emperor Xuanzong in the Tang Dynasty. Li Bai wished to visit him and become acquainted with him so that he could recommend Li Bai for an official post. Li Bai wrote a letter to him in which Li said, "Once the Dragon Gate is crossed, my status will rise ten times."

"Letter to Han Jingzhou"*

*A letter written by the great poet Li Bai (701-762) of the Tang Dynasty to Han Chaozong, governor of Jingzhou.

一夜十往

yī yè shí wǎng

一晚上去了十次；形容體貼周到地服侍病人。

東漢時，有個叫第五倫的人，任會稽太守，為人正直，辦事廉明。

有一次，有人問第五倫：“像你這樣，是不是可以說毫無私心了呢？”他回答說：“不。有個朋友，求官於我，送來了一匹駿馬，我雖然沒有接受，至今也沒有介紹他做官，可是每逢推薦人的時候，却總是想起這個人來。還有，我的侄兒病的時候，我一夜起來十次去看他，看過回來，照樣呼呼入睡；我的兒子生病的時候，我也同樣一次又一次地去看他，但看過之後，心裏總是牽掛着，整夜不能入睡。這樣看來，能說我毫無私心嗎？”

＊《後漢書》記載東漢歷史的著作，南北朝范曄（公元398－445年）撰。

Ten Visits in One Night

Describing meticulous care extended to a patient.

Di Wulun, prefect of Kuaiji in the Eastern Han Dynasty, was an upright man and honest official.

Once someone asked Di Wulun, "Can we say that a man like you is absolutely selfless?" "No," answered Wu. "A friend of mine once tried to give me good horse and wanted me to appoint him to an official post. I didn't take his horse, nor did I recommend him to an official post. But whenever I had to recommend somebody, this man always came to my mind. Again, when my nephew was ill, I got up ten times a night to see him. When I came back from him, I could go to sleep immediately. When my son fell ill, I also got up to see him several times in one night. But when I came back, I was always worried about him that I could not go to sleep. Can you say that I'm selfless?"

History of the Later Han Dynasty ＊

*Recording the events of the Eastern Han Dynasty (25-220), this book was compiled by Fan Ye (398-445) of the Southern and Northern Dynasties.

一筆勾銷

yī bī gōu xiāo

比喻一下子全部都取消。

宋代著名政治家和文學家范仲淹曾做過參政。有一次，他取出官吏名册，從頭至尾仔細看了一遍，然後拿起筆來，毫不留情地把不稱職的各路（路為地方行政區劃名）監司從名册上勾去。副職富弼看了，對范仲淹說：「您只是一筆勾掉了事，怎知被免職的官吏的一家會因此而痛哭呢！」范仲淹回答說：「一家哭就一家吧，免得他害得一路百姓哭！」於是就把各路不稱職的監司罷免了。

出自《五朝名臣言行錄》

Writing Off with One Stroke of the Pen

Meaning to cancel everything.

FAN Zhongyan, the famous statesman and writer of the Song Dynasty, once served as a Vice Prime Minister. One day, while reading through a roll of officials, he took up his pen and mercilessly struck out with one stroke all the names of prefectural supervisors who were incompetent. Fu Bi, his assistant, said to him, "You can strike out their names with one stroke of the pen, but don't you know the whole family of a dismissed official will weep bitterly?" "Let a whole family cry if they want to," answered Fan Zhongyan, "so that the people of a whole prefecture will not cry." Thus, he dismissed all the incompetent supervisors.

Words and Deeds of Famous
Officials of the Five Dynasties

一意孤行

yī yì gū xíng

堅持按自己的主張去做；常指不考慮客觀條件和別人的意見而獨斷專行。

14

西漢時，有個名叫趙禹的人，是太尉周亞夫的部下。吳楚七國之亂平定後，周亞夫升爲丞相，趙禹任丞相史，後來升任御史中大夫。

當時的官吏，大都養有一批食客。趙禹爲人廉潔，爲吏以來，門下沒有食客，孤立行意。公卿大夫們請他辦私事，都被他一一謝絕。《史記》作者司馬遷說他是"孤立行一意"。

出自《史記》

Insisting on Having One's Own Way

Implying that one is acting wilfully without regard to objective conditions and other people's opinion.

ZHAO Yu of the Western Han Dynasty was a subordinate of Grand Chancellor Zhou Yafu. After the revolt of the seven states of Wu and Chu, Zhou Yafu was promoted to the post of Prime Minister and Zhao Yu became Assistant to the Prime Minister and later the Imperial Censor.

All the high officials in those days kept a group of hangers-on in their houses. Zhao Yu was honest in performing his duties. Since the day he became an official, he had never kept any hanger-on in his house and he insisted on doing things in his own way. He refused to do any favour for the nobles and other officials in their personal affairs. Sima Qian, the author of the *Records of the Historian,* said that he "clung obstinately to his own course".

Records of the Historian

一髮千鈞

yī   fà   qian   jun

一縷頭髮上懸掛着千鈞（古制三十斤爲一鈞）的重量；比喻情況萬分危急。

西漢時，枚乘在吳王劉濞官府裏做郎中。劉濞想反叛朝廷，枚乘勸阻他說：“在一縷頭髮上掛着千鈞重的東西，上邊懸在沒有盡頭的高處，下邊垂在無底的深淵，這種情景是極其危險的。你要反叛，就像這縷頭髮一樣的危險啊！”枚乘的忠告，未得到劉濞的採納，他只好離開吳國到梁國去了。

後來，劉濞聯合其他六個諸侯國謀反，被大將周亞夫平滅。漢景帝知枚乘之賢，讓他任都尉之職，枚乘不想做官，不久就以多病爲理由辭去了。

出自《漢書》＊

＊《漢書》歷史著作，記載西漢二百三十年間的歷史，東漢班固（公元32－92年）作。

A Heavy Weight Hanging by a Hair

Meaning in a critical situation.

MEI Cheng of the Western Han Dynasty was General of the Guards of Liu Pi, the Prince of Wu. Liu Pi wanted to stage a revolt against the imperial court. Mei Cheng tried to dissuade him, saying, "It's like a heavy weight hanging by a hair from an infinite height over a bottomless abyss. Such a situation is extremely dangerous. If you stage a revolt, you'll be in danger just like that hair." His advice having been refused by Liu Pi, Mei Cheng had no alternative but to leave the state of Wu for the state of Liang.

Later, Liu Pi joined hands with six other princes and started a revolt and was destroyed by Grand Chancellor Zhou Yafu. Emperor Jing of the Han Dynasty thought Mei Cheng a virtuous man and wanted to appoint him to the post of commander-in-chief. Mei Cheng did not wish to be an official and declined the offer on the pretext of poor health.

History of the Han Dynasty*

*A history of the Western Han Dynasty of 230 years by Ban Gu (A.D. 32-92) of the Eastern Han Dynasty.

一曝十寒

yī pù shí hán

一天曝曬，十天受凍；比喻學習或工作時而勤奮，時而懈怠，沒有恒心。

孟子是戰國時期著名思想家，他善於運用比喻的方法說明道理。

當時，人們對齊王治理國家沒有成績很不滿意，甚至懷疑他的天資不夠聰明。孟子正在齊國遊歷，聽到這些議論，就說：“這不是聰明與不聰明的問題。比如拿培育植物來說，如果把它放到太陽下曬一天，然後又放在寒冷的地方凍十天，即使是最容易生長的植物，也一定生長不好。在齊王周圍的人中，像我這樣給他溫暖的人很少，我一走開，那些給他施加寒冷的人就紛至沓來。雖然有時齊王萌發幹事的念頭，但得不到支持也是很難成功的。”

出自《孟子》＊

＊《孟子》儒家經典著作，戰國孟軻（公元前372－前289年）著。

One Day of Sunning and Ten Days of Freezing

By Fits and Starts

Said of someone who lacks perseverance in his study or work.

THE famous thinker Mencius of the Warring States Period was good at using parables to explain his ideas.

At Mencius' time, people were discontented with the king of Qi who achieved nothing in his rule of the country. They even doubted if he was gifted with enough wisdom. Mencius was then touring the state of Qi. When he heard such talks, he said, "It's not a question of being wise or not wise. Compare it to growing a plant. If you put the plant in the sun for one day and leave it in a freezing place for ten days, even the most viable plant will not grow well. Among the people around the king of Qi, there are very few who can give him warmth as I do. As soon as I'm away, those who want to freeze him will come one after another. Although the king of

Qi sometimes wants to accomplish something, he can hardly succeed without support."

The Book of Mencius*

*A Confucian classic by Mencius (372-289 B.C.), who lived during the Warring States Period.

一顧之榮

yī gù zhī róng

回頭一看它，它就變得光榮；原比喻因被名人賞識而地位驟然提高，現常比喻因貴客光臨而引以爲榮。

春秋時，秦國有個叫孫陽的人，是一位著名的相馬專家，人們都稱他爲伯樂（中國古代神話傳說中稱管天馬的星宿爲伯樂）。有

19

一次，一個賣馬的人牽着馬在街市上出現過三次，沒有一個人理他。這個人找到孫陽，請他在街市上對自己的馬看一眼，臨走時再回過頭來看一眼。孫陽照辦了。於是這匹馬立刻被街市上的人們重視起來，售價一下子增加了十倍。

出自《戰國策》＊

＊《戰國策》戰國時期的史料滙編，經西漢劉向（約公元前77－前6年）校訂，按國別編成三十三篇。

Being Honoured by a Glance

Originally a metaphor for someone who has suddenly risen in status because of the good graces of a famous figure, it is now a metaphor for being honoured by the visit of a distinguished guest.

A man named Sun Yang of the state of Qin during the Spring and Autumn Period was a famous judge of horses. People called him Bo Le, the name of the star in charge of heavenly horses in ancient Chinese mythology. Once a man wanted to sell his horse. Although he took his horse to the market three times, nobody was interested in it. The man came to Sun Yang and asked him to come to the market and cast a glance at his horse and, before leaving the market, turn back and give the horse another glance. Sun Yang did what the man asked him to do. The horse immediately attracted attention and its price rose by ten times.

*Anecdotes of the Warring States**

*A collection of historical data about the Warring States Period (475-221 B.C.). Containing thirty-three chapters each covering a state, it was collated by the Western Han historian Liu Xiang (77-6 B.C.).

人人自危

rén rén zì wēi

人人都感到有危險，不安全。

公元前210年，秦始皇病死於沙丘。臨終前，秦始皇召見丞相李斯及宦官趙高，告訴他們要立公子扶蘇爲王。但秦始皇死後，趙高與李斯勾結篡奪了大權。他們僞造遺詔，逼使扶蘇自殺，立胡亥爲二世皇帝。

胡亥即位後，昏庸暴虐。他害怕人們識破他與趙高等人的陰謀，尋找借口先後殺了大將蒙恬、蒙毅，接着又殺害了十二個公子和十個公主，因受牽連而被殺害的人更是不計其數。由於秦二世的暴政，造成了羣臣人人自危，人人思變，促使秦王朝很快滅亡了。

出自《史記》

Everybody Finds Himself in Danger

Everybody feels that he is in danger and insecure.

BEFORE the First Emperor of Qin died in Shaqiu in 210B.C., he told Prime Minister Li Si and the eunuch official Zhao Gao that he wanted to put his eldest son Fusu in the throne. But after the death of the First Emperor, Zhao Gao and Li Si colluded in taking over the supreme power. They fabricated a death-bed decree, forcing Fusu to commit suicide and putting Huhai in the throne as the Second Emperor.

After becoming emperor, Huhai, who was both stupid and cruel, feared that people might find out the tricks he, Zhao Gao and others had played. On some pretext, he killed the generals Meng Tian and Meng Yi one after the other and then murdered twelve princes and ten princesses and a countless number of people who were involved. All the ministers found themselves in danger under the tyranny of the Second Emperor and they all wanted to have a change, which hastened the downfall of the Qin Dynasty.

Records of the Historian

人琴俱亡

rén qín jù wáng

人和琴同時失去；表示看到遺物，悼念死者的悲痛心情。

　　王獻之和王徽之都是東晉大書法家王羲之的兒子。王獻之也是東晉著名的書法家，與王羲之齊名。公元386年，兄弟二人都得了重病，弟弟王獻之先去世了。王徽之要了一輛車子趕去料理弟弟的喪事。

　　王獻之生前喜歡彈琴。王徽之非常悲痛地坐在弟弟的靈床上，取過弟弟生前彈過的琴來彈。但彈來彈去，總是調不準琴弦。王徽之把琴扔在地上，嘆道："子敬（王獻之的字）啊，子敬，你是人和琴都同時去了啊！"說罷，痛哭流涕，久久不能平靜。一個多月後，王徽之也死了。

出自《世說新語》*

* 《世說新語》南北朝時宋人劉義慶（公元403－444年）著，記載晉代士大夫的言談、軼事。

Both Man and Lute Have Perished

Said of the sadness felt at the sight something left behind by a deceased.

WANG Xianzhi and Wang Huizhi were the sons of Wang Xizhi, the great calligrapher of the Eastern Jin Dynasty. Wang Xianzhi was also a famous calligrapher whose name ranked on a par with his father's. In A.D.386, both brothers were seriously ill. The younger brother Wang Xianzhi died first. Wang Huizhi hired a carriage to look after his brother's funeral.

During his lifetime, Wang Xianzhi was fond of playing the lute. Sitting by his brother's coffin, Wang Huizhi was very sad. He took his brother's lute and plucked at the strings. But however he tried, he could not get the correct tunes. He threw the lute to the floor and said with a sigh, "Zijing (Wang Xianzhi's familiar name), Zijing, for you both the man and the lute have perished!" After saying so, he cried bitterly and for a long time could not calm down. Over a month later, Wang Huizhi also died.

*New Social Anecdotes**

*By Liu Yiqing (403-444) of the Southern and Northern Dynasties, it records the words and anecdotes of the scholars and officials of the Jin Dynasty.

干將莫邪

gān jiāng mó yé

干將劍與莫邪劍；比喻名劍。

春秋時，越王曾獻給吳王闔閭三把寶劍，這三把寶劍分別爲吳國有名的匠人歐冶子和干將鑄造。其中有名的干將劍和莫邪劍相傳有段故事：有一次，干將精選了不少靑銅來鑄劍，但費了整整三年功夫也不能將銅化開；這時他試將妻子莫邪的頭髮和指甲丟進爐中，又派了三百名童男童女拉風箱，這才將靑銅化開，鑄成了鋒利無比的雌雄二劍，並以夫妻的名字爲寶劍命名。從此，後人總喜歡

以 "干將莫邪" 比喻世上的名劍。

出自《吳越春秋》*

* 《吳越春秋》東漢趙曄（約公元40年前後在世）撰，敘述吳自太伯至夫差，越自無餘至勾踐的史事。

Gan Jiang and Mo Ye

Synonyms for famous swords.

THE king of the state of Yue of the Spring and Autumn Period gave He Lu, the king of the state of Wu, a gift of three swords made by Ou Yezi and Gang Jiang, two famous swordsmiths of Wu. There was a story behind two of the swords known as the Gang Jiang and the Mo Ye. Once Gan Jiang had selected some bronze for casting swords. But he spent three whole years and could not melt it down. One day, he threw his wife Mo Ye's hair and nails into the furnace and employed three hundred boys and girls to work the bellows. Only then was he able to melt the bronze and cast two swords of incomparable sharpness. The two swords, one male and the other female, were named after the husband and wife. People of later generations used "Gan Jiang and Mo Ye" as synonyms of famous swords.

*Annals of Wu and Yue**

*Compiled by Zhao Ye (flourished around A.D.40) of the Eastern Han Dynasty, it records the events of the state of Wu from Tai Bo to Fu Chai and of the state of Yue from Wu Yu to Gou Jian.

大器晚成

dà qì wǎn chéng

大才需要長時間才能成器；比喻才大的人成名往往較晚，也用來安慰長期不得志的人。

東漢初的馬援，十二歲便失去了父母，靠長兄馬況撫養長大。馬援少有大志，但生性並不聰明。當時有個叫朱勃的，十二歲便能口誦《詩經》、《尚書》。馬援自嘆不如，請求哥哥讓他到邊疆放牧，馬況勸弟弟說：朱勃僅是"小器速成"，他的才華就這麼多；而你是"大器晚成"，應該發憤圖強，將來定有出息。馬援從此不再自暴自棄，努力學習。後來他當了新城大尹、隴西太守，五十五歲時官拜伏波將軍，封新息侯。

出自《後漢書》

Great Vessels Take Longer to Complete

Great Oaks from Little Acorns Grow

Meaning a great mind takes longer to mature, it is used to describe people of great talents who often become famous in their later years and also to console people who have over long years failed to make a name for themselves.

MA Yuan of the early Eastern Han Dynasty lost his parents when he was twelve. It was his elder brother Ma Kuang who raised him. Ma Yuan was lofty minded even when he was young, but he was not particularly talented. There lived at the same time another boy named Zhu Bo, who could recite the *Book of Odes* and *Book of History* at twelve. Sighing over the fact that he was not as smart as Zhu, Ma Yuan asked his brother to send him to the frontier regions where he would spend his life herding. Ma Kuang advised his brother, saying, "For Zhu Bo it is a case of 'small vessels taking a short time to complete', because he only has that much of talents. For you it is a case of 'great vessels taking longer to complete'. You should make a firm resolution and work hard and you will definitely have a bright future." From then on, Ma Yuan no longer abandoned himself to despair and studied diligently. He later served as prefect of Xincheng and governor of Longxi. At fifty-five, he became General of Fupo and was made the Marquis of Xinxi.

History of the Later Han Dynasty

三顧茅廬

sān gù máo lú

三次光顧簡陋的草屋；比喻邀請賢能的誠意。

諸葛亮，三國時著名政治家和軍事家。東漢末年，他隱居隆中，但却留心世事。劉備聽說諸葛亮才能極高，便親自到諸葛亮的茅舍邀請他出來輔政。諸葛亮爲了試探劉備的誠意，前兩次都借故不見，第三次劉備來到他住的草屋求見，諸葛亮感動了，決定輔佐劉備，並提出佔據荊、益二州，聯合孫權，對抗曹操，進而一統天下的建議。從此，諸葛亮成了劉備的主要謀士。

出自 《三國演義》＊

＊《三國演義》長篇歷史小說，元末明初人羅貫中（約公元1330－1400年）撰。

Calling Thrice at the Thatched Cottage

Describing sincerity in enlisting the service of a man of talent.

ZHUGE Liang, the famous statesman and military strategist of the Three Kingdoms time, lived in seclusion in Longzhong at the end of the Eastern Han. But he kept a close watch on the development of the affairs of the state. When Liu Bei heard that Zhuge Liang was a man of extraordinary talents, he called in person at Zhuge Liang's thatched cottage to ask him to come out from his seclusion and assist him in running the government. To test Liu Bei's sincerity, Zhuge Liang deliberately avoided him during his first two calls. When Liu Bei called on him for the third time, Zhuge Liang was moved. He decided to help Liu Bei and proposed the plan of taking the prefectures of Jing and Yi and uniting Sun Quan against Cao Cao before unifying the whole country. From then on, Zhuge Liang became Liu Bei's principal advisor.

Tales of the Three Kingdoms*

*A historical novel by Luo Guanzhong (about 1330-1400) who lived at the end of the Yuan Dynasty and the beginning of the Ming Dynasty.

上下其手

shàng xià qí shǒu

向上舉起一隻手，接着又把手放下來；比喻通同作弊。

春秋時，楚國出兵攻打鄭國，鄭國守將皇頡被楚國的穿封戌（xū）俘獲。楚王之弟公子圍想冒功領賞，謊稱皇頡是他所獲。穿封戌和公子圍爭執起來，互不相讓，於是請了太宰伯州犁來裁判。伯州犁認爲事情簡單，只要問一下皇頡便知究竟。皇頡來後，伯州犁向上高舉起一隻手，恭敬地指着公子圍，對皇頡說：「這位是公子圍，我們國君的弟弟。」然後，把手放低，輕輕地指着穿封戌說：「這個人叫穿封戌，是我國邊境上的一個縣官。究竟是誰把你捉住的？」皇頡見伯州犁介紹時的手勢、語氣大不相同，心裏早已明白了他暗示的意思，便趁機逢迎，撒謊道：「我遇到公子，就大敗被俘。」

出自《左傳》*

* 《左傳》編年體歷史著作，記載春秋時期的重大歷史事件，相傳爲春秋時魯國人左丘明所撰。

Raising and Lowering the Hand

Working Hand in Glove

Meaning collusion in a fraud.

THE state of Chu in the Spring and Autumn Period launched an attack against the state of Zheng. Huang Jie, the garrison general of Zheng, was captured in battle by Chuan Fengxu. Prince Wei, brother of the king of Chu, who wanted to collect the reward claimed that it was he who had captured Huang Jie. An quarrel ensued between Chuan Fengxu and

Prince Wei and either party refused to give in. Prime Minister Bo Zhouli was invited to arbitrate. Bo thought it was a simple matter. They had only to ask Huang Jie to find out the truth. When Huang Jie came, Bo Zhouli raised his hand, pointed respectfully at Prince Wei and said to Huang Jie, "This is Prince Wei, brother of our sovereign." He then lowered his hand, pointed carelessly at Chuan Fengxu and said, "This is Chuan Fengxu, a petty county official from our frontiers. Now who was it that captured you?" From the gesture of Bo's hand when he made the introduction and the difference in the tone of his voice, Huang Jie immediately took the hint. Fawningly he lied, "When I met the prince, I was defeated and captured."

*Zuo Qiuming's Chronicles**

*Attributed to Zuo Qiuming of the state of Lu of the Spring and Autumn Period, this history book records important events of the Spring and Autumn Period.

千慮一得

qiān lǜ yī dé

愚鈍的人只要多方面用心考慮，也會偶有所得；常用於陳述見解時表示自謙。

春秋時，齊國相國晏嬰很有名望。有一天，齊景公派一位使者來見，這時晏嬰正在吃飯，他就把自己的飯菜分成兩份，請使者共進午餐，結果兩人都沒吃飽。使者回去後，把這一情況告訴了齊景公。齊景公立即派人送去千金，供晏嬰招待賓客時用。晏嬰不肯接受。齊景公又派人送回，晏嬰還是不收。當齊景公第三次派人來時，晏嬰仍然不肯收下，便和來人一起去面見齊景公。齊景公不願馬上收回成命，說：「對於應當接受的封賞，連管仲（齊國歷史上著名的賢相）也不推辭，你爲什麼一定要拒絕呢？"晏嬰說："聖人千慮，必有一失；愚人千慮，必有一得。在這件事上，也許管仲考慮得不夠周到，而我的想法却是對的。"齊景公聽了，只好作罷。

出自《晏子春秋》*

Hitting upon an Idea after Much Thought

A Fool May Be Wise for Once

The full form of this idiom means that even a fool may hit upon a good idea upon weighing the issue a thousand times. It is used to express modesty when voicing one's opinion.

YAN Ying, the Prime Minister of the state of Qi during the Spring and Autumn Period, was a man of great fame. One day, a messenger sent by Duke Jing of Qi came to see him while he was eating his meal. He divided his food into two portions and asked the messenger to share the dinner with him. But neither of them had enough to eat. Upon his return, the messenger told Duke Jing what had happened. The duke immediately sent someone to Yan Ying with a thousand pieces of gold for him to entertain his guests. Yan Ying refused to take the gold. The duke had the gold taken to him again. Yan Ying still refused to take it. When the man from Duke Jing came for the third time, Yan Ying went with him to see the duke without accepting the gold. Unwilling to countermand the order, the duke said, "Even a man like Guan Zhong (a famous minister in the history of Qi) did not refuse the reward he deserved. Why do you have to refuse it?" Yan Ying answered, "A wise man, weighing a matter a thousand times, may make a slip, while a fool, weighing the issue a thousand times, may hit upon a good idea. On this particular matter, Guan Zhong might not have carefully thought it over, while my idea may be correct." Duke Jing of Qi had to give up after hearing what he had said.

Anecdotes of Yan Zi

*A book recording the words and deeds of Yan Ying (?-500 B.C.) collated in the Warring States Period.

亡戟得矛

wáng   jǐ   dé   máo

丟了戟，得了矛；比喻得失相當。

春秋時，齊國和晉國發生戰爭。有一個來自平阿（在今安徽懷遠縣西南）的小兵在兩軍混戰中丟失了自己的戟，可是他又在戰場上撿到一枝矛。他想來想去不敢要，心裏很不痛快。這時，迎面走來了一個人，這個小兵問道：「丟失了一枝戟，要是撿回來一枝矛，可以歸隊不受處罰嗎？」那人說：「戟是兵器，矛也是兵器，丟失了一件兵器，撿回來一件兵器，正好相抵，為什麼不可以歸隊呢？」

出自《呂氏春秋》＊

＊《呂氏春秋》戰國末期秦相國呂不韋（ ？－公元前235年）召集門客編寫。

Losing a Halberd and Gaining a Spear

Meaning the loss is made up by the gain.

IN a war that broke out between the state of Qi and the state of Jin in the Spring and Autumn Period, a young soldier from Ping'e (southwest of today's Huaiyuan County, Anhui Province) lost his halberd in the confusion of a battle. He picked up a spear on the battlefield. As he was not sure if he should take the spear, he was very unhappy. A man happened to walk up to him. The young soldier asked him, "I've lost my halberd, but I've picked up a spear. Can I get away from being punished when I return to my unit?" "The halberd is a weapon, so is the spear," the man answered. "You've lost one weapon and picked up another. The loss has been compensated for by the gain. Why can't you return to your unit?"

*The Discourses of Lü Buwei**

*Compiled by Lü Buwei (?-235 B.C.), the Prime Minister of the state of Qin at the end of the Warring States Period, and a group of followers he had assembled.

天下無雙

tiān xià wú shuāng

世上獨一無二；形容出類拔萃。

戰國時，魏國的信陵君無忌竊得兵符，調動魏軍救趙國，戰勝了秦國，受到趙國上下的稱頌。但他擔心魏王追究竊取兵符之罪，便移居趙國。定居後，信陵君四處招納賢士。他聽說趙國的毛公、薛公素有賢才，便派人去召請，但他們有意躲避，不肯來見信陵君。信陵君打聽到毛公藏身於賭徒之中，便親自秘密地前去察訪，終於結識了毛公。後來又打聽到薛公藏身於賣酒人家，於是又獨自悄悄地到賣酒人家尋訪，終於也結識了薛公。

趙惠文王的兄弟平原君對自己的夫人說："以前聽說你弟弟信陵君為人出類拔萃，天下無雙；今天看來，只不過徒有虛名，實際上是個行為荒唐的人！"信陵君聽到這話後，認為平原君是一個不重才學，只重出身門第的人。後來，在平原君門下的一些人，認為信陵君精神境界高尚，便紛紛辭別了平原君，投奔在信陵君門下。

出自《史記》

Unequalled under the Sky

Said of somebody or something of unparalleled qualities.

DURING the Warring States Period, Wu Ji, Lord Xinling of the state of Wei, manoeuvred the Wei army on a stolen military tally and rescued the state of Zhao by defeating the army of the state of Qin. He was praised by people high and low in the state of Zhao. For fear of an inquiry by the king of Wei about the stolen military tally, he moved to the state of Zhao. After settling down there, he began to gather men of talents from all parts of the country. When he heard that Mao Gong and Xue Gong of the state of Zhao were talented men, he sent someone to invite them. But they avoided his messenger and did not come. Lord Xinling learned that Mao was hiding among a group of gamblers. So he went in person secretly to look for him and was able to make his acquaintance. Later, when he heard that Xue was hiding in the house of a wine seller, he again went alone to the wine seller and was able to make friends with Xue.

Lord Pingyuan, brother of King Huiwen of the state of Zhao, said to his wife, "In the past, I heard that your brother Lord Xinling was a man of outstanding quality unequalled under the sky. From what I've seen today, he has only an undeserved reputation and is actually a man of absurd behaviour." When his sister relaid these words to him, Lord Xinling realized that Lord Pingyuan was a man who attached no importance to talents and learning and all he cared was a man's family origin. Later, seeing Lord Xinling was a noble-minded man, followers of Lord Pingyuan left him one after another and went over to Lord Xinling.

Records of the Historian

木人石心

mù rén shí xīn

木頭人，石頭心；比喻意志堅定，不受誘惑。

西晉時，有一年春天，太尉賈充在京都洛陽遊春。忽然，他發現河邊小船上坐着一個很古怪的人，神情莊重，對周圍的熱鬧情景無動於衷。原來此人叫夏統，是個厭惡世俗濁流、潔身自守的隱士，因母親病重，從江南來京都買藥。

兩人交談後，賈充發現夏統節操高尚，不慕榮華，很有才氣，要保舉他做官。夏統一聽，勃然不悅，再也不願說話了。賈充心想：官職、地位、女色，誰見了能不動心呢？於是，他調來了一大羣美女，載歌載舞地把夏統團團圍住。然而，夏統對此全不理會，仍然穩坐船中，表情冷漠。見此情景，賈充等人議論道：“這傢伙真是木人石心啊！”說罷，無可奈何地離去了。

出自《晉書》＊

＊《晉書》記述晉朝史事的紀傳體著作，唐房玄齡（公元579－648年）等撰。

Man of Wood with a Heart of Stone

Said of a man of strong will unmoved by temptations.

ONE spring day, when Grand Counsellor Jia Chong of the Western Jin was on a excursion admiring spring scenery in the capital Luoyang, he saw a strange man sitting in a small boat near the bank of a river. Solemn in expression, the man seemed to be quite unperturbed by the sights and noises around him. The man was in fact named Xia Tong, a hermit who detested the vulgar practices of the mundane world and was determined to preserve his own purity. His mother was seriously ill and he had come to the capital to buy medicine.

After Jia Chong started a conversation with him and found that Xia Tong was a man of lofty ideals, talented and having no desire for honour and glory, he told Xia that he would like to recommend him for an official post. On hearing it, Xia suddenly became angry and refused to talk with him any more. Well, where is the man who is not attempted by position, honour and women, thought Jia Chong. So he called over a bevy of beautiful women, who began to sing and dance around Xia Tong. But Xia was quite unmoved, sitting steadily in the boat with an expression of indifference on his face. Jia Chong then said to his followers, "This fellow is really a man of wood with a heart of stone." Saying so, he had no alternative but to depart.

History of the Jin Dynasty ＊

＊By Fang Xuanling (579-648) and others of the Tang Dynasty, this history book consists mostly of biographies.

犬牙交錯

quǎn yā jiāo cuò

像狗的牙齒那樣參差不齊；比喻情況複雜，或雙方力量互有短長。

漢高祖劉邦建立漢朝之後，把被封在各地的異族王侯全部消滅，而把自己的兒子、弟弟、侄子等分封到各地爲王。到了漢景帝的時候，這些同姓王勢力強大起來，不斷與朝廷對抗，終於爆發了以吳王劉濞爲首的七個王侯聯合反叛的事件。但是，漢景帝沒有從中接受教訓，他又把自己的許多兒子分封爲王侯。

漢武帝即位後，許多大臣向武帝建議削弱這些王侯的勢力。王侯們知道後，大爲不滿，揚言說：“先帝給我們這些封地，就像犬牙那樣交叉在一起，是爲了讓我們互相支援，保衛京都，使劉家天下堅如磐石。”武帝是個有雄才大略的皇帝，先在表面上安慰他們一番，穩住他們，之後採取措施，把大王國變成許多小王國，並設置刺史，考察各國的政事，從而削弱了他們的勢力，鞏固了中央集權。

出自《漢書》

In an Interlocked Canine-Teeth Pattern

In a Jigsaw Pattern

Said of a complex situation with forces of two sides interlocked in a jigsaw pattern.

AFTER the founding of the Han Dynasty, Emperor Gaozu wiped out all the dukes and marquises not of his own clan who had been enfeoffed in various parts of the country. He then enfeoffed his sons, brothers and nephews as princes in all parts of the country. By the time of Emperor Jing, the princes of the Liu clan had grown powerful and rivalled incessantly with the imperial court, leading eventually to the outbreak of the revolt of seven princes headed by Liu Pi, the prince of Wu. However, Emperor Jing did not draw a lesson from the revolt and enfeoffed his many sons as princes.

When Emperor Wu came to the throne, many of his ministers advised him to weaken the power of the princes. When the princes heard about the advice, they were very displeased. They declared, "Our feoffs given to us by the former emperors lie in an interlocked canine-teeth pattern. The purpose was for us to support one another and safeguard the capital so that the Liu dynasty would be as solid as a rock." Emperor Wu was a man of great talent and bold vision. Outwardly he consoled them so as to steady them. But afterwards, he adopted measures to turn the large princedoms into many small princedoms and appointed governors to look into the affairs of each princedom. In this way he was able to weaken the power of the princes and consolidate the central government.

History of the Han Dynasty

不自量力

bù zì liàng lì

不能實事求是地估計自己的力量。

戰國時，孟嘗君田文是齊國貴族。有一次，他的封地薛邑（今山東省滕縣東南）遭楚國軍隊的進攻。正巧，齊國大夫淳于髠出使楚國回來，路過薛邑。孟嘗君對淳于髠說：“楚軍就要進攻薛邑，請先生爲我分擔憂愁，設法援救。”淳于髠安慰他說：“請放心，我回到都城臨淄面見君主後，一定爲足下請命。”

淳于髠回到臨淄後，齊王問：“在楚國見到什麼？”淳于髠巧妙地回答：“楚國人不大通情理，而我們的孟嘗君却有點不自量

37

力。"齊王問："先生說的是什麼意思？"淳于髡說："孟嘗君也不估計自己的力量能不能保衞自己的領地，就在那裏爲先王立了宗廟。現在，楚軍執意要攻打薛邑，先王的宗廟眼看要保不住了。"齊王聽了驚叫道："哎呀，原來先王的宗廟設在那裏呀！"於是他馬上派兵星夜趕到薛邑救援。楚國得知齊王已派援軍，便退兵回國，薛邑終於避免了災難。

出自《戰國策》

Overrating One's Own Strength

Overreaching Oneself

Said of someone who is not able to estimate his own strength or ability realistically.

LORD Mengchang was an aristocrat of the state of Qi in the Warring States Period. Once his enfeoffment Xueyi (southeast of today's Tengxian, Shandong Province) was threatened by the approaching Chu army. At the moment, a ranking official of Qi, Chunyu Kun, was passing Xueyi on his return from a mission to the state of Chu. Lord Mengchang said to Chunyu Kun, "The Chu army is about to attack Xueyi. May I ask Your Excellency to share my anxiety and secure help for me?" Chunyu comforted him, "Don't worry. When I return to the capital Linzi and see the king, I'll ask his help on your behalf."

"What did you see in the state of Chu?" the king of Qi asked Chunyu Kun on the latter's return. Chunyu answered ingeniously, "People in Chu are behaving unreasonably. But our Lord Mengchang is overrating his own strength." "What do you mean?" questioned the king. "Lord Mengchang didn't calculate if he's powerful enough to defend his enfeoffment before he built the ancestral temple of the former king," said Chunyu. "Now that the Chu army is about to attack Xueyi, the ancestral temple of the former king will soon fall into the hands of the enemy." The king was greatly alarmed. "Aiya," he exclaimed, "so that's where the ancestral temple has been built." He immediately ordered his army to march overnight to the rescue of Xueyi. When the king of Chu heard that the king of Qi had sent reinforcements, he ordered his forces to withdraw and Xueyi was saved from disaster.

Anecdotes of the Warring States

不寒而慄

bù hán ér lì

不是因為寒冷而發抖；形容極其恐懼。

義縱，是漢武帝時一個殘酷的官吏。他原是個盜賊，後因他姐姐得到太后的歡寵，才做起官來。在他當定襄太守時，一到任就逮捕了二百多人，把他們判處死刑。許多人的家屬和朋友到監獄去探望，也被逮捕，並以"為死罪開脫"的罪名全部處死。他一下子就殺死四百多人。消息傳開，人們非常恐懼，個個心驚膽戰，像在冷風中一樣瑟瑟發抖。

出自《史記》

Shivering All Over though Not Cold
Trembling with Fear

Said of someone experiencing an extreme horror.

YI Zong was a cruel official during the reign of Emperor Wu of the Han Dynasty. He had been a bandit, before he became an official because his sister had won the favour of the Empress Dowager. As soon as he assumed office as prefect of Dingxiang, he arrested more than two hundred people and sentenced all of them to death. When family members and friends of many of these people came to the prison to see them, they were arrested, too and executed for the crime of "pleading for capital offences". Altogether, more than four hundred people were killed in one go. When news spread, people were terrified. They trembled with fear as if they were standing in the cold wind.

Records of the Historian

不覺技癢
bù júe jī yǎng

表示擅長某種技藝，極想表演一下，好比發癢一樣。

高漸離，戰國時燕國人，善彈奏樂器。他的好朋友荆軻應燕國太子丹的請求，到秦國去行刺秦王。當他們在易水之濱分手時，高漸離彈筑（一種樂器），荆軻唱着歌，兩人揮淚而別。荆軻刺秦王失敗後，高漸離改名換姓，逃到一個偏僻的地方，給人家當了傭工。

有一次，主人家來了一位客人，席間彈筑。高漸離聽後，不覺技癢，也當眾演奏起來。他那高超的演奏技巧，受到主人和在座賓客的一致稱讚。從此，主人待之如上賓，不再讓他當傭工了。

出自《風俗通義》＊

＊《風俗通義》東漢應劭（約公元178年前後在世）撰。

Itching to Show One's Skill

Itching to Have a Go

Said of someone who is eager to show his skill.

GAO Jianli of the state of Yan in the Warring States Period was a good performer of musical instruments. At the request of Prince Dan of Yan, his good friend Jing Ke was about to depart for the state of Qin to assassinate the Qin king. Before they bid farewell by the River Yishui, Gao Jianli played an instrument named Zhu and Jing Ke sang. They parted their way with tears in their eyes. After Jing Ke had failed in his attempt to assassinate the Qin king, Gao Jianli changed his name and fled to an out-of-the-way place, where he worked as a servant in a family.

One day, when the master of the house was entertaining some guests, one of the guests played the instrument Zhu. When Gao Jianli heard it, he itched to show his skill. When he performed in front of the guests, his superb skill won the praise of the master of the house and all the guests. From then on, the master of the house treated him as an distinguished guest and no longer looked upon him as a servant.

Explanations of Customs＊

*By Ying Shao who lived around A.D. 178 in the Eastern Han Dynasty.

水深火熱

shuǐ shēn huǒ rè

處於深水和熱火之中；比喻處境困難，難於生存。

戰國時，燕王噲將王位讓給相國子之，將軍子被和太子平不服，起兵攻打子之，於是爆發了一場內戰。齊宣王趁燕國混亂之機，派匡章帶領大軍攻打燕國，並很快攻下了燕國國都。燕王噲自殺，子之也被殺害。

這時，齊宣王問孟子：“有人勸我不要併吞燕國，也有人勸我併吞它，究竟該怎麼辦，我想聽聽您的意見。”孟子說：“如果燕國的人民高興你佔領，你就佔領，古人這樣做過，周武王便是；如果燕國的人民不高興你佔領，那就不要佔領，古人也有這樣做的，周文王便是。當你進軍的時候，如果燕國的人民用食物和茶水來歡迎你的軍隊，這說明那裏的人民想擺脫困苦的境地。如果你佔領燕國，燕國人民反而覺得災難像水越來越深，像火越來越熱，那麼，燕國人民就只好離開你，逃到別的地方去了。”

出自《孟子》

Deep Water and Hot Fire

An Abyss of Sufferings

Describing the deepest misery in which it is impossible to live.

KING Kuai of the state of Yan in the Warring States Period passed his throne to Prime Minister Zi Zhi. General Zi Bei and Prince Ping refused to accept the new king and launched an attack on Zi Zhi. A civil war thus ensued. Taking advantage of the confusion in the state of Yan, King Xuan of the state of Qi sent Kuang Zhang with a large army against Yan and soon occupied the capital of Yan. King Kuai of Yan committed suicide and Zi Zhi was killed.

King Xuan of Qi then asked Mencius, "Some people advised me not to annex the state of Yan while others urged me to do it. What shall I do? I would like to hear your opinion." Mencius said, "If the people of Yan are pleased that you've occupied their country, you can do it. The ancients have done it. King Wu of the Zhou Dynasty was one of them. If the people of Yan are not pleased with your occupation, then you must not occupy their country. The ancients have also done the same. King Wen of the Zhou Dynasty was one of them. If the people of Yan welcomed your army with food and drinks when you marched into their country, it showed the people there wanted to be lifted out of misery. If the people of Yan think your occupation of Yan is a disaster like water of increasing depth and fire of increasing heat, they'll have to leave you and flee to other places."

The Book of Mencius

水滴石穿

shuǐ dī shí chuān

水不住地滴下來，把石頭滴穿；比喻只要堅持不懈，即使力量很小，也能做出看來很難辦到的事情。

從前，有個叫張乖崖的人，在崇陽做縣令。一天，他在衙門周圍巡行，看見一個管理錢庫的小吏慌慌張張地從府庫中出來，鬢旁頭巾下藏着一枚銅錢，經過查問，小吏搪塞不過，承認是從府庫中偷來的。

　　張乖崖派人將小吏押回大堂拷打，小吏不服，大聲嚷道："一枚錢有什麼了不起，你便這樣打我！你只能打我，難道還能殺我！"張乖崖見小吏如此頂撞，毫不猶豫地拿起朱筆批道："一日一錢，千日千錢，時間長了，繩子能鋸斷木頭，水能滴穿石頭。"然後將筆一擲，手提寶劍，親自斬了小吏。

出自《鶴林玉露》*

　*《鶴林玉露》南宋羅大經（約公元1224年前後在世）撰，雜記讀書所得，多引南宋道學家之語，也評論詩文。

Constant Dripping Wears Away the Stone

Little Strokes Fell Great Oaks

Meaning that even an infinitesimal force can accomplish a seemingly impossible feat with persistance.

ZHANG Guaiya was the magistrate of Chongyang. One day, while making a round of inspection of the government building, he saw a junior keeper slipping out of the coffers building in a flurry with a copper coin hidden under his turban. Having been questioned, the keeper, who could not get away with a vague answer, admitted that he had stolen the coin from the coffers.

Zhang Guaiya had the keeper taken to the courtroom and beaten. Pleading not guilty, the keeper cried out, "What does a copper coin amount to? Now you're beating me. I would like to see you kill me for it." Angered by his defiance, Zhang Guaiya promptly picked up a red-inked writing brush and wrote: "A copper a day makes a thousand coppers in a thousand days. A hemp rope can saw up wood and drips of water can penetrate a rock." Throwing down the writing brush, he drew his sword and killed the keeper with his own hand.

*Forest of Cranes and Dews of Jade**

**A collection of reading notes with many quotations from Taoists of the Southern Song Dynasty and literary reviews by Luo Dajing (fl. around 1224) of the Southern Song Dynasty.

月下老人

yuè xià lǎo rén

月光下的老人；稱呼主管婚姻的神或媒人的代稱。

唐代時，有個名叫韋固的青年，路過宋城，見一老人倚着背囊在月光下翻看一本書。韋固感到奇怪，前去問其究竟，老人回答說：“看的是天下人的姻緣簿，背囊中放的是專門拴繫夫妻兩人的脚的紅繩子。”韋固和老人來到街市上，見一盲眼老婦抱着一個三歲多的女孩，老人對韋固說：“這女孩是你將來的妻子。”韋固聽後，認爲老人是在有意戲弄他，便命家奴刺了女孩一刀。

十四年後，相州刺史王泰將女兒許配給韋固爲妻，韋固見這女子很美，但眉間有一傷疤。詢問之後，方知十四年前曾在街市上被人刺過一刀，一切情況竟同韋固的經歷一樣。

出自《續玄怪錄》*

*《續玄怪錄》傳奇小說專集，唐李復言（約公元831年前後在世）著。

The Old Man under the Moon

A synonym for the god of matrimony or a match-maker.

IT happened in the Tang Dynasty. A young man named Wei

45

Gu was passing the city of Songcheng, where he saw an old man leaning on his pack reading a book in the moonlight. Being amazed at it, Wei Gu walked up and asked what he was doing. The old man answered, "I'm reading a book of marriage listing who is going to marry whom. In my pack are red cords for tying the feet of husband and wife." When Wei Gu and the old man came together to a marketplace, they saw a blind old woman carrying a three-year-old little girl in her arms. The old man said to Wei Gu, "This little girl will be your wife one day." Thinking the old man was making fun of him, Wei Gu ordered his servant to stab the girl with his knife.

Fourteen years later, Wang Tai, the governor of Xiangzhou, gave Wei Gu his daughter in marriage. The daughter was a beautiful young woman, but Wei Gu found that there was a scar between her eyebrows. When he asked what had happened, he was told that she had been stabbed by a man in the marketplace fourteen years before.

*More Strange Tales**

*A collection of strange tales by Li Fuyan (fl. around 831) of the Tang Dynasty.

46

手不釋卷

shǒu bù shì juàn

手裏經常拿着書不放；形容刻苦用功。

三國時，吳國大將呂蒙，行伍出身，讀書很少。吳王孫權見他年輕有爲，而且身居要職，勸他多讀些書，增長知識。呂蒙認爲讀書是文人學者的事，武官只要能打仗就行了，不用讀書，便推托說：“軍隊裏事情太多，哪有時間讀書啊！”孫權聽後嚴肅地說：“你說事情忙，難道比我還要忙嗎？我過去讀過一些經書，後來主持國家軍政大計，還是在百忙中讀了一些史書和兵書，自己覺得很有長進。漢光武帝領兵打仗很緊張，仍然手裏拿着書本不放，你爲什麼不刻苦讀書呢？”呂蒙很受感動，從此以後，他勤奮讀書，進步很快。後來，呂蒙做了吳國的主將，有勇有謀，屢建奇功。

出自《三國志》

Always Having a Book in One's Hand

Said of someone who is studying assiduously.

GENERAL Lü Meng of the state of Wu during the Three Kingdoms period had worked his way up from among the ranks and files and had very little book learning. Seeing that he was young and capable and was occupying an important position, Sun Quan, the king of Wu, advised him to read more books and broaden his knowledge. Lü Meng thought that book reading was the business of the scholars. A military officer did not have to read as long as he could fight battles. He therefore tried to excuse himself, saying, "There're too many things to do in the army. How can I find time to read?" After hearing what he had said, Sun Quan said sternly, "You said that you were too busy. Are you much busier than I am?

I've read some classics in the past. After I began to supervise the military and political affairs of the state, I still find time to read some history and military books however busy I am. I find I've improved myself a great deal. Although Emperor Guangwu of the Han Dynasty was very busy commanding troops and fighting battles, he always had a book in his hand. Why shouldn't you read and study hard?" Lü Meng was deeply moved. From then on, he studied diligently and made rapid progress. He later became the chief general of the state of Wu with both courage and wisdom and repeatedly performed outstanding services.

History of the Three Kingdoms

分道揚鑣

fēn　dào　yáng　biāo

分開道路，揚起馬口中銜的鐵環；比喻目標、志趣不同，各走各的道路。

南北朝時，北魏孝文帝遷都洛陽，派元志做洛陽令。有一天，元志乘車外出，在路上和御史中尉李彪的車馬相遇。按規定，百姓要爲官員讓路，下級官員要爲上級官員讓路。可是元志毫不謙讓，李彪非常生氣，雙方爭執起來，一直鬧到孝文帝那裏，並要他斷定哪一方對。李彪說："我是朝廷近臣，元志只是地方長官，哪有與我抗衡的道理？"元志說："皇帝任命我管理京城，凡是居住在洛陽的人都編在我的戶籍裏，爲什麼要我給你讓路呢？"孝文帝看看二人，不好評判是非，只好說："你們就分開道路，驅馬而行吧！"從宮廷出來，元志找來標尺，在街道上測量劃線，從此，他們就各走道路的半邊。

出自《北史》＊

＊《北史》記載從北魏到隋朝歷史的著作，唐李延壽撰。

Going Separate Ways

Meaning literally each urging his horse on and going his own way. It is said of people who go their own ways because of their different aims and different interests.

YUAN Zhi was appointed governor of Luoyang when Emperor Xiaowen of the Northern Wei Dunasty moved his capital to Luoyang during the period of the Southern and Northern Dynasties. One day when Yuan Zhi went out, his carriage met head-on with that of Li Biao, the Imperial Censor. According to regulations, common people were to give way to officials and officials of lower ranks to officials of higher ranks. But Yuan Zhi refused to give way. Li Biao was very angry. The two of them started to quarrel and together they went to see Emperor Xiaowen and asked him to say which side was right. "I'm an official of the court while Yuan Zhi is only a local official. What right does he have to block my path?" said Li Biao. "The emperor has appointed me to govern the capital. All the people living in Luoyang are listed in my census register. Why do I have to give way?" countered Yuan Zhi. Finding it difficult to say which side was right, Emperor Xiaowen said, "Divide the path so that each of you can go along different ways." When they came out of the court, Yuan Zhi found a measuring rod and divided the road in the middle. From then on, each of them travelled along a different path.

*History of the Northern Dynasties**

*By Li Yanshou of the Tang Dynasty, it covers the history from the Northern Wei Dynasty to the Sui Dynasty.

牛衣對泣

niú yī duì qì

披着蓑衣，對視而泣；形容共守窮困的境況。

西漢成帝時，有一個叫王章的人，任京兆尹，他能直言勸諫皇上的過失，頗受人們尊敬。可是，王章沒做官時，却生活窮困。有一次，王章身患重病，無被子可蓋，只好將蓋牛的蓑衣用來代替。此時此刻，王章頹廢萬分，覺得自己再也沒有出頭之日，不禁對着妻子嗚咽起來。妻子雖也難過，但覺得頹廢無濟於事，還是振作起來爲好，於是鼓勵王章說：「目前，京城做官的人，誰能比得上你的才華！這點小病和困難，怎能摧垮你的意志而對前途失去信心呢？」從此以後，王章振作精神，刻苦攻讀，終於一舉成名。

出自《漢書》

Crying Face to Face in an Ox Cape

Said of people sharing misery together.

DURING the reign of Emperor Cheng in the Western Han Dynasty, Wang Zhang, the prefect of the capital, was respected by people for being honest in pointing out the faults of the emperor. But before he became an official, Wang Zhang had lived in poverty. Once when he was seriously ill, he had to cover himself with the straw cape for covering an ox because he did not have a warm quilt. Wang Zhang was very disheartened then, thinking that he would never be able to make a name for himself. As he thought so, he could not refrain from crying face to face with his wife. His wife also felt very sad, but she could see that feeling dejected would not help them in any way and that they should exert themselves. She encouraged Wang Zhang, saying, "None of the officials in the capital is as talented as you are. How can you allow yourself to be discouraged by some minor illness and difficulties?" From then on, Wang Zhang began to pluck up and studied hard until he eventually came to fame.

History of the Han Dynasty

牛鼎烹鷄

niú dīng pēng jī

用煮牛的大鍋煮鷄；本意爲大器小用，後用來比喻大材小用。

東漢末年，有個叫邊讓的人，能詩善賦，寫一手好文章，很有些名氣。大將軍何進將他招來，命他做史令官。不久，朝廷的議郎蔡邕聽說邊讓在何進那裏，心想："邊讓才學不凡，應該做個大官。"於是，蔡邕親自來到何進家裏，勸說他把邊讓推薦出去，說："我看邊讓這個人是難得的奇才啊！俗話說，用煮牛的大鍋來煮一隻小鷄，水放多了，味道沒了，就不好吃；水放少了，則煮不熟，更不能吃。我現在憂慮的是，這個煮牛的大鍋沒有用來煮牛，希望將軍考慮，使邊讓施展他的才能！"何進認爲蔡邕說得對，便推薦邊讓在朝廷做了大官。

出自《後漢書》

Cooking a Chicken in a Cauldron for Stewing an Ox

Originally meaning using a large instrument for minor work, it now means putting a man of great talents on a petty job.

BIAN Rang of the end of the Eastern Han Dynasty enjoyed

some fame for composing poems, rhymed proses and good essays. Grand General He Jin employed him as a recorder of events. Later, when Imperial Advisor Cai Yong heard that Bian Rang was serving under He Jin, he thought Bian was a man of unusual talents and should be appointed to an important official post. Thereupon, he came to He Jin's house and said to him that he should recommend Bian to work in another place. "I think Bian Rang has rare talents. As the saying goes, when you use a cauldron for stewing an ox to cook a chicken, it will be tasteless if you put too much water in it and it can't be cooked in too little water. What I'm worrying is that the cauldron has not been used for stewing an ox. I hope that you can give him an opportunity to use his talents." Being convinced that what Cai Yong said was right, He Jin recommended Bian to serve as an ranking official at the imperial court.

History of the Later Han Dynasty

心腹之患

xīn fù zhī huàn

心臟和腹部的疾病；比喻隱藏在內部要害處的禍害。

春秋末年，吳越兩國相互攻伐。在一次戰爭中，吳軍圍困越國都城會稽（今浙江紹興），越王勾踐向吳王夫差乞降求和。勾踐表面上順從，暗中卻圖謀報仇復國。有一次，吳國準備發兵攻打齊國，勾踐帶領臣子前來朝拜夫差，說了許多恭維的話，並贈送了厚禮。大夫伍子胥對越國一直懷有戒心，他看出了勾踐的真正目的，極力勸告夫差說：「戰勝了齊國，好比得到一塊像石頭一樣不長莊稼的土地，而越國對我們來說，正像隱藏在心臟和腹部的疾病一樣啊！」可是，夫差根本聽不進伍子胥的勸告。後來，吳國果然被越國打敗，夫差也自殺身亡了。

出自《左傳》

A Disease in the Vital Organs

Meaning a hidden danger or disaster.

THE states of Wu and Yue were constantly at rivalry towards the end of the Spring and Autumn Period. In one of their wars, the army of Wu surrounded Guaiji (today's Shaoxing in Zhejiang Province), the capital of Yue, and Gou Jian, the king of Yue, surrendered to Fu Chai, the king of Wu, and sued for peace. Outwardly Gou Jian was obedient, but he secretly plotted for revenge and for restoring his country. Later, when the state of Wu was making preparations for an attack against the state of Qi, Gou Jian came with his ministers to pay respect to Fu Chai. He said many flattering words and presented the Wu king with expensive gifts. Wu Zixu, a ranking official of Wu who had always been on guard against the state of Yue, saw the real motive of Gou Jian. He tried hard to warn Fu Chai, saying, "The conquest of Qi means winning a stretch of land as barren as a rock. But to us the state of Yue is like a disease in the vital organs." But Fu Chai refused to take his advice. As it was expected, the state of Wu was later defeated by the state of Yue and Fu Chai committed suicide.

Zuo Qinming's Chronicles

心懷叵測

xīn huái pǒ cè

心裏藏着難以猜測的主意；形容存心險惡，不可推測。

東漢末年，曹操準備率兵南征，但他擔心大軍南下後，涼州太守馬騰會襲擊京都洛陽。於是，他採納了謀士荀攸的建議，封馬騰為征南將軍，引他進京，然後殺掉。

馬騰接到詔書後，和幾個子姪商量去還是不去。兒子馬超主張去，姪兒馬岱主張不去。馬岱說：「曹操陰險毒辣，心懷叵測，叔父如果去了，恐怕會遭致殺害。」馬騰沒有聽馬岱的話，帶着五千兵馬來到京都，後來果然被曹操殺害。

出自《三國演義》

Harbouring Evil Designs

Said of someone with unpredictable evil intentions.

AT the end of the Eastern Han Dynasty, before Cao Cao started an expedition against the south, he feared that Ma Teng, governor of Liangzhou, might attack his capital Luoyang during his absence. On the suggestion of his advisor Xun You, he conferred the title of General of the Southern Expedition on Ma Teng with the intention of luring him into the capital and then killing him.

When Ma Teng received the edict, he discussed with his

son and nephew whether he should go to the capital or not. His son Ma Chao said that he should go while his nephew Ma Tai advised against it. Ma Tai said, "Cao Cao is a treacherous fellow who harbours evil designs. If you go you will probably meet death at his hand." Unheeding Ma Tai's warning, Ma Teng led five thousand soldiers and went to the capital, where he was indeed murdered by Cao Cao.

Tales of the Three Kingdoms

引錐刺股

yǐn zhuī cì gǔ

用錐子刺大腿；比喻發憤讀書，刻苦求知。

蘇秦，戰國時人，少有大志。但由於學識淺薄，得不到重用，甚至家裏的人都瞧不起他。這使他很難過，並受到很大刺激。他決心發憤讀書，增長學識。蘇秦經常讀書到深夜，疲倦了，難免打瞌睡。爲了振作精神，他拿了一把錐子，一打瞌睡，就猛刺大腿。後來，他終於成爲一個政治家、軍事家，游說齊、楚、燕、韓、趙、魏六國合縱抵抗秦國。

出自《戰國策》

Pricking One's Thigh with an Awl

Describing someone who studies assiduously with a firm determination.

SU Qin who lived during the Warring States Period was a young man with high aspirations. As he did not have much learning, he was never given any work of importance. Even people in his own family looked down on him. He felt miserable and deeply upset. So he made up his mind to study hard and improve himself. As he often read deep into the night, he sometimes found himself dozing off. To bestir himself, he placed an awl near him. Whenever he began to doze off, he would prick his thigh with it. He eventually became a statesman and military strategist going from place to place advocating a united front of the six states of Qi, Chu, Yan, Han, Zhao and Wei against the state of Qin.

Anecdotes of the Warring States

巧取豪夺

qiǎo   qǔ   háo   duó

以巧妙的办法骗取，用强力去掠夺；形容以欺骗和强力去夺取别人的珍贵物品。

宋代有個書畫家叫米芾，他只要打聽到誰家有古字畫，就以觀賞爲名借來臨摹，然後把臨摹品"歸還"人家，而自己留下眞品；有時他還故意把原本和摹本混在一起讓主人挑選，主人分辨不清，往往把摹本當作原本收回。有一次，米芾在船上遇見一個叫蔡攸的人，蔡攸把收藏的晉代書法家王羲之的眞迹給他看。米芾邊看邊盤算，對蔡攸說："我很喜歡它，想用一幅名畫跟您交換，可以嗎？"蔡攸毫不客氣地拒絕了。於是米芾就跑到船頭說："你如果不交換，我就跳河死在你面前！"蔡攸無奈，只好答應了。後來，人們把米芾這種行爲，叫做"巧取豪奪"。

出自《清波雜志》*

* 《清波雜志》宋周煇（公元1126年－？）撰，記述宋人雜事。

Seizing by Trick or by Force

Meaning to obtain valuable things of others by cheating or forcible means.

MI Fu was a painter and calligrapher of the Song Dynasty. Whenever he heard somebody owning an ancient work of calligraphy or an ancient painting, he would borrow it on the pretext of admiring it and make a copy of it. He would then return the copy to the owner and keep the genuine work himself. Sometimes he even deliberately took the original and the copy to the owner and asked the owner to pick it out. Being unable to tell the original from the copy, the owner sometimes mistakenly took the copy. Once Mi Fu met a man named Cai You on a boat. Cai showed him a masterpiece of the calligrapher Wang Xizhi of the Jin Dynasty in his collection. Mi Fu calculated as he looked at the calligraphy and then said to Cai You, "I like this calligraphy very much. I would like to exchange a famous painting for it." Cai You flatly refused him. Mi Fu then walked to the bow of the boat and said to Cai, "If you don't exchange it with me, I'll jump into the river and kill myself before you." Cai You had no alternative but to agree to the exchange. Later, people described Mi Fu's behaviour as "seizing by trick or by force".

Miscellaneous Notes on Qingbo*

*Notes on miscellaneous things and events of the Song Dynasty by Zhou Hui (1126-?) of the Song Dynasty.

未能免俗

wèi néng miǎn sú

指不能免於世上的習俗。

晉初名士阮咸，和他的叔父阮籍都是當時曠達不羈的文人。他們叔侄倆住在路南，阮家同族的其他人家住在路北。凡住在路北的人都很富有，住在路南的都很貧寒。當時有個風俗，每逢七月七日，大家都要曬衣服。有一年的這一天，路北阮姓人家大張旗鼓地曬衣服，都是些綾羅綢緞。阮咸沒有什麼好衣服，便用竹竿挑起一條粗布短褲曬在院子裏。有人看見，感到奇怪，問其究竟，阮咸回答說：「不能免於世俗，我也表示個意思吧！」

出自《世說新語》

Unable to Break Away from the Conventions

Meaning that one has to follow the worldly ways.

THE well-known scholar Yuan Xian of the early Jin Dynasty and his uncle Yuan Ji were both broad-minded and unconventional men of letters. They lived on the southern

58

side of a road while the other members of the Yuan clan lived on the northern side. Most of the people living on the northern side were rich and those on the southern side were poor. There was then the tradition of sunning clothes on the seventh day of the seventh month. On that day one year, when families on the northern side all put their silks and satins in the sun in a big display of colour, Yuan Xian sunned his short pants at the end of a bamboo pole because he had no good clothing. People were puzzled and asked him why. "Because I'm unable to break away from the conventions, I've to do this for appearance sake," answered Yuan Xian.

New Social Anecdotes

瓜田李下

guā tián lǐ xià

在瓜田裏和李樹下；比喻易於引起嫌疑和誤會。

　　古樂府《君子行》中有這樣幾句：“君子防未然，不處嫌疑間；瓜田不納履，李下不正冠。”意思是說：君子潔身自愛，不但平日要敦品勵行，而且要處處避免他人誤會。當經過瓜田時，即使鞋子掉了也不要彎腰去穿它，以免別人誤會偷瓜；在李樹下面走過時，即使帽子歪了也不要舉手去正它，因爲這可免除別人懷疑偷李子。

　　　　　　　　　　出自古樂府《君子行》＊

＊《君子行》樂府《平調曲》名。古辭今存。

In a Melon Plot and under a Plum Tree

Meaning circumstances that tend to give rise to suspicion and misconstruction.

AMONG the old folk songs is one called *Song of the Gentleman,* which has these lines: "A gentleman must prevent possible troubles and not place himself under suspicious circumstances. He is not to fasten his shoes in a melon plot or adjust his hat under a plum tree." It means that a gentleman must make himself respectable and regulate his conduct so as to avoid being misunderstood by others. When he walks by a melon plot, he is not to fasten his shoes even when they have come loose, and when he passes a tree laden with plums, he is not to raise his hands to adjust his hat even if it has become crooked so that no one will suspect him of trying to steal melons or plums.

Song of the Gentleman *

*The name of a song to the tune of *Ping Diao Qu* from the Music Bureau ballads.

生吞活剝

shēng tūn huó bāo

比喻生硬地搬用別人的言論或文辭。

唐朝時，棗強（今河北冀縣）縣尉張懷慶，不學無術，專愛抄襲別人詩句，冒充雅士。朝中大臣李義府寫了一首"鏤月爲歌扇，裁雲作舞衣"的五言詩。張懷慶便把這首詩照抄下來，只在每句前面硬添兩個字，湊成"生情鏤月爲歌扇，出性裁雲作舞衣"的七言詩。人們讀了張懷慶"創作"的詩，不知道是什麼意思，無不嘩然

大笑。有人根據他常常抄襲當時名人張昌齡、郭正一作品的行為，
譏笑他是："活剝張昌齡，生吞郭正一。"

出自《大唐新語》＊

＊《大唐新語》唐劉肅（約公元820年前後在世）撰，記載唐初至大歷末年
士大夫的政治生活、著作活動等。

Swallowing Raw and Skinning Alive

Meaning copying mechanically the views and writings of others.

ZHANG Huaiqing, the constable of Zaoqiang County (today's Jixian, Hebei Province) in the Tang Dynasty was a man who had neither learning nor skill. He made a habit of plagiarizing the poems of others and passing himself off as a refined scholar. Minister Li Yifu at the imperial court wrote a poem which began with these two lines: "Carving the moon into a fan for singer; Sewing the clouds into a dress for dancer." There were five characters in each line. Zhang Huaiqing copied the poem and mechanically added two more characters before each line, making it a poem with seven characters in each line. The two lines thus read: "With emotion, carving the moon into a fan for singer; out of nature, sewing the clouds into a dress for dancer." When people read the poem Zhang Huaiqing had "created", they split their sides with laughter because they could make neither head nor tail of it. As Zhang often copied the works of the famous Zhang Changling and Guo Zhengyi of the time, people ridiculed him as "skinning Zhang Changling alive and swallowing Guo Zhengyi raw".

*New Anecdotes of the Great Tang**

*By Liu Su (fl. around A.D.820) of the Tang Dynasty, it records the political and literary activities of ranking officials from the beginning of the Tang Dynasty to the end of the Dali reign (618-766).

外強中乾

wài qiáng zhōng gān

外表強壯，內裏虛弱；形容表面上強大，內部空虛。

春秋時，秦國和晉國之間發生了戰爭，秦穆公領兵打到了晉國的韓地，晉惠公率兵抵抗。晉惠公叫人給他的戰車套上鄭國產的駿馬，大臣慶鄭勸告說：「自古以來，打仗時都用本國的好馬，因為它適應本國的水土，熟悉道路，聽從使喚。如今您却使用外國的馬，這種馬外表看起來很強壯，實際上並沒有什麼能耐，打起仗來一緊張，就會亂踢亂叫，不聽指揮。到那時候，進退不得，您一定會後悔的！」晉惠公沒有聽從慶鄭的勸告。結果，戰鼓一響，鄭國馬就驚慌起來，無法駕馭，戰車陷入泥坑，想進不能，要退不得，晉軍大敗，連晉惠公也被秦軍捉去，當了俘虜。

出自《左傳》

Outwardly Strong but Inwardly Shrivelled

Meaning powerful in appearance but hollow inside.

A war broke out in the Spring and Autumn Period between the state of Qin and the state of Jin. When Duke Mu of Qin led his army to Han in the state of Jin, Duke Hui of Jin prepared to resist with his army and had a fine horse from the state of Zheng harnessed to his chariot. His minister Qing Zheng advised him, "Since ancient times, people have always used horses of their own country to fight battles because they are adapted to the local conditions, know the roads and answer to bidding. But you are now using a foreign horse. It looks outwardly strong but inwardly shrivelled. It'll bolt and neigh in the confusion of a battle and refuse to heed your directions. I'm sure you'll regret it when you find yourself being unable to advance and withdraw." Duke Hui did not accept Qing Zheng's advice, and as soon as the drums of battle began to sound, the horse from the state of Zheng became alarmed and uncontrollable. The chariot was bogged down in a quagmire and could neither advance nor retreat. The Jin army was utterly defeated and Duke Hui himself was captured by the Qin army.

Zuo Qinming's Chronicles

包藏禍心

bāo cáng huò xīn

心裏藏着壞主意。

春秋時，鄭國想同楚國交好，鄭國大夫公孫段將女兒許配楚國公子圍爲妻。公元前541年，公子圍借到鄭國迎親的機會，帶兵偸襲鄭國。鄭國掌握政務的子產見楚國人不懷好意，便派子羽對他們說：“我們鄭國城小，容納不了你們這麼多人，婚禮請在城外舉行吧！”楚國人不肯，要求入城。子羽回答說：“我們鄭國和你們楚國聯姻，本想依靠大國的保護而使國家安定，可是貴國却包藏禍心，打算暗攻我們吧！”公子圍見鄭國已有了戒備，於是放棄了偸襲的計劃。楚國人答應不帶武器，才被允許進城。

出自《左傳》

Having Secret Evil Intentions
With Evil Intent

IN the Spring and Autumn Period, as the state of Zheng wished to establish friendly relations with the state of Chu,

Gongsun Duan, a high official of Zheng, married his daughter to the Chu prince Wei. In the year 541 B.C., Prince Wei intended to take the opportunity of wedding in the state of Zheng to launch a surprise attack on Zheng. When Zi Chan, the official in charge of political affairs in Zheng, saw that the Chu people did not have good intentions, he sent Zi Yu to them and told them, "The capital city of Zheng is too small to hold so many of your people. The wedding will be held outside the city." When the Chu people insisted on marching into the city, Zi Yu said to them, "We thought with a marriage between Zheng and Chu we could obtain the protection of a big country to keep our country secure. We now find that you have secret evil intentions and want to launch a secret attack on us." When Prince Wei saw that the state of Zheng is on his guard, he abandoned his plan for a surprise attack and promised to go into the Zheng capital without carrying arms.

Zuo Qiuming's Chronicles

半途而廢

bàn tú ér fèi

半路上就停了下來；比喻做事沒有恒心，有始無終。

從前，有個讀書人叫樂羊子，離家去遠方拜師求學，可是過了一年就回來了。他的妻子正在織布，見丈夫回來，便問："你完成學業了嗎？"樂羊子回答說："沒有。走後我非常想念你，所以回來看看。"妻子一聽，很是生氣，就拿起一把剪刀對樂羊子說："你看，這用蠶繭做成的絲綫，由織布機一絲一綫地編織起來，日積月累才能織出成匹的絹布。現在我如果把它剪斷，豈不是前功盡棄，白費了時日！你出外求學也是這樣，知識要日積月累，如果半路就停下來，不是和剪斷絲綫一樣嗎？"樂羊子聽了妻子的話很受感動，於是重新出外求學，一去七年，直到完成學業才回來。

出自《後漢書》

Giving Up Halfway

Said of someone who lacks constancy of purpose to carry a job through to the end.

ONCE there was a scholar named Le Yangzi, who left home to study under a teacher in a faraway place. When he returned home a year later, his wife who was sitting at the loom weaving cloth asked him. "Have you finished your studies?" "No. But I missed you so much that I've come back to see you," answered Le Yangzi. His wife was angry. She took a pair of scissors and said to him, "The cocoons are unreeled and spun into yarns. The loom then weaves the yarns one by one into cloth. It takes months to finished a bolt of silk cloth. Now if I cut it with a pair of scissors, all I've done before will be wasted. It is all the same with your studies. Knowledge has to be accumulated day after day and month after month. If you give up halfway, isn't it like cutting the yarns with scissors?" Le Yangzi was deeply moved by what his wife had said. He left again and did not come back until he finished his studies seven years later.

History of the Later Han Dynasty

立錐之地

lì zhuī zhī dì

插錐的地方；形容極小的空間。

春秋時，楚國有個能歌善舞的藝人，名叫優孟。令尹孫叔敖深知優孟是位賢良的人才，待他很好。孫叔敖病危時對他的兒子說："我做了幾年官，沒積下什麼財產。我死後，你將會受窮，那時你可去找優孟想辦法。"幾年後，孫叔敖的兒子果然窮得靠賣柴度日。有一天，他在路上碰到優孟，便把父親臨終時的話說了一遍。優孟答應替他想辦法。

優孟回家後，摹仿孫叔敖的聲音笑貌，經過一年，已學得很像了。一天，楚莊王舉行宴會，優孟就裝扮成孫叔敖前去獻酒。莊王見了，大吃一驚，以為孫叔敖又復活了，便請他做楚國的令尹。優孟說要回去和妻子商量一下。三天後，優孟對莊王說："我的妻子叫我不要做楚國的令尹。她說，孫叔敖忠心耿耿，廉潔奉公，幫助莊王做了天下的霸主，但他死後，兒子卻窮得連插一根錐子的地方都沒有，只能靠賣柴度日。如果落得這樣的下場，還不如死了的好！"莊王聽了，明白話中的意思，立即答應照顧孫叔敖的兒子。

出自《史記》

A Place to Stick an Awl
A Foothold

Meaning a very small space or piece of land.

YOU Meng was an excellent singing and dancing artist of the state of Chu during the Spring and Autumn Period. He became a good friend of Minister Sunshu Ao, who knew that You Meng was an honest person. Later, when Sunshu Ao was critically ill, he said to his son, "I've served as an official for a few years, but I haven't amassed any property. When I die, you may suffer from poverty. You can then go to You Meng and ask him to find a way out for you." A few years after his father's death, Sunshu Ao's son became so poor that he had to sell firewood for a living. He met You Meng on the street one day and repeated to him what his father had said to him. You Meng promised to help him.

After returning home, You Meng began to learn to mimic Sunshu's voice and gesture. After a year's practice, he became very successful. One day, Duke Zhuang of Chu gave a banquet and You Meng disguised himself as Sunshu Ao and went up to the duke to offer a drink of wine. The duke was greatly surprised for he thought Sunshu Ao had come back to life. He told You Meng that he could serve as his minister. But You Meng said that he had to go back and consult with his wife. Three days later, You Meng said to Duke Zhuang, "My wife told me not to serve as a minister of Chu. She said that Sunshu Ao was a loyal, honest and upright official. He helped Duke Zhuang to have achieved hegemony. But after he died, his son became so poor that he didn't even have a speck of land to stick an awl. He had to make a living by selling firewood. It's better to die than to end up like that." On hearing it, Duke Zhuang saw what he meant and immediately promised to help Sunshu Ao's son.

Records of the Historian

司空見慣

sī kōng jiàn guàn

"司空"看得習慣了；形容經常見到，不足爲奇。

唐代著名詩人劉禹錫，曾做過蘇州刺史。有一天，司空（掌管工程的官）李紳請他喝酒，並叫歌女作陪。劉禹錫喝得大醉，即席賦詩一首："鬢髻梳頭宮樣裝（一作"高髻雲鬟宮樣裝"），春風一曲《杜韋娘》。司空見慣渾閒事，斷盡江南刺史腸。"這首詩的頭兩句描寫美麗的舞姿和動人的歌聲；後兩句是說：你這位司空看慣了這種奢華綺靡的場面，覺得極爲平常，可我這個蘇州刺史却難得見到這種場面，因而，實在太激動了。

＊《本事詩》唐孟啓作，所記多爲唐人詩的本事。

A Common Occurence

Meaning literally that the thing in question is a common occurence or sight for Sikong, or Minister of Works.

THE famous poet Liu Yuxi of the Tang Dynasty once served as governor of Suzhou. One day Li Shen, the Minister of Works, invited him to a drinking feast accompanied by singing-girls. Liu Yuxi was thoroughly drunk and composed an impromptu poem which reads:

> Her hair is done in the beautiful palace style,
> Her song *Maiden Du Wei* drifts like spring breeze;
> A common sight for the Minister of Works
> Moves the southern governor to deep emotions.

The first two lines describe the attractive singing-girl and her beautiful song while the last two lines say that the splendid sight, though commonplace to the Minister of Works, had greatly agitated the governor of Suzhou, who had hardly seen a similar thing.

*Narrative Poems**

*A collection of Tang narrative poems compiled by Meng Qi of the Tang Dynasty.

成也蕭何，敗也蕭何

chéng yě xiāo hé，bài yě xiāo hé

成功在蕭何，失敗也在蕭何；比喻事情的成敗都由於同一個人。

劉邦在做漢王時，韓信投奔到他門下當了一名小官，因沒法施展他的軍事才能，便逃走了。丞相蕭何聽說韓信走了，帶了隨從連夜追趕。追回以後，蕭何推薦韓信做了大將軍。從此，韓信南征北戰，馳騁疆場，為劉邦完成統一大業、建立漢朝立下了累累功勳。

劉邦做了皇帝以後，對韓信却不放心了，就解除了他的兵權，改封為楚王，後又降為淮陰侯。後來，劉邦去討伐代相陳豨。因韓信與陳豨曾有交往，有人乘機向劉邦的妻子呂后告密說，韓信見陳豨事敗，正在謀劃造反。呂后聽了，與蕭何商量出一個計策，把韓信騙進宮中，當場殺害。

當初，極力推薦韓信做大將的是蕭何；後來設計殺韓信的也是蕭何。所以，人們說："成也蕭何，敗也蕭何"。

出自《容齋續筆》*

* 《容齋續筆》筆記，南宋洪邁（公元1123－1202年）撰。筆記分《隨筆》、《續筆》、《三筆》、《四筆》、《五筆》五集。

It Was Done by Xiao He and Undone Also by Him

Meaning that the success and failure of a thing has been caused by one and the same person.

WHEN Liu Bang was the king of Han, Han Xin served under him as a minor official and had no opportunity to display his military talents. So he left without saying goodbye. When Prime Minister Xiao He heard that Han Xin had gone, he took some followers with him and gave chase. After he caught up with Han Xin, he recommended him to serve as the

Grand General. From then on, Han Xin fought south and north on the battlefield and rendered an outstanding service to Liu Bang's unification of the country.

After Liu Bang became emperor, he could not trust Han Xin. He stripped Han Xin of his military command and enfeoffed him as the Duke of Chu and later demoted him to the Marquis of Huaiyin. Liu Bang later launched an expedition against the acting Prime Minister Chen Xi. Because Han Xin had contact with Chen Xi, somebody informed against him to Liu Bang's wife, Queen Lü, saying that knowing Chen Xi had been defeated, Han Xin was plotting for a revolt. Queen Lü consulted with Xiao He and they set a trap to lure Han Xin into the palace and killed him then and there.

Since it was Xiao He who recommended Han Xin to serve as the Grand General and it was also Xiao He who set the trap to kill Han Xin, people said, "It's done by Xiao He and also undone by Xiao He."

*More Notes from Rong Studio**

*By Hong Mai (1123-1202) of the Southern Song Dynasty, the notes are in five parts: Random Notes, More Notes, Third Volume of Notes, Fourth Volume of Notes and Fifth Volume of Notes.

有恃無恐

yǒu shì wú kǒng

有了依仗，什麼都不怕；形容那些依仗勢力而胡作非為的人。

　　春秋時，齊孝公乘魯國受災之機，率軍攻打魯國。魯僖公得知，派大夫展喜勸說齊孝公罷兵。展喜對齊孝公說："我們國君聽說您親臨我國，特派我前來慰勞。"齊孝公以為魯國正在鬧饑荒，一定怕打仗，便問："魯國人害怕了嗎？"展喜答道："個別見識短淺的人害怕，但魯國多數人却沒有絲毫畏懼。"齊孝公輕蔑地說："你們國庫空虛，田裏連青草都不長，依仗什麼不害怕呢？"展喜說："依仗先王的賜命！從前魯國的祖先周公和齊國的祖先姜太公同心協力輔佐周成王，成王對他倆十分感激，讓他們立盟說，後世子孫要友好，不要互相侵害。誰廢棄祖宗的盟約，誰就對不起祖宗，就要受到懲罰。我們魯國就是憑着這一點才不害怕的。"齊孝公被說得無話可答，只好班師回國。

出自《左傳》

Undaunted on Account of Powerful Backing

Applied now to someone who does evil under powerful protection.

DUKE Xiao of the state of Qi in the Spring and Autumn Period took the opportunity that the state of Lu was struck by a natural disaster and launched an attack on the latter. When Duke Xi of Lu heard the news of the coming attack, he sent a high official named Zhan Xi to try to persuade Duke Xiao to stop the attack. Zhan Xi said to Duke Xiao of Qi, "Our sovereign's heard that you're coming to our country. He sent me to bring gifts of welcome to you." Thinking that the state of Lu is suffering from the natural disaster and must be afraid of starting a war, Duke Xiao asked Zhan Xi, "Are the people of Lu scared?" Zhan Xi answered, "Some shortsighted men might be scared, but most of the Lu people are unafraid." Duke Xiao said disdainfully, "Your government coffers are empty and even grass doesn't grow in your fields. What is it that makes you unafraid?" To this, Zhan Xi said, "We have the backing of the former kings. Duke Zhou, the ancester of Lu, and Duke Jiang, the ancester of Qi, had worked together to assist King Cheng of the Zhou Dynasty. King Cheng was grateful to them and asked them to make a pledge that their sons and grandsons in the later generations would always be friendly to one another and never hurt one another. Whoever breaks the pledge, he will be punished for letting our ancestors down. This is what makes us unafraid." Duke Xiao was quite at a loss what to answer and had to withdraw his troops and went back to his country.

Zuo Qiuming's Chronicles

老蚌生珠

lǎo bàng shēng zhū

老蚌生出了珍珠；比喻年老得子。

東漢老將韋端，有兩個兒子，大的叫元將，小的仲將，都是很優秀的人才，並且和當時的名人孔融關係密切。有一次，孔融寫信給韋端說："前天元將來，我見他學問高深，才華橫溢，意志堅強，度量很大，將來必定是一個有本領，能創立偉業的人才；昨天仲將又來，我看他做事有條理，資質聰明，思維敏捷，心地敦厚老實，待人熱情誠懇，將來一定是位能繼承家業的好子弟。想不到你這位老蚌生出了一對寶貴的珍珠。"

出自《與韋端書》*

* 《與韋端書》漢末文學家孔融（公元153－208年）寫給韋端的一封信。

An Old Oyster Yields Pearls

A euphony for begetting offspring at old age.

THE old general Wei Duan of the Eastern Han Dynasty had two sons. The elder one was named Yuanjiang and the younger one, Zhongjiang. Both of them were fine young men and close friends of the famous Kong Rong. In a letter to Wei Duan, Kong Rong wrote, "Yuanjiang came to see me the day before yesterday. I find that he is well learned and brimming over with talent. He is firm in his determination and broad-minded. I am sure he will carve out a brilliant career for himself. Zhongjiang came to see me too yesterday. He is systematic and clever. He has a quick mind and is honest and warm-hearted to others. I am sure he will be a fine son for inheriting the family property. I never expected that an old oyster like you could brought forth two precious pearls.

Letter to Wei Duan*

*By Kong Rong (A.D.153-208), a man of letters at the end of the Han Dynasty.

老當益壯
lǎo dāng yì zhuàng

表示年老而志氣更加壯盛。

東漢人馬援，自幼就胸懷去邊疆從事放牧的志向。長大以後，馬援在郡裏當上了小官吏。有一次，他在押解犯人時，覺得犯人可憐，半路上便把犯人釋放了，自己逃到北地郡躲藏起來，在那裏放牧，實現了自己的志願。他常說："做個大丈夫，越窮困，志向越要堅定；年紀越大，志氣應該更加壯盛。"後來，馬援成為東漢名將，立下許多戰功。

出自《後漢書》

Old but More Spirited

Hale and Hearty

Said of someone who is vigorous in spirit though advanced in years.

MA Yuan of the Eastern Han Dynasty made up his mind to herd animals in the frontier regions even when he was very young. He became a minor official in a prefecture when he grew up. Once when he was escorting some prisoners to another place, feeling pity for the prisoners, he set them free on the way, while he himself fled to a northern prefecture, where he herded animals as he had always wished to do. He often said, "The poorer a great man becomes, the firmer his determination should be; the older he grows, the more spirited he should become." Ma Yuan later became a famous general of the Eastern Han Dynasty and distinquished himself in many battles.

History of the Later Han Dynasty

老驥伏櫪

lǎo jì fú lì

伏於馬槽的老馬；比喻人雖年老，但仍有雄心壯志。

公元207年，曹操率領大軍北征烏桓，在取勝回師途中，路經面臨滄海的碣石山下。他滿懷勝利的喜悅，揮鞭跳馬，登山眺望，而後寫下了著名的詩篇《步出夏門行‧龜雖壽》。其中有四句說：「老驥伏櫪，志在千里；烈士暮年，壯心不已。」當時，曹操五十三歲，已到暮年。北方雖已統一，但南方的孫權和西蜀的劉備仍各據一方，詩句表達了他統一全中國的雄心壯志。

出自《魏武帝集》＊

＊《魏武帝集》三國時政治家、軍事家、詩人曹操（公元155－220年）作。原集久佚，現有《曹操集》。

An Old Horse at the Trough

Meaning someone who is old but still have boundless aspirations.

IN the year A.D.207, Cao Cao launched an expedition against the Wuhuan in the north. After his truimphant return from the expedition, he passed the Jieshi Hill by the sea. With the joy of victory, he climbed to the top of the hill on his horse and there composed his famous poem *Coming Out of the Summer Gate*. There are these four lines in the poem: "An old horse at the trough, Still aspires to travel long distances. A hero in his old age, Never gives up his lofty ideals." Cao

Cao was then fifty-three years old. Although he had unified the north, the south was still controlled by Sun Quan and Liu Bei. The poem expressed his determination to unify the whole country.

Collected Works of Emperor Wu of Wei*

*A collection of the works of Cao Cao (A.D.155-220), a statesman, military strategist and poet of the Three Kingdoms period. The original book was lost and only the *Collected Works of Cao Cao* is extant.

仰人鼻息

yǎng rén bí xī

仰賴別人鼻子裏呼出來的氣息；形容依仗別人才能生存，或看別人的臉色行事。

東漢末年，一些州、郡的官吏各佔地盤，互相攻伐，形成軍閥割據的局面。

漢獻帝時，渤海太守袁紹想攻佔冀州，謀士逢紀向他獻計：一面寫信給北平太守公孫瓚，鼓動他引兵南下，進攻冀州；一面派荀諶、高干等人去冀州對刺史韓馥說：“公孫瓚南下，袁紹也有所行動，看來你已經處在十分危險的境地了！爲你着想，不如主動把冀州讓給袁紹，這樣，旣可以獲得讓賢的美名，又可以保住自家性命，實在是兩全之策。”無能的韓馥竟然同意了。可是韓馥的部下極力反對，勸韓馥說：“冀州有强兵百萬，糧草充足，而袁紹不過是窮軍孤客，依賴我們的鼻息而活着，就像吃奶的孩子，斷了奶汁，立刻就會餓死，我們憑什麼把冀州讓給他呢？”但韓馥不聽，派自己的兒子將冀州牧的印綬送給了袁紹。

袁紹得了冀州，軍力大增。韓馥後來却被他逼得自殺了。

出自 《後漢書》

To Be Dependent on the Whims of Others

Meaning to depend on others for one very existence or to be under someone's thumb.

TOWARDS the end of the Eastern Han Dynasty, some of the prefectural governors marked out their territories and attacked one another, carving the country into a number of warlord regimes.

At the time of Emperor Xian, as Yuan Shao, governor of Bohai, wanted to seize Jizhou, his advisor Feng Ji devised a stratagem for him. On the one hand, he wrote a letter to Governor of Beiping Gongsun Zan encouraging him to move his army southward in an attack on Jizhou, and on the other hand, he sent Xun Chen and Gao Gan to Jizhou to inform Governor Han Fu of the attack. "Gongsun Zan is moving southward. Yuan Shao is also on the move," they said. "You're in grave danger. It's for your own good to hand over Jizhou to Yuan Shao. You'll not only have a good reputation for handing over the reins to someone who's competent, but also save yourself and your family. It's a way out to satisfy both sides." To everyone's surprise, the weakling Han Fu agreed to their suggestion despite the fact that his subordinates were deadly against it. They said to Han Fu, "Jizhou has a million soldiers and more than enough grain and fodder while Yuan Shao is a needy man who had to depend on us for a living like a baby fed with milk. Once the flow of milk stops, he'll die. Why should we hand over Jizhou to Yuan Shao?" But Han Fu would not listen to them. He sent his son over to Yuan Shao with the seal of the governor of Jizhou.

After Yuan Shao gained possession of Jizhou, his army grew greatly in size. Han Fu was eventually forced to commit suicide.

History of the Later Han Dynasty

行屍走肉

xíng shī zǒu ròu

可以走動的屍體，沒有靈魂的肉體；比喻庸碌無能，只具形骸，缺乏生活意義的人。

東漢時，有個名叫任末的人，常常勉勵自己說：「人要成才，就要刻苦學習。」任末到十四歲時，還沒有一位固定的老師，只得經常揹着書箱到遠處多方求教。有時，他在樹林裏用茅草搭起棚子住下，把荊條削尖作筆，刻出樹汁作墨，勤奮學習寫字；夜晚，映着月光讀書，沒有月光時則點着蒿草照明。讀書如有所得，便連忙寫在衣服上。這樣日復一日，年復一年，任末終於成了學問家。不少人慕名而來，拜在他門下求學。

任末臨終時，告誡他的學生說：「假如一個人能夠勤奮學習，就是死了，也好像還活着；不學習的人，即使活着，也只不過是一個可以走動的屍體和沒有靈魂的軀殼罷了！」

出自《拾遺記》＊

＊《拾遺記》志怪小說集，東晉王嘉（公元？－390年左右）作。

A Walking Corpse

A Man of Straw

Said of someone who is utterly worthless and to whom life has no meaning.

REN Mo of the Eastern Han Dynasty often urged himself, "If a man is to become a useful person, he must study diligently." But by the time he was fourteen, he hadn't yet had a regular teacher. He had to travel a long distance with his book chest to ask for advice. Sometimes, he lived in a straw shed in the woods and used a twig as a pen and tree sap as ink to write with. At night, he read by the moonlight. When there was no moon, he would light a torch. When he found inspirations from his reading, he would write them down on his clothes. Day after day and year after year, Ren Mo eventually became a very learned man. Out of admiration, many people came to him and became his students.

Before he died, he admonished his students, "For a man who studies hard, even when he dies, he still seems to be alive. For a man who doesn't study, even when he's alive, he's only a walking corpse, a shell without a soul."

*Collection of Lost Stories**

*A collection of supernatural stories by Wang Jia (?-c.390) of the Eastern Jin Dynasty.

各自爲政

gè zì wéi zhèng

各人處理各人的政事；表示各人按各人的主張辦事，不顧整體。

春秋時，鄭國攻打宋國，宋國大將華元率兵抵抗。決戰前夕，華元爲了鼓舞士氣，特地宰羊設酒犒勞將士。將士們吃着羊肉，喝着美酒，一片歡騰。唯獨不讓駕車的羊斟參加宴會。他呆呆地坐在一旁，饞涎欲滴。

決戰開始，華元命令羊斟把戰車趕向鄭軍右方兵力薄弱的地方，以便指揮宋軍向這裏突破，可是羊斟却反向而馳，將戰車趕往鄭軍左方兵卒密集的地方。華元大叫："停車！停車！"羊斟得意地回答說："先前吃羊的事你作主，今日趕車的事我作主！"說完，揮鞭把戰車趕到鄭軍陣地。一羣鄭兵趁機蜂擁而上，把華元捉住。宋軍見主將被俘，軍心大亂，很快便敗下陣來。

出自《左傳》

Each Following His Own Policy

Meaning each person doing things his own way in disregard of the overall situation.

IT happened in the Spring and Autumn Period. The state of Zheng started an attack against the state of Song. The Song general Hua Yuan resisted with his army. On the eve of the decisive battle, Hua Yuan gave a feast of mutton and wine to his soldiers to raise their morale. The feast went on with much merry-making. But Yang Zhen, the driver of Hua's chariot, was not allowed to come to the feast. He had to sit lonely on the side with his mouth watering.

When the decisive battle began, Hua Yuan ordered Yang Zhen to drive the chariot to the weak right flank of the Zheng army so that the Song army could make a breakthrough there. But Yang Zhen drove the chariot in the opposite direction to the left flank of the Zheng army where there was a large concentration of soldiers. "Stop the chariot! Stop the chariot!" cried Hua Yuan. "It was you who decided who was to eat mutton. It's now my turn to decide where the chariot is to go!" answered complacently Yang Zhen. As he said so, he drove the chariot right to the positions of the Zheng army. The Zheng soldiers swarmed over and captured Hua Yuan. When the Song soldiers saw that their general had been taken prisoner, their morale was greatly shaken and they were soon defeated by the enemy.

Zuo Qiuming's Chronicles

州官放火

zhōu guān fàng huǒ

形容上層統治者的蠻橫無理。

宋朝時，有個名叫田登的州官。爲了維護他的尊嚴，下令不准人們用"燈"字。誰要是用了，不挨竹板打，就受皮鞭抽。鬧得州裏人說話、寫字，都要格外小心。

有一年燈節快要到了，州裏要放燈三天，管燈火的官員發了愁。因爲按慣例要先寫個告示，讓大家早知道。他在告示上不敢寫"燈"字，只得寫："本州依照慣例，放火三天！"告示一貼出，人們看了不禁啼笑皆非。

出自《老學庵筆記》＊

＊《老學庵筆記》記載遺聞軼事、考訂詩文和民間傳說。宋陸游（公元1125－1210年）作。

The Magistrate Sets Fire

Describing the rudeness and unreasonableness of the rulers.

THERE was a magistrate named Tian Deng in the Song Dynasty. To safeguard his personal dignity, he decreed that no one was allowed to use the word "lantern" which is a homonym of his name Deng. People had to be very careful for whoever inadvertently used the word "lantern" in his speech or writing they would be beaten with a bamboo pole or lashed with a leather whip.

People then had the tradition of celebrating the Lantern Festival by lighting fancy lanterns for three days. When Lantern Festival was near that year, the official in charge of the celebration found himself in a dilemma because he had to write a notice to inform the public. Not daring to use the word "lantern", he wrote a notice which read: "According to the usual practice, the prefecture is to set fire for three days." Having read the notice, people did not know whether to laugh or cry.

Notes from the Old Scholar's Hamlet*

*A collection of anecdotes, textual criticism of poems and essays, and folk tales by Lu You (1125-1210) of the Song Dynasty.

休戚相關

xiū qī xiāng guān

喜悦和悲哀互相關聯着；形容雙方關係密切，利害一致。

春秋時代，晉厲公在位的時候，晉襄公的曾孫姬周不在晉國，而在周朝的貴族單襄公家裏做家臣。他雖然離開祖國，但每當聽到晉國有喜慶事情，就笑容滿面；如果聽到晉國發生了什麼災禍，便十分憂愁。單襄公臨終時對兒子單頃公說：“姬周能同晉國共享歡樂，共分憂愁，眞是不忘其本！他將來回到晉國後，一定會受到人們的愛戴，你要誠懇地待他呀！”後來，晉國發生動亂，晉厲公被殺，晉國派人把姬周請回國，擁立爲國君。

出自《國語》＊

＊《國語》歷史書籍，記載西周末到春秋時的歷史，相傳爲春秋左丘明作。

Sharing Joys and Sorrows
In Weal or Woe

Said of two parties that have close ties and identity of interests.

WHEN Duke Li was reigning in the state of Jin during the Spring and Autumn Period, Ji Zhou, the great grandson of Duke Xiang of Jin, was away from home serving as a retainer in the house of Duke Shanxiang, an aristocrat of the Zhou Dynasty. Although he was away from his native country, he was all smiles when he heard goods news of the state of Jin and laden with anxieties when he heard bad news about the state of Jin. Before his death, Duke Shanxiang said to his son, "Ji Zhou shares joys and sorrows with the state of Jin and never forgets his country. When he goes back to the state of Jin in the future, he will surely be loved and supported by the people. You must treat him sincerely." A riot later broke out in Jin and Duke Li was killed. The state of Jin asked Ji Zhou to go back and put him in the throne.

*Anecdotes of the States**

*A book of history recording events from the end of the Western Zhou Dynasty to the Spring and Autumn Period and usually attributed to Zuo Qiuming of the Spring and Autumn Period.

名落孫山

míng　luò　sūn　shān

名字落在孫山後面；比喻考試、比賽落選。

宋朝時，蘇州有個叫孫山的書生，他生性幽默，言談風趣，人稱"滑稽才子"。有一年，孫山去投考，一位同鄉請他帶着自己的兒子一同應試。發榜時，同鄉的兒子沒有考取，孫山的名字列在榜上最後一名。回到家裏，當那位同鄉打聽自己的兒子是否考中時，孫山隨口謅了兩句詩："解名盡處是孫山，賢郎更在孫山外。"同鄉知道兒子沒有考中，便快快走開了。

出自《過庭錄》＊

＊《過庭錄》筆記，宋范公偁（約公元1147年前後在世）撰。

Falling behind Sun Shan

Meaning having failed in a competitive examination or a contest.

IN the Song Dynasty, there was a scholar named Sun Shan in Suzhou. Being a man full of charm and wit, he was known as the Humorous Scholar. One year, Sun Shan went with the son of a fellow townsman to take the imperial civil examination. When the list of successful candidates was published, Sun Shan found that the son of his fellow townsman had failed while his own name was at the end of the list. When he went back, his fellow townsman asked him if his son had been successful. He answered with an impromptu verse of two lines: "At the end of the list is Sun Shan; And your son is behind Sun Shan." His fellow townsman realized that his son had failed, and left unhappily.

Notes of Guoting *

*By Fan Gongcheng (fl. around 1147) of the Song Dynasty.

多難興邦

duō nàn xīng bāng

患難多反而能使國家振興；常用於激勵人們去克服困難，從而取得成就。

西晉末年，國勢衰弱。北方的少數民族乘機向晉朝進犯，先後擄去晉朝的兩個皇帝。當時，左丞相司馬睿鎮守建康（今南京）。他是晉朝的宗室，又掌握着軍政大權。祖逖、劉琨等將領，一面領兵北伐，一面遣使上書，勸司馬睿繼任帝位，把國家大事擔當起來，並且說：“國家遭到這麼多的危難，但只要從中吸取教訓，奮發圖強，反倒可以復興晉朝，使國家強盛起來。”後來，司馬睿果然這樣做了，當了皇帝，建立了東晉。

出自《晉書》

Many Hardships May Rejuvenate a Nation

This is often used to encourage people to achieve success by overcoming difficulties.

AT the end of the Western Jin Dynasty, the strength of the country was dissipated. The minority nationalities in the north took the opportunity to make encroachments upon the Jin Dynasty and captured one after the other two Jin emperors. Sima Rui, the Left Minister, was then commanding the garrison of Jiankang (today's Nanjing). He was a member of the Jin imperial clan and held both military and political power. Zu Ti, Liu Kun and some other generals, while leading their armies in an northern expedition, wrote a petition to

87

Sima Rui urging him to succeed to the throne and take the responsibilities of managing the affairs of the state. They also wrote, "The country is experiencing many dangers and hardships. But if we can draw lessons from them and work with a will, the Jin Dynasty may be rejuvenated and the country may become strong and prosperous." Sima later followed their advice and became emperor with the establishment of the Eastern Jin Dynasty.

History of the Eastern Jin Dynasty

亦步亦趨

yì bù yì qū

跟着走，跟着快走；比喻事事追隨和摹仿他人。

春秋時，孔子的學生顏回對老師十分崇拜，事事追隨摹仿，連走路的姿態，說話的腔調，都要學孔子的樣子。有一回，顏回對孔子說：「老師慢步走，我也跟着慢步走；老師快步走，我也跟着快步走；老師跑，我也跟着跑；老師飛奔，我只能驚異地瞪着眼睛，從老師脚步揚起的灰塵中看着您的背影了！」

出自《莊子》*

*《莊子》莊周（公元前369－前286年）及其弟子撰寫。莊周為道家學派的創始人之一。

Following Someone at Every Step

Meaning following or imitating someone in every thing.

AT Spring and Autumn time, Confucius' student Yan Hui adored his teacher with so much devotion that he imitated him in every thing he did, including even his gait and the way he spoke. Once Yan Hui said to Confucius, "When my teacher walks in slow steps, I follow in slow steps; when my teacher walks in quick steps, I follow in quick steps; when my teacher runs, I run after him. But when my teacher dashes forward, I can only stare in surprise and watch his back disappearing in a cloud of dust kicked up by his feet!"

The Book of Zhuang Zi*

*By Zhuang Zhou (369-286 B.C.), one of the founders of the Taoist school of philosophy, and his disciples.

安步當車

ān bù dàng chē

不慌不忙地步行，代替坐車子。

戰國時，齊國有個很有才能的人叫顏斶（Chù）。有一次，齊宣王召見他，說："顏斶，過來！"顏斶却說："大王，過來！"齊宣王見他這樣傲慢，很不高興。左右的大臣們也很生氣，質問顏斶："大王是君，你是臣，國王讓你過來，你不但不遵命，反而讓他過來，這成何體統！"顏斶回答說："你們太不明白事理了。要是我走過去，說明我仰慕權勢，大王如果到我這裏來，說明他禮賢下士。與其讓我仰慕權勢，倒不如讓大王落個禮賢下士的好名聲。"齊宣王聽後問道："到底是國王高貴，還是賢士高貴？"顏斶笑道："我看還是賢士高貴。"宣王問他為什麼，顏斶說："過去秦國攻打齊國時，曾命令全軍：有敢在賢士柳下季的墓地伐一棵樹者，處以死刑；有能得到齊王首級者封萬戶侯，賜千金。由此看來，君王的頭還不如柳下季墓地上的一棵樹。"

齊宣王無言以對，客氣地說："顏先生果然名不虛傳。今天聽了您的話，十分欽佩。您到我這兒來吧，每餐有肉，出門乘車，榮華富貴享受不盡！"顏斶淡淡地說："謝謝大王的厚恩，我還是回去吧！我覺得，餓了吃粗茶淡飯比肉還香；不慌不忙地步行比坐車子還舒服；這樣的生活多麼自在自樂，無憂無慮啊！"顏斶說完，又向齊王道了聲"謝謝"，轉身就走了。

出自《戰國策》

Strolling Rather than Riding in a Carriage

Meaning that strolling leisurely is just as comfortable as riding in a carriage.

YAN Chu was a man of great talent in the state of Qi during the Warring States Period. Once King Xuan of Qi summoned him to an interview and said to him, "Come here, Yan Chu!" But Yan Chu said, "Come here, Your Majesty!" King Xuan was displeased by his arrogance. The court officials present were also angry. "His Majesty is the sovereign and you are his subject. How could you ask His Majesty to come over instead of you obeying His Majesty? This is downright outrageous!" they called Yan Chu to account. "How can you be so insensible?" Yan Chu countered. "If I go over, it will show that I'm looking up to power and glory. If His Majesty comes over, it will show that he treats a scholar with courtesy. Why not give His Majesty a good reputation for treating a scholar with courtesy instead of letting me looking up to power and glory?" King Xuan then asked him, "Who is more valuable, a king or a scholar?" Yan Chu smiled and said, "I think the scholar is more valuable." When the king asked him why, Yan said, "When the state of Qin launched an attack against the state of Qi in the past, an order was issued to the whole army: Anyone who dared to fell a tree at Scholar Liu Xiaji's grave was to be punished by death, and anyone who could cut off the head of the Qi king would be given a fief of ten thousand households and a thousand pieces of gold. This shows that a king's head is worth less than a tree at Liu Xiaji's grave."

Overwhelmed by Yan Chu's eloquence, the king said politely, "You truly deserve your reputation. I wholly admire what you've said today. Come and join my staff. You'll be served meat at every meal and a carriage when you go out. There'll be more honour and glory than you can ever enjoy!" But Yan Chu said lukewarmly, "I'm grateful for Your Majesty's generous offer, but I would rather go home. To me, plain tea and simple food are more delicious than meat when I'm hungry, and strolling leisurely is more comfortable than riding in a carriage. The life I live is wholly satisfactory and completely carefree." When he finished, he thanked the king, turned round and left.

Anecdotes of the Warring States

江郎才盡

jiāng　láng　cái　jìn

江淹的才智用完了；比喻才思減退。

　　南北朝時，梁朝人江淹，年輕時好學不倦，寫出不少精彩的詩文，成為當時有名氣的文學家，人稱"江郎"。可是，他到晚年，才思減退，詩文平庸。傳說，有一次，他做了個夢，夢見一個自稱郭璞（晋代著名文學家）的人，對他說："我有一支筆放在你這兒多年了，現在可以還給我了。"江淹向懷中一摸，果然有一支五彩筆，便還給了這個自稱郭璞的人。從此以後，江淹再也寫不出優美的詩文了，所以人們說他的才智已經用完。

出自《南史》

Master Jiang Has Exhausted His Talent

Meaning that one's talent and creativeness have degenerated.

JIANG Yan of the Liang Dynasty during the period of the Southern and Northern Dynasties studied diligently when he was young, and earned considerable literary fame on account of the brilliant poems and essays that he had written. People called him "Master Jiang". But when he reached old age, his talent seemed to have deteriorated and his writings became rather mediocre. It was said that he once had a dream. In his dream, a man who claimed to be Guo Pu (a famous writer of the Jin Dynasty) said to him, "I left a pen with you many years ago. I want it back now." Jiang Yan put his hand into his pocket, and indeed there was a multi-coloured pen there. Jiang returned the pen to the man who called himself Guo Pu. From then on, Jiang Yan was never able to write any beautiful poems and essays. That was why people said that Master Jiang had exhausted his talent.

History of the Southern Dynasties

好好先生

háo háo xiān shēng

事事都説好的人；指誰也不敢得罪，只求相安無事。

東漢末年，有個叫司馬徽的人，從來不議論別人的短處，與人說話不管好壞，總是說好。有一次，他在路上遇到一個熟人，那人問他："先生，你好嗎？"他回答說："好。"又有一次，有個老朋友到他家來，十分傷心地談起自己的兒子死了，誰知司馬徽也說："太好了。"等那位朋友走後，妻子責備他說："人家以爲你是個有德操的人，所以相信你，把心裏話講給你聽，可是，你爲什麼聽人家說兒子死了，反而竟說'太好了'呢？"司馬徽聽了妻子的話，不慌不忙地說："好，你說的話也很好哇！"從此，人們都稱司馬徽"好好先生"。

出自《古今譚概》*

*《古今譚概》筆記，明馮夢龍（公元1574－1646年）作。

Mr. Fine

Said of someone who shows approval to everything and tries not to offend anybody for the sake of peace.

A man named Sima Hui who lived at the end of the Eastern Han Dynasty was known to have never spoken ill of anybody. Whatever the others spoke about, he always said that it was fine. Once he met an acquaintance on the street. The man asked him, "How are you, sir?" He said, "Fine." At another time, an old friend came to his home and brokenheartedly told him that his son had died. He was surprised to hear that Sima Hui said, "That's fine." After the man had left, Sima's wife rebuked him, saying, "He thought you were a man of virtue and trusted you. That's why he told you what was on his mind. Why did you say 'It's fine' when he told you that his son had died?" After hearing his wife's words, Sima said unhurriedly, "Fine. What you said is fine." From then on, Sima Hui became known as Mr. Fine.

*Anecdotes Past and Present**

*A collection of anecdotes by Feng Menglong (1574-1646) of the Ming Dynasty.

如火如荼

rú huǒ rú tú

像火一樣紅，像荼花一樣白；比喻氣勢旺盛。

春秋末年，吳、晉兩國互相爭奪霸主地位，吳王夫差打算用武力來壓服晉定公。一天夜晚，夫差命令全軍將士出營列隊，共擺了三個萬人方陣。中軍穿着白色衣裳，白色鎧甲，打着白色旗幟，帶着白色羽毛裝飾的弓箭，遠遠望去，好像原野上盛開的荼花。左軍穿着紅色衣裳，紅色鎧甲，打着紅色旗幟，帶着用紅色羽毛裝飾的弓箭，遠遠望去，如同熊熊的火焰。右軍也是這樣，全是黑色打扮，遠看好似天空佈滿烏雲。

第二天清早，夫差親自擂鼓，命令進兵，三軍將士齊聲吶喊，驚天動地。晉軍看到吳國軍隊這樣整齊雄壯，心裏非常害怕，晉定公更是膽戰心驚。於是，連忙與吳國訂立盟約，讓夫差做了霸主。

出自《國語》

Raging like a Fire

Meaning literally red like a fire and white like reed flowers, this describes a great momentum.

AT the end of the Spring and Autumn Period, the states of Wu and Jin rivalled with each other for hegemony. Fu Chai, the king of Wu, wanted to use force to coerce Duke Ding of Jin into submission. One night, Fu Chai ordered his generals and soldiers to form into three square formations with ten thousand men in each. The men in the central unit were dressed in white uniform and white armour and carried white flags and bows and arrows decorated with white feathers. From a distance they looked like a patch of blooming reed flowers. The men in the left unit were dressed in red uniform and red armour and carried red flags and bows and arrows decorated with red feathers. From a distance they looked like a field on fire. The men in the right unit were similarly dressed and armed in black. They looked like a rain cloud in the sky.

The following morning, Fu Chai, beating the drum himself, ordered his army to advance. The men in the three units shouted at the top of their voice which shook heaven and moved earth. Seeing the Wu army in neat formations, the Jin army was very frightened. Duke Ding was also in the jitters. He hastily signed an alliance with the state of Wu and acknowledged Fu Chai's hegemony.

Anecdotes of the States

如鳥獸散

rú niǎo shòu sàn

像鳥獸那樣飛奔四散；比喻潰敗逃散。

西漢時，匈奴經常興兵騷擾漢朝的邊境。公元前99年，漢武帝派騎都尉李陵領兵攻打匈奴。李陵所率五千兵馬，一到浚稽山就被三萬匈奴騎兵團團包圍。由於寡不敵衆，加之漢軍箭枝已用完，李陵知道大勢已去，便命令士兵們把旗幟和值錢的東西埋了起來，對士兵們說：「要是有幾十枝箭，我們可能再衝殺一陣，但現在箭用完了，刀、戟都已折斷，到了天明，大家都得作俘虜。不如現在趁着天黑，大家乾脆像鳥獸一樣各自逃命去吧，如能有幾個人逃回去報告皇上也是好的。」

出自《漢書》

Scattering like Birds and Beasts

Describing defeated soldiers fleeing helter-skelter from the enemy.

DURING the Western Han Dynasty, the Huns often encroached upon the frontiers of the Han. In 99 B.C., Emperor Wu of Han sent General Li Ling with an army to attack the Huns. As soon as the five thousand soldiers led by Li Ling reached Mount Junji, they were surrounded by thirty thousand Huns on horseback. Being helplessly outnumbered, the Han army soon exhausted their supply of arrows. Seeing that defeat was innevitable, Li Ling told his men to bury the flags and valuables. He then said to them, "If we had even a few dozen more arrows, we could launch another assault. But we've used up all our arrows and our swords and spears are broken. Instead of waiting until daybreak and becoming captives, let's take advantage of the darkness of the night and flee for our lives like birds and beasts. If some of us can slip off, they'll go back and report to the emperor what has happened."

History of the Han Dynasty

束之高閣

shù zhī gāo gé

捆起來放在高高的閣樓上；比喻對人或事置之不理或放棄不用。

東晉時，有個將軍叫庾翼，鎮守武昌，握有兵權。有人向他推薦玄學家殷浩和杜乂，說這兩個人很有才幹，可以當官。庾翼却認為他們有名無實，不能重用，並鄙視地說：「像殷浩、杜乂這樣的人，只能把他們當作無用的東西一樣，捆起來放在高高的閣樓上，等天下太平了，再考慮給他們做點什麼事。」

出自《晉書》

To Be Pigeonholed

Meaning literally to tie something up and put it in the attic and figuratively to neglect or abandon somebody or something.

GENERAL Yu Yi of the Eastern Jin Dynasty was commander of the garrison of Wuchang. Somebody recommended the two metaphysicists Yin Hao and Du Yi to him and told him that the two men were talented and could serve as officials under him. But Yu Yi thought the two were men of talent in name but not in reality and could not be given any important work to do. Disdainfully he said, "Men like Yin Hao and Du Yi can only be tied up and placed high in the attic as we do with all other useless things. They may be given something to do after peace returns to the country."

History of the Jin Dynasty

投筆從戎

tóu bǐ cóng róng

扔下筆去從軍；比喻棄文就武。

　　東漢人班超，從小刻苦好學，立志報效國家。公元62年，他隨同哥哥班固來到京都洛陽。那時，他家境貧困，常替官府抄寫文件，掙錢供養老母。班超很不滿意這種平庸的生活。有一次，他把筆猛地一扔，嘆息道：“大丈夫應像傅介子、張騫那樣，立功異地，怎能長期在筆硯之間混日子呢？”不久，他就扔下筆桿從軍去了。在軍隊裏，班超英勇作戰，屢建功勳，還奉命出使西域，成為歷史上著名的軍事家和外交家。

出自《後漢書》

Throwing Down the Pen and Joining the Army

Meaning giving up desk work to fight on the battlefield.

BAN Chao of the Eastern Han Dynasty studied diligently when he was young, and determined one day to serve his country. In A.D.62, he moved to Luoyang, the capital, with his brother Ban Gu. His family was then very poor. He had to copy documents for government offices to provide for his old mother. Ban Chao was very dissatisfied with the kind of humdrum life. One day, throwing down his pen, he sighed: "A true man should perform outstanding services in distant places like Fu Jiezi and Zhang Qian. How can he spend long years in company with pen and ink?" Before long, he really laid down his pen and joined the army. He fought heroically in the army and won honours on many occasions. He later served as an ambassador to the Western Regions and became a famous military strategist and diplomat in history.

History of the Later Han Dynasty

投鞭斷流
tóu biān duàn liú

將馬鞭子投入長江，截斷水流；形容人馬眾多，兵力強大。

公元357年，前秦的苻堅自稱大秦天王，佔據北方，並不斷向南擴展，與東晉王朝相對峙。公元382年，他召集羣臣聚會，說："我稱王二十多年了，四方安定，唯有南方的晉未被征服，想到此事，我吃不下飯，睡不好覺。現在，我們已有精兵九十七萬，我準備親自率兵去滅晉，不知你們意見如何？"大臣權翼說："目前晉雖不強大，但他們君臣和睦，上下一心，又有大將領兵，眼下滅晉很難。"大臣石越也勸阻說："晉佔據着長江天險，這對他們有利，我們應該先把兵養好，等待機會。"苻堅不以為然，說："長江天險算什麼！憑我們這麼多軍隊，只要每人把馬鞭子投入江中，就足以截斷江水！"苻堅一意孤行，決定大舉南下，結果，在淝水之戰中被晉軍打得大敗。

出自《晉書》

Throwing in Whips and Stopping a River

Describing a vast and power army that if each man flings his whip into the Yangtze, the flow of the river may be stopped.

IN A.D.357, Fu Jian of the Former Qin Dynasty proclaimed himself to be the Heavenly King of the Great Qin. He occupied the northern part of the country and continued to push southwards, rivalling the Eastern Jin Dynasty in the south. In A.D.382, he called his ministers to a meeting and said to them, "I've been in the throne for more than twenty years. People in the whole country now live in peace and security. Only the Jin in the south hasn't been conquered. Whenever I think about this, I can't eat and sleep well. Now we have a powerful army of 970,000 strong. I want to take command of the army myself in a campaign against the Jin to destroy it. I would like to hear your opinion about it." Minister Quan Yi said, "The Jin is not very powerful at the moment. But their emperor and subjects work in harmony and with one mind. They also have great generals commanding their troops. It's very difficult to destroy the Jin right now." Minister Shi Yue also tried to stop Fu Jian. He said, "The Jin has the Yangtze River, which is a natural barrier to their advantage. We should train our army and wait for an opportunity." But Fu Jian thought otherwise. "What is the Yangtze River to us?" said he. "If each of us flings his whip into the river, the flow will be stopped!" He refused to listen to advice and launched a great campaign against the Jin in the south. In the end, he was utterly defeated by the Jin army in the Battle of Feishui.

History of the Jin Dynasty

車載斗量

chē zài dǒu liáng

用車載，用斗量；形容數量極多。

三國時，吳國有一個叫趙咨的中大夫，他不但博學多識，還有一副好口才。有一次，吳王孫權派他出使魏國。魏文帝曹丕輕蔑地問：「你們吳王有學問嗎？」趙咨回答說：「吳王胸懷雄才大略，閒時，閱讀各種書籍，研究歷史經驗。」曹丕又問：「吳國可能被征服嗎？」趙咨毫不畏懼地答道：「大國有征伐的武力，小國也有抵禦的良策。」曹丕又追問：「吳國怕魏國嗎？」趙咨泰然答道：「吳國有雄兵百萬，又有長江、漢水的天險作屏障，有什麼可怕的呢！」趙咨對答如流，有理有據，使曹丕大為嘆服。於是，他改變了態度，客氣地問趙咨：「像先生這樣有才能的人，吳國有多少？」趙咨笑着回答說：「特別聰明的有八、九十人，至於像我這樣的人，多得可以用車載，用斗量，數也數不清。」

出自《三國志》

Cartloads and Bushelfuls

Meaning a vast number.

ZHAO Zi was a middle-ranking official of the state of Wu during the Three Kingdoms period. He was a learned man and an eloquent speaker. Once, Sun Quan, the king of Wu, sent him as an envoy to the state of Wei. "Is your king a man of learning?" Cao Pi, Emperor Wen of Wei, asked contemptuously. "The king of Wu is a man of great talent. Whenever he has time, he reads all kinds of books and studies historical experience," answered Zhao Zi. "Can the state of Wu be conquered?" asked Cao Pi again. "A big country has the military strength to launch attacks. But a small country has good ways of defending itself," answered Zhao without showing the least sign of fear. "Is the Wu afraid of the Wei?" asked Cao Pi. "The state of Wu has an army of a million men and is protected by the natural barriers of the Yangtze and the Han. What is there to be afraid of?" answered Zhao Zi calmly. Cao Pi was greatly impressed by Zhao's fluent answers and convincing argument. With a changed attitude, he asked politely, "How many people are there as talented as you are in the state of Wu?" Zhao Zi smiled and said, "There are about eighty or ninety men of great wisdom. As for people like me, there are cartloads and bushelfuls of them, too numerous to be counted."

History of the Three Kingdoms

吳牛喘月

wú niú chuǎn yuè

吳地的牛見到月亮就發喘；比喻過度畏懼。

晉代武帝時，尙書令滿奮，平時最怕風。有一次，他去見晉武帝司馬炎，武帝叫他坐在北面窗戶旁的座位上，後面立着幾扇透明的琉璃屏風，看起來好像有空隙會透風。滿奮臉上流露出畏難的神色。武帝見他這副樣子，笑了起來，問他什麼原因，滿奮回答說：「我好比吳地的牛，見到月亮誤認爲太陽，感到酷熱而發喘。」

出自《世説新語》

The Buffalo of Wu Pants at the Sight of the Moon

Said of someone who is nervously scared of something.

MINISTER Man Fen during the reign of Emperor Wu of the Jin Dynasty was a man who was afraid of exposing himself to wind. Once during an interview with Sima Yan, Emperor Wu, the emperor told him to sit by a window facing north. There were several transparent screen shielding the seat from wind. But as they were transparent, it looked as if wind was blowing in from the window. Man Fen hesitated to take the seat. Fear was written on his face. Emperor Wu smiled at the sight of him and asked him why. Man Fen said, "I'm like a water buffalo from Wu that mistook the moon for the sun and panted for the heat it felt."

New Social Anecdotes

呆若木雞

dāi rùo mù jī

呆得像木頭做的雞一樣；形容因驚恐而發愣的神情。

鬥雞，是古代一種娛樂活動。春秋時期，有位叫紀渻（xǐng）子的人，是有名的鬥雞專家。有一次，他為齊王訓練鬥雞。十天後，齊王催問道：「訓練成了嗎？」紀渻子說：「不行，它見到別的雞，就躍躍欲試，很不沉着。」

又過了十天，齊王又問：「現在該練成了吧？」紀渻子回答說：「不成，它心神還不安定，火氣還沒有消除。」

又過了十天，齊王又問：「難道還不成嗎？」紀渻子說：「現在差不多了。它驕氣沒有了，心神也安定了；別的雞叫，它好像沒有聽到似的，不論遇見什麼突然的情況，它都十分沉着，不驚不動，看上去，好像是一隻木頭做的雞。別的雞看見它，準會轉身就跑，不敢同它鬥。」試鬥結果，果真如此。齊王非常高興。

出自《莊子》

Dumb like a Wooden Cock

Meaning to be struck dumb with fear.

COCKFIGHT was an amusement in ancient times. A man named Ji Xingzi in the Spring and Autumn Period was a famous cockfight expert. Once he began to train a gamecock for the king of Qi. Ten days later, the king asked "Have you finished training it?" Ji Xingzi answered, "No. When it sees another cock, it is too eager to have a go and not steady enough."

Another ten days passed and the Qi king asked again, "How about now?" Ji Xingzi said, "I'm afraid it is still not cool enough. Its hot-headedness has to be removed."

After ten more days, the king asked, "Is it not ready yet?"
Ji Xingzi said, "It is about ready. Its arrogance is gone and it
is cool-headed. When another cock crows, it seems not to have
heard it. It remains cool and undisturbed in any emergencies.
It is like a wooden cock. When other cocks see it, they will
turn and run and will never dare fight with it." This was
exactly what happened when they tried it in a cockfight. The
king of Qi was very pleased.

The Book of Zhuang Zi

見怪不怪

jiàn guài bù guài

看到奇怪的事，並不大驚小怪。

相傳壽春城裏有個名叫姜七的人，專做接待過路客商的營生。
有年春天，姜七總聽到家中後園內有隱隱哭聲，但開門細看，却一
無所見。兩個月後，他接待的五位販藥客商，夜間也聽到悲切的哭
聲，出去一看，原來是猪圈裏的一頭母猪在哭泣。客商大聲喝問：
"畜生，爲何在此作怪？"不意母猪竟口吐人言說："我本是姜七
的祖母，生前以飼養母猪出賣仔猪爲業，因此撐起了家當。我死之
後，受罰投生爲猪，如今真是後悔莫及……"客商大爲吃驚，次日

晨將所見告姜七，勸他好好奉養這頭母豬。姜七却惱怒地說："畜生的話何足爲信。見怪不怪，其怪自壞，何必大驚小怪？" 商人再三相勸，姜七就是不聽。兩天後，姜七突然得病，他疑心是母豬作怪，乾脆命屠夫把那頭母豬縛去，殺了賣錢。從此以後，姜七一病不起，臨死前，竟發出一陣陣豬的慘叫聲。

出自《夷堅志》*

*《夷堅志》爲筆記小說集，內容多爲神怪故事和異聞雜錄。南宋人洪邁（公元1123－1202年）撰。

Facing the Uncanny with No Fears

Meaning not to be alarmed by a thing that is seemingly strange.

IT was said that in the town of Shouchun there was a man named Jiang Qi, who ran an inn that hosted travelling businessmen. One spring, he often heard someone sobbing quietly in his backyard. But when he opened his backdoor, he could see nothing. Two months later, when five merchants of medicine stayed in his inn, they too heard the dismal sobbing. They went out and saw it was a sow that was sobbing in the pigpen. "Swine, how dare you make the strange noise?" one of the merchants shouted at her. They never expected that the sow spoke to them in human language. "I was Jiang Qi's grandmother," said the sow. "I made a living by keeping sows and selling their piglets. When I died, I was punished to reincarnate as a pig. It's too late to regret now...." The merchants were utterly astonished. The following morning, they told Jiang Qi what they had seen the previous night and advised him to take good care of the sow. But Jiang Qi was angry. He said, "How are we to believe the words of a swine? Face the uncanny with no fears, the uncanniness will disappear. There's no need to become alarmed." Again and again, the merchants tried to persuade him, but Jiang Qi would not listen. Two days later, Jiang Qi suddenly fell ill. He suspected that it was the sow that was playing a trick on him. He told a butcher to tie up and kill the sow and sold it for meat. From then on, Jiang never recovered from his illness. Just before he died, he was often heard wailing piteously like a pig.

*Records of Strange Happenings**

*A collection of strange tales of supernatural beings and strange happenings by Hong Mai (1123-1202) of the Southern Song Dynasty.

芒刺在背

máng   cì   zài   bèi

尖刺扎在背上；比喻心中惶恐，坐立不安。

漢代大司馬大將軍霍光，是漢武帝的託孤重臣，輔佐八歲的小兒劉弗陵繼位，稱漢昭帝。漢昭帝只活到二十一歲就病死了，由漢武帝的孫子劉賀繼位。劉賀非常浪蕩，整天吃喝玩樂，把皇宮鬧得烏煙瘴氣。霍光憂心忡忡，與大臣們商量後，把他廢掉，立漢武帝的曾孫劉洵爲帝，即漢宣帝。

漢宣帝即位後由霍光陪同前去拜祭高祖廟。年輕的皇帝早就聽說霍光威嚴權重，現在看到他身材高大，面容嚴峻，目光烔烔，感到非常畏懼，惶恐不安，坐在車中，猶如針芒刺在背上那樣不自在。後來，霍光病死，漢宣帝親自執政，他出遊時，則由車騎將軍張安陪同。張安沒有霍光那樣威嚴可怕，宣帝感到無拘無束，不再惶恐不安了。

出自《漢書》

108

A Thorn in One's Back

A Thorn in One's Side

Said of something that keeps troubling one and making one uneasy.

GRAND Marshal Huo Guang of the Han Dynasty was an important court official to whom Emperor Wu, in his death-bed, had entrusted his son. Huo Guang assisted the eight-year-old Liu Foling to succeed to the throne and become Emperor Zhao. Emperor Zhao died of illness when he was twenty-one and Emperor Wu's grandson Liu He came to the throne. But Liu He spent all his days in pleasure-seeking, turning the palace into a madhouse. Huo Guang was very worried. After consulting with other important court officials, he dethroned Liu He and put Emperor Wu's great grandson Liu Xun in the throne. When Liu Xun became Emperor Xuan, Huo Guang accompanied him to offer sacrifices to the shrine of Emperor Gaozu. The young emperor had heard that Huo Guang was a man of severe dignity. Now when he saw his tall stature, solemn expression and sparkling eyes, he felt fearful and perplexed. Sitting in the carriage he felt as uneasy as having a thorn in his back. Later, when Huo Guang died of illness, Emperor Xuan took over the executive power. When he went out on excursions, he was accompanied by General Zhang An who was not as fearful as Huo Guang and Emperor Xuan no longer felt restrained and uneasy.

History of the Han Dynasty

別無長物

bié wú cháng wù

沒有多餘的東西；形容貧窮或沒有像樣的東西。

王恭，東晉人，他有個朋友叫王忱。他倆都曾擔任過太子的老師。有一次，王恭隨同父親遊盛產竹蓆的會稽（今浙江紹興）後回到都城（今南京），王忱去看望他，見王恭坐的那張新竹蓆很漂亮（晉人習慣不坐櫈子），便問王恭索要。王恭當即應允，就把那張竹蓆送給了他。其實，王恭只買了這張竹蓆，送給了王忱，自己就只好坐舊草蓆了。

後來，王忱知道此事，連忙到王恭家，向他表示歉意。他對王恭說：「我以為你從會稽帶回來的竹蓆不會就這一張。」王恭笑着說：「我平生無長物。」

出自《世說新語》

Having Nothing to Spare

Down at Heel

Said of someone who is poor or does not have a thing of value.

WANG Gong of the Eastern Jin Dynasty and his friend Wang Chen had been teachers of the crown prince. Wang Gong once went with his father on a trip to Kuaiji (today's Shaoxing in Zhejiang), a famous producing centre of bamboo mats. On his return to the capital (today's Nanjing), Wang Chen came to see him and saw him sitting on a beautiful brand-new bamboo mat. Wang Chen asked him if he could have the bamboo mat. Wang Gong promptly agreed and gave the mat to Wang Chen as a gift. The bamboo mat was in fact the only one Wang Gong had. Having given it to Wang Chen, he had to use his old straw mat.

Later, when Wang Chen learned about this, he hurriedly came to Wang Gong's place and apologized. He said to Wang Gong, "I thought you must have brought back more than one bamboo mat from Kuaiji." Wang Gong smiled and said, "I've never had anything to spare all my life."

New Social Anecdotes

含沙射影

hán shā shè yǐng

含着沙子噴射人的影子；比喻用心險惡，暗中傷人。

　　傳說，古時候有一種動物叫"蜮"。它形狀奇怪，像鱉，但只有三條腿。蜮平時躲在水中，見有人來，就口含沙粒，朝人噴去。被它噴到的人，就會生瘡或得病，即便是噴在人的影子上，此人也要得病。

出自《經典釋文》＊

＊《經典釋文》記述中國古代經學傳授源流及解釋各類經學著作。唐陸德明（約公元550－630年）撰。

Attacking by Innuendo

Meaning literally holding sand in the mouth and spitting it on someone's shadow.

IT was said that in ancient times there was an animal known as Yu. Strangely shaped, it looked like a turtle but had only three legs. Hiding at the bottom of the water, it would pick up some sand in its mouth and spit it on a man who happened to pass by. The man hit by the sand would be infected with sores or fall ill. He would become ill even if the sand had hit his shadow.

*Explanations of Classics**

*By Lu Deming (around 550-630) of the Tang Dynasty, it is a book on the origin of the ancient Chinese Confucian classics and of annotations of those classics.

作法自斃

zuò fǎ zì bì

自己立法自己受害。

商鞅是戰國時期著名的政治家，他做秦國丞相時，在秦孝公的支持下，改革舊的制度，推行新法，使秦國轉弱爲强。秦孝公爲此賜他封地，封他爲商君。但秦國的貴族和大臣則對他很不滿意。

秦孝公死後，秦惠王即位。此時有人向惠王誣告商鞅謀反。惠王對商鞅素無好感，便下令逮捕他，商鞅不得已而潛逃。他逃到邊關時，天已黑，投宿的客店主人不肯收留他，說："這是商君的法令，如留下身份不明的旅客要治罪的。"商鞅聽後，長嘆一聲說："我自己主張變法，訂出種種法令，結果反而把自己害了。"

出自《史記》

Making Laws to Bind Oneself

Meaning to fall foul of a law of one's own making.

SHANG Yang was a famous statesman of the Warring States Period. When he was the Prime Minister of the state of Qin, he carried out reforms of the old system and instituted new laws with the support of Duke Xiao of Qin, transforming Qin from a weak state into a powerful one. Duke Xiao enfeoffed him and made him Lord Shang. But the aristocrats and ranking officials were displeased with him.

After the death of Duke Xiao, Duke Hui succeeded to the throne. Shang Yang was falsely accused for conspiring against the state. As Duke Hui had never liked him, he ordered the arrest of Shang Yang. Shang had no choice but to flee. When he reached the border checkpoint, it was already dark. He came to an inn, but the innkeeper refused to let him stay, saying, "It's a law laid down by Lord Shang. I shall be punished for hosting a traveller of unknown identity." Shang Yang drew a deep sigh and said to himself, "I stood for reforms and laid down all kinds of laws and decrees. I've now fallen foul of them myself."

Records of the Historian

每況愈下
měi kuàng yù xià

形容情況愈來愈糟。

莊子是戰國時道家著名的代表人物。有一次，東郭子向莊子請教所謂道都表現在什麼地方。莊子回答說："什麼地方都存在。"東郭子說："你能不能說得具體一點？"於是莊子從螻蟻說起，一直說到稗草、磚頭瓦片、大小便等，並指出這都是“道”所在的地方。東郭子見莊子越說越低下，乾脆不問了。莊子說：“要滿足你的要求，把道的真象說清楚，就像市場上賣豬的經紀人用腳踏豬來估量它的肥瘦一樣，越靠下踏，踏到豬的腳脛上，就越能知道它是否真肥，因為腳脛是最難肥的部位。這個道理叫‘每下愈況’。”即愈細微的地方，肥瘦愈明顯。

後來人們習慣叫做“每況愈下”。意思也變為形容境況愈來愈不妙。

出自《莊子》

Getting Steadily Worse

ZHUANG Zi was a famous representative of the Taoists in the Warring States Period. Once Dong Guozi asked him where Tao was manifested. "It exists everywhere," answered Zhuang Zi. "Can you make it more specific?" said Dong Guozi. Thereupon, Zhuang Zi started from crickets and ants and dwelled on grass and straw, brick and tile, defecating and urinating and told him that these were all where Tao was to be found. Seeing that Zhuang Zi was getting steadily coarser, Dong Guozi refused to ask any more questions. So Zhuang Zi continued, "To satisfy what you want and to give a clear picture of Tao, we can compare it to a pig dealer on the market who steps on a pig to find out if it is fat or lean. He starts from the upper part and moves downward to the shin. The lower he goes, the easier it is for him to find out if the pig is really fat, because the shin is the most difficult part to grow fat. The reason behind this method is called "getting steadily worse". It means that the lower the part, the easier to find the fat and the lean. Later, people called it "getting steadily worse when circumstances are going from bad to worse.

The Book of Zhuang Zi

言過其實

yán guò qí shí

言論浮誇，超過實際能力；現多指說話誇張失實。

三國時，蜀國參軍馬謖，才氣過人，好論軍事。在軍師諸葛亮南征時，他曾建議採取攻心的策略，被諸葛亮採納，因此深得諸葛亮的器重。但主公劉備對馬謖另有看法，曾告誡諸葛亮："馬謖這個人言論誇張超過了實際才能，千萬不可重用。"諸葛亮對劉備的告誡，却不以為然。公元228年，諸葛亮攻魏，馬謖被任命為先鋒，駐守要塞街亭。由於馬謖獨斷專行，將軍隊駐扎在不利的地形，結果被魏軍團團圍住，遭到慘敗，丟失了街亭。按照軍法，馬謖被判刑，並死在獄中，時年三十九歲。

出自《三國志》

To Exaggerate

Meaning to overstate beyond the fact.

MA Su, the general of the state of Shu of the Three Kingdoms period, was a man of unusual ability who liked to talk about military strategy. During Military Advisor Zhuge Liang's southern expedition, he suggested adopting the strategy of winning the hearts of the enemy, Zhuge took his advice and thought highly of him. But Liu Bei, the king of Shu, had a different view of him and had warned Zhuge that Ma Su tended to overstate beyond his actual ability. Zhuge Liang did not quite agree with Liu Bei. In A.D.228 when Zhuge Liang attacked the state of Wei, Ma Su was appointed as the vanguard of the army to defend the strategic Jieting. Acting arbitrarily, Ma Su stationed his troops at an unfavourable terrain. As a result he was surrounded by the enemy and suffered a crushing defeat. He was punished according to military law for the loss of Jieting and died in prison when he was thirty-nine.

History of the Three Kingdoms

忍辱負重

rěn rǔ fù zhòng

忍受屈辱，擔負重任。

三國時，西蜀主公劉備率領大軍向東吳西部邊境進發，吳王孫權任命年輕有為的陸遜為大都督，帶領五萬人馬前去迎擊。隨同的將領，有的是孫權的哥哥孫策的舊將，有的是宮室貴戚，這些人個個驕傲，不肯聽從主帥陸遜的指揮。陸遜十分着急，一天，他召集眾將議事，手按着寶劍厲聲說道：「劉備天下知名，連曹操都怕他，現他帶領大軍進入我國，希望諸位將軍以大局為重，和睦團結，共同滅敵，這樣才對得起國家。我雖是個書生，但是主上任命我為統管全軍的大都督，因為我能夠忍受屈辱擔負重任。從現在起，每個人都要各負其責，不得推辭，違反命令者，按軍法從事！」後來，陸遜巧用計謀，大破蜀軍，使東吳諸將十分佩服。

出自《三國志》

Enduring Humiliations in Order to Perform an Important Duty

LIU Bei, the king of Shu of the Three Kingdoms period, mobilized a great army to march on the western borders of the state of Wu. Sun Quan, the king of Wu, appointed the young and capable Lu Xun as the commander-in-chief to

116

resist the invasion with fifty thousand men. Among the generals were those who had fought with Sun Ce, Sun Quan's brother, as well as relatives of the royal family. They were all proud and would not obey Lu Xun's command. Deeply worried, Lu Xun one day assembled all the generals to a conference. With his hand on the sword, he said sternly, "Liu Bei's name resounds throughout the country. Even Cao Cao is afraid of him. He's now leading a great army against us. I hope all of you will take the overall situation into consideration, unite and work in harmony to destroy the enemy so as to be worthy of our country. A mere scholar as I am, the king has appointed me commander-in-chief of the army because I can endure humiliations in order to perform an important duty. From now on, all of you are to perform your duty and not to shrink your responsibility. Anyone who disobeys orders will be punished by military law." Later, Lu Xun utterly defeated the Shu army by stratagem. He won the admiration of all the Wu generals.

History of the Three Kingdoms

防微杜漸

fáng wēi dù jiàn

把出現的錯誤或壞事，杜絕在萌芽狀態；指防患於未然。

東漢和帝任命丁鴻爲司徒，他博覽羣書，能言善辯，很受人們敬重。當時，竇太后主持朝政，她的一班皇親國戚，依仗權勢，幹盡壞事，文武大臣對此敢怒而不敢言。一次，丁鴻在和帝面前，列數這班人的罪狀，並說：「任何事物在剛開始發生變化時就加以禁止，比較容易，到後來就難了；如果處理事情，不注意細微的變化，任其發展下去，就難收拾。」他向和帝建議，應該親自料理朝政，把壞事杜絕在萌芽狀態。後來，和帝採納了他的意見，親自主持朝政，除掉這班壞人，得到大臣們的擁護。

出自《後漢書》

Checking a Bad Thing at the Outset

Nipping in the Bud

Meaning to prevent something before it takes place.

DING Hong was appointed as the prime minister during the reign of Emperor He of the Eastern Han Dynasty. Being a learned man and a gifted speaker, Ding was highly respected by others. At that time, the government affairs were supervised by the empress dowager Dou. Relying on her power and influence, a group of her relatives committed all manner of crimes. The civil and military officials were furious but no one dared to speak out against them. It was Ding Hong who recounted their crimes to Emperor He and said, "It's easier to prevent a change at the outset than later. If things are allowed to change even in minute degrees, it will be difficult to put it back in order later." He advised Emperor He to manage the government affairs himself and check a bad thing at the outset. Emperor He took his advice and began to supervise the government himself. He eliminated the group of evil-doers and won the support of all the ministers.

History of the Later Han Dynasty

青出於藍而勝於藍

qīng chū yú lán ér shèng yú lán

靛青是從蓼藍中提煉出來，但它却比蓼藍藍得更深；比喻學生勝過老師或後人勝過前人。

南北朝時，李謐拜孔璠爲師，過了幾年，他的學問超過了他的老師孔璠，孔璠對此很是高興。有時，孔璠有了疑難問題還向李謐請教，而李謐對老師的請教則覺得很不好意思。孔璠很誠懇地對他說：「你不要覺得不好意思。凡在某一方面有學問的人，都可以做我的老師，何況是你呢！」

孔璠虛心向學生求教的佳話傳出後，人們深受感動。有人編了一首短歌，頌揚孔璠不恥下問的精神

青成藍，藍謝青，

師何常，在明經。

意思是說，靛青這種染料，是從蓼藍中提煉出來的，然而它却比蓼藍更藍。同樣，師生關係也不是固定不變的，誰的知識多，誰就可以當老師。

出自《北史》

The Blue Dye Extracted from Indigo Is Bluer than Indigo

Said of a student who excels his teacher or of a late-comer who overtakes his predecessor.

AFTER studying for a few years under his teacher Kong Pan, Li Mi of the Southern and Northern Dynasties excelled his teacher in his learning. Kong Pan was very pleased with it. Sometimes when he had a problem, he even asked Li Mi for advice. But Li Mi felt embarrassed. Kong Pan said to him with all sincerity, "Don't be embarrassed. Anyone who knows more than I do in any field can be my teacher, let alone you."

This story of Kong Pan asking his student for advice soon spread far and wide and people were deeply moved. Someone composed a short verse in praise of Kong Pan who did not feel ashamed to ask advice from his student:

Indigo is turned into blue,
And blue is grateful for the indigo.
There is no eternal teacher,
The teacher is the one who knows more.

History of the Northern Dynasties.

東山再起

dong shan zài qǐ

從東山再出來；比喻隱居後再出來任職或失敗後捲土重來。

　　東晉時，有個名叫謝安的人，年輕時就很有才氣，名聲很大。朝廷屢次召他做官，他都回絕了。他隱居在會稽的東山，經常與王羲之等人遊山玩水，寫詩作文。

　　後來，征西大將軍桓溫請謝安作司馬，他不得已才答應出山任職，此時，他已四十多歲了。在謝安出征的時候，朝中文武百官都來送行，有人同他開玩笑說：「你過去高臥東山，多次違背朝廷旨意，不肯出來做官，想不到，今天到底出來了。」謝安聽了，甚感羞愧。桓溫死後，謝安升爲尙書僕射，位同宰相。

出自《晋書》

Rising Again from the East Mountain

Making a Comeback

Said of someone who resumes public office after reclusion or stages a comeback after a defeat.

XIE An of the East Jin Dynasty was talented and enjoyed great fame even when he was young. Many times the court appointed him to public offices, but he declined each time. He lived in reclusion in Kuaiji's East Mountain and spent his time enjoying nature and composing poems and essays with Wang Xizhi and others.

Later, Huan Wen, Grand General of the Western Expedition, asked him to serve as a military governor. As he found it hard to refuse, Xie An agreed to take the post. At the time, he was well over forty. When Xie An departed for the expedition, all the civil and military officials came to bid him farewell. "Several times you disobeyed the court and refused to be an official. We never expected you to rise again from the East Mountain, " someone joked with him. Xie An was both embarrassed and ashamed. After the death of Huan Wen, Xie An was promoted and became the prime minister.

History of the Jin Dynasty

東窗事發

dōng　chuāng　shì　fā

　　在東窗下密謀的事，已被揭發；指作姦犯科的人，事機敗露，被緝法辦。

南宋時，宰相秦檜在他家的東窗下與妻王氏密謀陷害抗金大將岳飛的奸計。後來，岳飛果然被害。秦檜死後，他的兒子熺不久也死去。王氏請方士爲秦檜父子招魂，方士看見熺戴着鐵枷，就問：「太師在何處？」熺說：「在酆都。」於是方士前往酆都，見秦檜和他的同夥都戴着鐵枷在受刑。秦檜對方士說：「請快告訴王氏，東窗之事，已被揭發了。」

出自《西湖遊覽志餘》＊

＊《西湖遊覽志餘》明田汝成（約公元1540年前後在世）撰，書中記述了西湖名勝及人物掌故等。

The Plot at the East Window Has Been Exposed

The Game Is Up

Said of evil-doers whose plot has been exposed and who are being hunted down.

QIN Hui, the prime minister of the Southern Song Dynasty, hatched a plot at the east window of his house with his wife Wang to frame up General Yue Fei who was resisting the Jin invasion. Yue Fei was indeed killed on the false charge they had framed. Shortly after Qin Hui died, his son Xi also died. His wife Wang asked a necromancer to pacify the souls of father and son. The necromancer saw Xi wearing an iron cangue and asked him, "Where's the prime minister?" Xi said, "In the netherworld." The necromancer then went to the netherworld and there he saw Qin Hui and his cohorts in iron cangues being tortured. Qin Hui said to the necromancer, "Please rush back and tell Wang that the plot at the east window has been exposed."

玩物喪志

wán wù sàng zhì

迷戀於所玩賞的事物，以致喪失進取的志向。

周武王滅商後，各諸侯國都向周朝稱臣納貢。一天，西方的旅國派來一位使者，獻給周武王一隻獒（巨犬），它身體高大，匍伏武王面前，俯首行禮。武王大喜，收下這稀有的貢品，重賞了使者。

退朝後，太保召公奭（shì）寫了一篇《旅獒》呈給武王，文內寫道：輕易侮弄別人，會損害自己的德行；迷戀於所玩賞的事物，會喪失進取的志向。創業艱難，不要讓它毀於一旦！

武王讀了《旅獒》後，下令把貢品都分賜給諸侯和功臣，自己精心治國，使周朝的統治得到了鞏固。

出自《尚書》*

* 《尚書》中國上古歷史文件和部分追述古代事迹著作的滙編。相傳由儒家創始者孔子（公元前551－前479年）編選，爲儒家經典之一。

Riding a Hobby Ruins One's Will

Meaning to be excessively devoted to a pastime so as to weaken the will to make progress.

AFTER King Wu of Zhou overthrew the Shang Dynasty, all the vassal states acknowledged allegiance and delivered tributes to the Zhou Dynasty. One day, an envoy from the state of Lü in the west presented King Wu with a mastiff. The large dog lay prostrate in front of King Wu and nodded its head in salute. King Wu was very pleased. He took the rare tribute and generously rewarded the envoy.

After the court session, Grand Guardian Lord Zhao of Shi wrote an essay entitled "The Mastiff of Lü" and presented it to King Wu. The essay said: To humiliate others hurts one's own virtue; to ride a hobby ruins one's will. A great cause started with difficulty must not be allowed to be destroyed overnight.

After reading "The Mastiff of Lü", King Wu ordered that all the tributes be distributed among the princes and officials who had rendered outstanding services. He devoted all his energy to the affairs of the government. As a result, the rule of the Zhou Dynasty was consolidated.

*The Book of History**

*A collection of historical documents and anecdotes of remote times. It is a Confucian classic usually attributed to Confucius (551-479 B.C.).

招搖過市

zhāo yáo guò shì

張揚炫耀地走過大街或鬧市；形容故意虛張聲勢，炫耀自己。

春秋末期，魯國人孔子爲了推行他的政治主張，曾帶領弟子，走訪各國。他首先到了衞國。衞國的國君衞靈公不管國事，大權操在夫人南子手裏。據傳這位夫人品德、名聲不太好。她接見孔子時，把衣裙上的珠玉飾物弄得叮噹響，外屋的人都能聽得很清楚。

在一個崇尚禮教的國家，又是在接見孔子的時候，發生這件事，當然要引起種種議論。弟子子路也很不滿意，孔子只得解釋一番。

　　一個多月後，衞靈公和南子同遊街市，又邀孔子同乘一車，在大街上昂然巡遊，招搖過市，街道兩旁居民，很不以爲然，引起的議論就更多了。孔子更覺尷尬，於是發着牢騷離開了衞國。

出自《史記》

Parading through the Busy Streets

Making an Ostentatious Display

Said of someone who seeks to attract attention by conspicuous behaviour.

TO win acceptance of his political views at the end of the Spring and Autumn Period, Confucius from the state of Lu started a tour of the various states with his disciples. He first came to the state of Wei, where Duke Ling, the sovereign, ignored the affairs of the state and power was in the hand of his wife Nan Zi, who was known to be a woman of imperfect virtue. When she received Confucius, people in the next room heard distinctly the tinkling of the jade ornaments on her skirt. The fact that this happened in a state known for its strict observance of rites when she received Confucius gave rise to all kinds of gossips. Even his disciple Zi Lu was very displeased. Confucius had to make explanations.

Over a month later, Confucius again rode in the same carriage with Duke Ling and Nan Zi and paraded themselves through the busy streets. People along the streets did not like it and there were more gossips. Finding himself in an awkward position, Confucius left the state of Wei while expressing discontent.

Records of the Historian

其貌不揚

qí mào bù yáng

形容人或物的外貌醜陋、不端正。

春秋時，鄭國有位賢人叫然明，他的相貌長得十分醜陋。有一次，晉國大夫叔向來到鄭國。然明隨着侍從混進叔向的住處，站在堂下，想一睹叔向的風采。叔向正在飲酒，聽到堂下有人說話，心想，是誰講話如此有學問有敎養？這必定是然明了。他急忙走下堂去，一問果然是然明，敬佩地說：「你的相貌醜陋、不端正，如果你不開口，我幾乎發現不了你。」從此，他們兩人成了非常好的朋友。

出自《左傳》

Undistinguished in Appearance

Said of someone or something ugly in appearance.

RAN Ming of the state of Zheng in the Spring and Autum. Period was a learned scholar, but his features were rather repulsive. Once when Shu Xiang, a ranking official of the state of Jin, came to Zheng, Ran Ming followed his retinue and managed to slip into the residence of Shu Xiang. He stood outside the hall and wanted to have a look at Shu Xiang. At the time, Shu Xiang was drinking in the hall. When he heard people talking outside, he thought the man must be Ran Ming because from the way Ran spoke he could tell Ran was a man of learning and culture. He hurried out of the hall and found, after questioning, it was indeed Ran Ming. He said to him with admiration, "You don't have a distinguished look. If you had not spoken, I probably might not have been able to find you." From then on, the two became fast friends.

Zuo Qiuming's Chronicles

抱薪救火

bào xīn jiù huǒ

抱着柴草去救火；比喻用錯誤的方法去消滅災害，反而使災害擴大。

戰國時，一些小的諸侯國先後被大國吞併，最後只剩下齊、楚、燕、韓、趙、魏、秦七國。其中秦國實力最強，不斷向其他六國進犯。公元前273年，秦軍大敗魏、韓、趙三國軍隊，魏國將軍段干子很害怕，請魏安釐王將南陽割送秦國以求和。大臣蘇代反對，對魏安釐王說：「魏國的地方沒有割完以前，秦國是不會罷休的，用割地的方法去求和，猶如抱着柴草去救火一般，柴草沒燒完，火是不會滅的。」魏安釐王不聽勸告，終於被秦國所滅。

出自《史記》

Carrying Faggots to Put Out a Fire
Pouring Oil on the Fire Is Not the Way to Quench It

Meaning trying to save a bad situation with a wrong method and ending up by making it worse.

AFTER the smaller princely states had been annexed in the Warring States Period, there remained only seven powers — Qi, Chu, Yan, Han, Zhao, Wei and Qin. The Qin, being the most powerful of the states, made continuous raids into the six other states. In 273 B.C., the Qin army won a big victory over the armies of Wei, Han and Zhao. The Wei general Duan Ganzi was scared. He asked Prince Anxi of Wei to cede Nanyang to Qin in order to sue for peace. Minister Su Dai was against it. He said to Prince Anxi, "The Qin will not be satisfied before all the Wei territory was ceded to them. To sue for peace by ceding territory is like to carry faggots to put out a fire. The fire can't be put out before the faggots are burnt up." Prince Anxi refused to take the minister's advice and the state of Wei was eventually subjugated by the Qin.

Records of the Historian

臥薪嘗膽

wò xīn cháng dǎn

睡在草堆上，品嘗苦膽的滋味；比喻刻苦自勵，發奮圖強。

春秋末年，越王勾踐曾被吳王夫差俘獲，在吳國受盡了屈辱。回國後，他決心報仇雪恥。爲了不忘恥辱，他每晚都睡在草堆上，還在房梁上吊一隻苦膽，每當吃飯和飲水的時候，都要嘗一嘗膽的苦味。勾踐在國內採取賢明政策，發展生產。他親自扶犁種田，夫人紡紗織布；他不吃特殊的飯菜，不穿艷麗的衣服，同百姓同甘共苦。這樣，越國漸漸強大起來。後來，勾踐終於滅掉吳國，並乘勝北進中原，成爲春秋末期的一個霸主。

出自《史記》

Sleeping on Straw and Tasting Gall
Through Hardship to the Stars

Meaning to make a determined effort and going through hardships to make oneself strong.

GOU Jian, the king of Yue, was taken prisoner by Fu Chai, the king of Wu, at the end of the Spring and Autumn Period. After suffering endless humiliations in the state of Wu, Gou Jian returned to his own country and was determined to take revenge. Gou Jian slept on a pile of straw every night and suspended a gall from the beam of his room so that he would not forget his humiliations. He tasted the bitterness of the gall every time he ate his meal and when he drank water. He adopted wise policies and developed production in his country. He ploughed the fields and his wife wove cloth. He shared weal and woe with the ordinary people, never eating anything special or wearing clothes of gorgeous colour. The state of Yue grew steadily stronger and eventually subjugated the state of Wu. Gou Jian marched north to the Central Plains and became a powerful chief of the princes.

Records of the Historian

虎口餘生

hǔ   kǒu   yú   shēng

從老虎口裏逃命；比喻經過危險，僥倖保存了性命。

宋朝，在湖州有個叫朱泰的人，家裏很窮，靠打柴度日。一天，他上山砍柴，忽然遇到一隻老虎，迎面撲來咬住他。朱泰大叫：“我死了不要緊，但家有老母無人照顧，太可憐哪！”這一叫，老虎似有所悟，扔下他走了。鄉親們聽說後，都說：“朱泰眞是虎口餘生啊！”

出自《宋書》*

* 《宋書》南朝梁人沈約（公元441-513年）撰，共一百卷。

Being Saved from the Tiger's Mouth

A Narrow Escape from Death

IN the Song Dynasty, there lived a man named Zhu Tai in Huzhou. Being very poor, he had to make a living by cutting firewood. One day, on his way up a hill to cut firewood, he crossed the path of a tiger. The tiger rushed at him and sank its teeth into him. Zhu Tai cried out in a loud voice, "It's all right for me to die. But I've an old mother at home. She'll be miserable with nobody looking after her!" The tiger seemed to understand what he said. It turned and left. After hearing his story, his neighbours all said, "Zhu Tai has indeed been saved from the tiger's mouth!"

*Book of the Song Dynasty**

*Compiled by Shen Yue (441-513) of the Southern Dynasties in 100 volumes.

咄咄怪事

duō duō guài shì

形容使人驚訝的怪事。

　　晉代人殷浩，曾做過刺史，後來，受到朝廷信任，在北征後秦時，擔任中軍將軍，統管揚州、豫州、徐州、兗州、青州五個州的軍事。殷浩雖有學問，但不善打仗，結果北征失利，被撤職流放到信安（今浙江衢縣）。他被流放後，從不抱怨，但常用手指在空中寫寫畫畫。有人發現他對空寫的是"咄咄怪事"幾個字。原來，殷浩是借此抒發內心的不滿和煩悶。

出自《世說新語》

A Strange Business

Used to describe something which is flagrantly absurd.

YIN Hao of the Jin Dynasty had served as a military governor before he was appointed by the court to lead the northern expedition against the Later Qin Dynasty. As General of the Central Army, he had jurisdiction over the military affairs of the five prefectures of Yangzhou, Yuzhou, Xuzhou, Yanzhou and Qingzhou. Although Yin Hao was a learned man, he was not a good soldier on the battlefield. For his defeat in the northern expedition, he was removed from office and banished to Xinan (today's Quxian in Zhejiang). During his exile, he never complained but often wrote characters with his finger in the air. People discovered that the characters he wrote meant "A strange business", with which Yin Hao vented his discontent and grievance.

New Social Anecdotes

金石爲開

jīn shí wéi kāi

像金子那樣堅硬的石頭都能被切開；比喻只要下苦功，任何困難都能克服。

周時楚人熊渠子是個射箭能手。一天夜裏，他行經山路，在黑暗中，見路邊有一隻老虎伏在那裏。他一箭射去，那老虎一動也不動。走近一看，才知是一塊大石頭。箭射進了石頭，連箭翎都幾乎看不見了。人們議論說，這不僅是因爲熊渠的力氣大，而且是由於他精神集中，以必勝的信心去制服對方，才出現了金石爲開的奇迹。

出自《新序》*

* 《新序》西漢劉向（公元前77－前6年）撰，書中記載了許多歷史故事。

Even Metal and Stone Can Be Pierced

Meaning that any difficulty can be overcome through hard work.

XIONG Quzi was an archer from Chu in the Zhou Dynasty. One dark night, while travelling along a mountain path, he saw a tiger on one side of the path. He shot an arrow at it, but the tiger did not stir at all. He walked up and saw that it was actually a big stone. The arrow had almost been shot into the stone. Even the feathered end was invisible. People said that the miracle of an arrow piercing into a stone occurred because Xiong Quzi was such a powerful man and because he concentrated so much and was fully confident in overcoming his opponent.

*New Prologue**

*A collection of many historical stories by Liu Xiang (77-6 B.C.) of the Western Han Dynasty.

金城湯池

jīn chéng tāng chí

金屬鑄造的城郭，滾燙的護城河；形容城防堅固，難以攻破。

前秦蒯通，很有辯才。當時，農民起義領袖陳勝的部將武臣，攻下了趙國大部分土地，並兵逼范陽（今河北易縣）。蒯通去拜訪了范陽縣令徐公，對他說："你死在眼前，故前來弔喪；不過，今天遇到了我，又可免於一死，所以該向你賀喜。"

徐公感到蹊蹺，便向蒯通作揖，請求講明其中道理。蒯通先講了將死的道理："你為官多年，殺了許多人，有人要給你一刀並不難，只是害怕秦朝的刑法罷了。如今，天下大亂，刑法無用，你不是馬上要挨刀子了嗎？"之後，他又說了可以免死的道理："武臣知道我有點名氣，必定想來聽聽我的意見，我準備這樣說：'如果攻打每個城池都靠硬攻，恐怕不是高明的辦法，不如採用不攻而破的策略。比如范陽城池，本可堅守，但縣令怕死，準備投降。投降後，你如殺了他，其他城鎮官吏，定然互相傳告——范陽令投降了仍不免一死，還不如固守。於是所有城池都成了金城湯池，就很難攻下了。不如優待范陽令，讓他帶着文告到燕、趙各地去，各城鎮定會紛紛投降。'武臣一定會聽從我的意見，所以你就可以免於一死。"

徐公聽後，立即備了車馬，讓蒯通去見武臣，武臣果然採納了他的建議。不但徐公免死，燕、趙等地三十多個城鎮，也主動宣告起義。

出自《漢書》

A City of Metal with Boiling Moats

Describing a strongly fortified city invulnerable to attacks.

KUAI Tong of the Former Qin Dynasty was an eloquent speaker. One year, Wu Chen, a general under Chen Sheng, the leader of a peasant uprising, had occupied most of the territory of the state of Zhao and was leading his army towards Fanyang (today's Yixian in Hebei Province). Kuai

Tong called on Lord Xu, the magistrate of Fanyang, and said to him, "Your death is imminent and I've come to mourn you. But since you've met me today, you can avoid death. So I should congratulate you."

Lord Xu was puzzled. Making a deep bow, he asked Kuai Tong to tell him why. Kuai Tong first told him why he was about to die: "You've been the magistrate for many years and have put many people to death. It's not difficult to cut you down with a sword. The fact that nobody has done so was because people were afraid of the penal code of the Qin Dynasty. The whole country is now in a tumult and the penal code cannot be enforced. Isn't it very likely that you'll soon have a taste of the sowrd?" He then went on to explain how he could avoid death: "Wu Chen knows that I am a man of some fame here. He'll surely want to hear my opinion. I've planned to say to him: 'To attack every city by sheer force, I'm afraid, is not a clever method. It's better to employ a tractic that will enable you to take a city without launching an attack. Take the city of Fanyang for example. The city can be stubbornly defended. But the magistrate, being afraid to die, is ready to capitulate. After he surrenders, if you kill him, news will be relaid to other cities and the officials there will tell one another: The magistrate of Fanyang's life was not spared even after he had surrendered. It's better to defend our cities as best as we can. The cities will then become cities of metal with boiling moats which are very difficult for you to take. It's better to treat the magistrate of Fanyang nicely and ask him to take proclamations to the various places in Yan and Zhao. The cities and towns will certainly surrender.' I'm sure Wu Chen will follow my advice, and your life will be spared."

After hearing him out, Lord Xu immediately prepared a horse and carriage and asked Kuai Tong to see Wu Chen. The latter indeed adopted Kuai Tong's suggestion. Not only was Lord Xu's life spared, but also more than thirty cities and towns in Yan and Zhao declared allegiance to the uprising.

History of the Han Dynasty

所向無敵

suǒ xiàng wú dí

所到之處，沒有對手；形容威力很大，無人能抵禦。

三國時，北方魏國的曹操，勢力最大，他曾威脅東吳的孫權，要他把兒子送去作"人質"。孫權主將周瑜勸孫權不要屈服，對孫權說："我們兵精糧足，物產富饒，交通便利，人心安定，只要充分利用這些條件，奮發圖強，定可'所向無敵'，爲什麼你要把曹操當作頭，而把自己當作他的尾巴呢？"

出自《三國志》

Unrivalled Anywhere

Said of a tremendous force that cannot be resisted.

CAO Cao of the state of Wei in the north was the most powerful of the Three Kingdoms. He once threatened Sun Quan of the state of Wu, demanding that Sun Quan deliver his son to him as a "hostage". Zhou Yu, the chief general of Sun Quan, advised Sun not to yield to his threat. He said to Sun Quan, "We have a fine army, sufficient food, abundant produce and a convenient transport system. The minds of our people are at rest. As long as we can make full use of these conditions and work hard for the prosperity of the country, we shall certainly become unrivalled anywhere. Why let Cao Cao act as the head while you serve as his tail?"

History of the Three Kingdoms

狗尾續貂

gǒu wěi xù diāo

貂尾不足，用狗尾代替；常比喻以壞續好。

晉武帝時，司馬倫被封爲趙王。晉惠帝時，他篡奪了皇位，大封其親屬和同黨，甚至連家奴、差役也封給爵位。每逢朝會，大臣們戴着用貂尾裝飾的帽子，把殿堂擠得滿滿的。由於封爵太濫，市上貂尾不足，受封的人買不到貂尾，就用狗尾代替。因此，人們編了句諺語，諷刺說：“貂不足，狗尾續。”

出自《晉書》

Attaching a Dog's Tail to a Sable

Meaning adding a poor sequel to an excellent work.

SIMA Lun, who was made the Prince of Zhao by Emperor Wu of the Jin Dynasty, usurped the throne during the reign of Emperor Hui. He enfeoffed all his relatives and cohorts. Even his house slaves and servants were granted titles of nobility. At every court session, the palace was crowded with nobles wearing hats decorated with sables' tails. Because so many people were given titles of nobility, there was a shortage of sable tails on the market. Some of those who had acquired titles were unable to get sable tails. They had to use dog tails instead. People thus devised a sarcastic saying: "When sables are in short supply, use dog tails instead."

History of the Jin Dynasty

返老還童

fǎn lǎo huán tóng

由老年返回到童年;形容由衰老恢復青春。

西漢時,淮南王劉安一心求仙學道,尋找長生不老術。一天,有八個白髮老人求見,說有"却老之術",願意當面奉獻。侍衛通報後,劉安說:"他們自己都已老成這個樣子,哪來什麼却老之術,分明是欺騙,不見!"八個老者聽說後,把自己變爲八個小娃娃,笑道:"淮南王嫌我們年老,這樣總可以了吧!"

出自《神仙傳》 *

* 《神仙傳》道教書,晉葛洪(公元284－364年)撰,記述中國古代傳說中的神仙故事。

Recovering the Youthful Vigour

IN the Western Han Dynasty, Liu An, the Prince of Huainan, had set his mind on seeking the help of immortals and mastering the Tao so that he could stay forever youthful. One day, eight white-haired old men requested an interview with him, saying that they had the "anti-senility art" and would like to offer it to him in person. When the guard reported it to Liu An, Liu said, "They themselves have become so old. How can they have the anti-senility art? They're clear frauds. I won't see them." When his words were relaid to the eight old men, they transformed themselves into eight small children. Smiling, they said, "The Prince of Huainan dislikes us for being too old. How about now?"

Tales of Immortals*

*A collection of ancient Chinese Taoist fairy tales by Ge Hong (A.D. 284-364) of the Jin Dynastty.

非驢非馬
fēi lǘ fēi mǎ

不像驢，也不像馬；形容不像樣子。

漢時，西域有個小國叫龜茲。國王絳賓對漢朝十分友好，多次來漢朝訪問。一次，他來訪後，被漢宣帝留住了一年。絳賓很喜歡漢朝的宮廷生活。回去後，他的宮殿式樣，器物陳設，嬪妃、侍從服飾，朝拜儀式，無不摹仿漢朝。西域其他國家，見龜茲不加選擇地摹仿漢朝，而且學得走了樣子，就說它是"驢非驢，馬非馬，倒像一頭騾子！"

出自《漢書》

Neither a Donkey nor a Horse

Neither Fish, Flesh, nor Fowl

Describing something that is unseemly.

DURING the Han Dynasty, there was a small country named Guizi in the Western Region. Its king Jiang Bin was very friendly to the Han and often came for a visit. Once Emperor Xuan invited him to stay for a whole year. He liked life in the Han court so much that upon his return he imitated the Han in everything, including the style of the palace buildings, their interior decoration, the system of consorts and servants, and the court dress and etiquette. The other countries in the Western Region, seeing that Guizi had distorted the Han style in its blind imitation of the Han, said that Guizi was "neither a donkey, nor a horse, but rather like a mule."

History of the Han Dynasty

河東獅吼

hé dōng shī hǒu

河東獅子叫；比喻嫉妒、撒潑的婦女。

宋朝有個叫陳慥（zào）的人，自稱龍丘居士，生性好客，妻子柳氏則嫉妒成性。陳慥宴客時，如有歌女陪伴，柳氏則用棍敲打牆壁大吼，賓客只得散去。陳慥很怕柳氏。他的好友宋代著名詩人

140

蘇東坡曾為此寫過一首開玩笑的詩："龍丘居士亦可憐，談空說有夜不眠。忽聞河東獅子吼，柱杖落手心茫然。"

出自《容齋三筆》*

*《容齋三筆》南宋洪邁（公元1123-1202年）撰。

The Lioness Roars on the East Bank

A Tigress

Said of a jealous shrewish woman.

CHEN Zao of the Song Dynasty called himself the Lay Buddhist of the Dragon Hill. Being a hospitable man, he often invited guests to his house. But his wife Liu was by nature a jealous woman. Sometimes when there were girl entertainers at the dinner parties given by Chen, his wife in the next room would knock on the wall with a stick and roar. Chen Zao thus became known as a henpecked man. His good friend Su Dongpo, the famous poet of the Song Dynasty, once wrote a jocular verse which reads:

The Lay Buddhist of the Dragon Hill is a pitiable man,
Deep into the night he chatted with his friends,
When suddenly the lioness roared on the east bank,
His heart was in a flutter and his stick dropped from his hand.

*Third Collection of Notes from Rong Studio**

*By Hong Mai (1123-1202) of the Southern Song Dynasty.

空洞無物

kōng dòng wú wù

空空洞洞，沒有東西；形容文辭沒有內容或不切實際。

公元318年，東晉元帝司馬睿即位後，王導作爲有功之臣，被任命爲丞相。當時，有個叫周顗的人，善於幽默，談吐詼諧，頗有名望。一次，周顗去王導家作客，兩人談得十分投機。談着談着，王導忘形地把頭枕在周顗的膝上，指着他的肚子問道："這裏面有什麼？"周顗挺挺身子，摸着肚子說："這裏面空空洞洞，什麼也沒有，但像你這樣的人，可以裝下幾百個。"王導聽後，先是一怔，接着哈哈大笑不止。

出自《世說新語》

Hollow and Devoid of Content

Used to describe a writing that has no substance or is divorced from reality.

WHEN Sima Rui ascended the throne and became Emperor Yuan of the Eastern Jin Dynasty in 318, Wang Dao, for his outstanding service, was made the prime minister. Zhou Yi was a man of some fame for his humorous talks. Once Zhou Yi was a guest at Wang Dao's house. The two had a very agreeable chat. As they talked on, Wang Dao jokingly rested his head on Zhou Yi's knees and, pointing at Zhou's stomach, asked, "What are there in here?" Zhou Yi stretched himself, put his hands on his stomach and said, "It's hollow and devoid of substance. But it can hold hundreds of men like you." Puzzled at first, Wang Dao roared with laughter when he saw the joke.

New Social Anecdotes

門可羅雀

mén kě luó què

門前可以落鳥雀；形容時過境遷，登門拜訪的人家家無幾。

西漢文帝時，有個廷尉官叫翟公。人們見他有權有勢，都來拜訪他，家裏常常賓客盈門。後來，他被免職，就誰也不來了。門前冷冷清清，簡直可設捕雀的網了。等翟公又恢復了官職，許多人又來拜訪他，翟公十分感慨，寫了幾句話貼在大門上："一死一生，乃知交情，一貧一富，乃知交態。一貴一賤，交情乃見。"

出自《史記》

One Can Catch Sparrows at the Door

Meaning that as a result of changed circumstances, few callers come to the door.

LORD Zhai was a court official at the time of Emperor Wen of the Western Han Dynasty. As he was powerful and influential, people called on him frequently. His house was often filled with guests. Later, when he was removed from office, people stopped coming. His front door was so quiet that one could set up a net and catch sparrows. When Lord Zhai was reinstated in his post, people started to come again in large numbers. Sensing the difference, Lord Zhai wrote these words on his front door: "Friendship and cordial relations are revealed by the change from life to death, from poverty to wealth and from nobility to humility."

Records of the Historian

門庭若市

mén   tíng   ruò   shì

門前和院子裏熱鬧得像集市一樣；形容來人很多，非常熱鬧。

戰國時，齊國相國鄒忌的妻妾、客人都誇他比當時有名的美男子徐公還漂亮，有一日，他見到徐公，發現自己並不如徐公漂亮，於是悟出一個道理，便進宮朝見齊威王說："我並不如徐公漂亮，可是妻子出於偏愛我，侍妾由於懼怕我，客人有求於我，所以他們都說我比徐公漂亮。如今我們國土廣大，城池眾多，宮中上下，誰不順從您，滿朝文武，誰不懼怕您，全國百姓，誰不有求於您。照這樣看來，您所受的蒙蔽實在太深了！"齊威王聽後，恍然大悟，於是通令全國："無論官員百姓，凡能當面指搞我的過失的，受上等獎；送上書信奏章規勸我的，受中等獎；在街頭巷尾議論我而讓我聽到的，受下等獎。」通令一下達，提意見的人來得很多，宮門前、庭院裏，熱鬧得像集市一樣；幾個月後，進諫的人雖然有，但越來越少；一年以後，即使想要進諫，也沒有什麼可說了。

出自《戰國策》

The House Is like a Marketplace

Describing a place overflowing with people coming and going.

DURING the Warring States Period, Zou Ji, the prime minister of the state of Qi, was told by his wife, concubines and guests that he was more handsome than the famous handsome man Lord Xu. When he saw Lord Xu one day, he found he was not as handsome as Xu. From this he came to see a truth. He went to the palace and said to King Wei of Qi, "I a partiality for me, my concubines are afraid of me and my guests need me for one thing or another, they all say I am more handsome than Lord Xu. Now we have a vast territory and many cities, everybody in the palace obeys Your Majesty. All the civil and military officials of the court are afraid of Your Majesty. The people in the whole country need one thing or another from Your Majesty. From this I can see that Your Majesty has been deeply hoodwinked." Upon hearing what Zou Ji said, the king suddenly realized what had happened. He therefore issued a decree to the effect that anyone, official or non-official, who could point out his errors to his face would be given a first-class award; anyone who could write a letter or a memorial offering advice would be given a second-class award; and those who talked about him would be given a third-class award. When the decree was made known to the people, many people came to give their opinions and the palace became like a marketplace. A few months later, though there were still people who came to offer their advice, they were steadily fewer in number. A year later, even there were people who came to offer advice, they actually did not have much to say.

Anecdotes of the Warring States

孟母三遷

mèng mǔ sān qiān

孟子的母親三次遷移住地；比喻父母注意對子女進行良好的教育。

　　戰國時，儒家學派著名人物孟子的母親對他幼時的教育非常注意。起初，孟母帶着幼年的孟子住在一所公墓附近。孟子看見人家哭哭哀哀埋葬死人，他也學着玩。孟母說：“我的孩子住在這裏不合適！”就立刻搬家，搬到集市的附近。孟子看見商人自吹自誇地賣東西賺錢，他又學着玩。孟母說：“我的孩子住在這裏也不合適！”就又立刻搬家，搬到了學堂附近。這時，孟子學習禮節和要求上學了。孟母說：“這裏才是適宜我的孩子居住的地方！”於是，就在這裏住下了。

出自《烈女傳》*

* 《烈女傳》西漢人劉向（公元前77－前6年）著，共八篇。

Mencius' Mother Moved House Three Times

Said of parents who give their children a good education.

THE mother of Mencius, the famous Confucian scholar of the Warring States Period, paid particular attention to the education of her son. The young Mencius and his mother at first lived near a cemetery. When Mencius saw people mourning at the burial of their dead, he started to imitate them to play. Mencius' mother said, "This is not a place for my son to live." They immediately moved to a place near a market. When Mencius saw vendors bragging about what they wanted to sell and making money, he started again to imitate them. Mencius' mother said, "This is also not a suitable place for my son to live." Again they moved immediately to a place near a school. Here Mencius began to learn manners and wanted to go to school. His mother said, "This is a suitable place for my child to live." It was here that they finally settled down.

Biographies of Virtuous Women*

*A collection of eight biographies by Liu Xiang (77-6 B.C.) of the Western Han Dynasty.

147

殃及池魚

yang jí chí yú

池塘中的魚遭到了災殃；比喻飛來橫禍，無辜受牽連。

春秋時，宋國的司馬（官名，掌管軍事）桓魋（tuí）得到了一顆寶珠。宋國的國君知道了，想奪取它，桓魋拒絕交出寶珠，國君派人去抄家，也無所得。追問桓魋把寶珠藏到何處，桓魋說："扔到魚池裏了。"他們把魚池裏的水汲乾了，還是沒有找到，而池裏的魚却因此遭到意外的災難。最後，國君就以私藏國寶為名，將桓魋驅逐出境。

出自《呂氏春秋》

Disaster Spreads to the Fish in the Pond

Meaning an unexpected disaster in which the innocents are involved.

HUAN Tui, the Minister of War of the state of Song during the Spring and Autumn Period, came into possession of a precious pearl. When the king of Song heard about it, he wanted to seize it for himself. Huan Tui refused to hand over the pearl. The king then sent people to search his house but they could not find it. They questioned Huan Tui as to where he had hidden the pearl. Huan Tui told them that he had thrown it into the fish pond. They drained the fish pond but still could not find it. The fish in the pond however suffered an unexpected disaster. The king accused him for secretly concealing a treasure of the state and threatened to banish him from the country.

The Discourses of Lü Buwei

148

畏首畏尾

wèi shǒu wèi wěi

怕前怕後；比喻膽小怕事，顧慮重重。

春秋時，晉靈公在鄭國的扈邑約會一些諸侯。鄭穆公因有顧慮，沒有赴會。晉靈公懷疑鄭國要投靠南方大國楚國，於是準備出兵攻打鄭國。鄭國得知後，去信說：“鄭國地小勢弱，對晉國一向不敢怠慢，極為尊重，但你們却懷疑我們，還想欺侮我們。鄭國寧可滅亡，也不能再忍受了。古人說：‘如果頭也怕，尾也怕，全身還剩下什麼？’”又說：“鹿到生命危急時，就無暇選擇藏身之所了。我們小小鄭國臨到滅亡時，也會像鹿一樣，隨便找個躲避的地方，那就只好去投靠楚國了。”晉國見鄭國態度强硬，出兵不一定有利，便派人前往鄭國，進行和談了事。

出自《左傳》

Fearing the Head and Fearing the Tail

Said of someone who is timid and overcautious and was full of misgivings before and after doing something.

IN the Spring and Autumn Period, Duke Ling of the state of Jin held a meeting with the dukes of the other princely states at Huyi in the state of Zheng. But Duke Mu of the state of Zheng, being doubtful of the purpose of the meeting, did not go. Duke Ling of Jin suspected that the state of Zheng was going to yield its allegiance to the state of Chu, and planned to launch a military attack against Zheng. When the state of Zheng learned of the coming attack, it wrote a letter to Duke Ling, declaring, "The state of Zheng, being a small and weak country, never dares to slight the state of Jin, but holds it in full respect. Yet you are suspicious of us and want to bully us. The state of Zheng will rather perish than endure any longer. The ancients said, 'If one fears the head and fears the tail, what else does one have of the whole body?' They also said, 'When a deer's life is in danger, it has no time to choose where to hide itself.' When this small Zheng State of ours faces subjugation, it will act like a deer and find a possible place to hide itself and will have no choice but to go over to the state of Chu." Seeing that the state of Zheng took an uncompromising stand, the state of Jin concluded that it would not gain anything from a military attack and sent someone to Zheng to negotiate for peace.

Zuo Qiuming's Chronicles

苟延殘喘

gǒu yán cán chuǎn

暫且延續一下臨死前的喘息；比喻暫時維持生存。

東郭先生趕着一頭毛驢去中山謀職，途中遇到一隻被獵人追捕受傷的狼。狼向東郭先生擺尾，苦苦哀求："先生是願意拯救世間萬物的，請您讓我鑽進布袋中，使垂危的生命暫且得到延續。"東郭先生動了惻隱之心，答應了它的要求，讓它躲過獵人的追捕。誰知狼從袋中出來後，馬上顯出原形，竟要吃掉東郭先生。這時，來了個老農，東郭先生和狼向他訴說了經過，請他裁決。老農沉思片刻，出謀引誘惡狼重新進入布袋，幫助東郭先生打死了這隻惡狼。

出自《中山狼傳》*

*《中山狼傳》傳奇小說。明馬中錫（？－約公元1512年）撰。

Lingering On before Dying

Being on One's Last Legs

Meaning to drag out one's feeble existence.

MASTER Dongguo, driving a donkey with him, was on his way to Zhongshan to look for a job when he met a wolf wounded by hunters who were close on its heels. The wolf wagged its tail and begged Dongguo, "I know the Master is willing to save the lives of all creatures. Please allow me to get into the cloth bag to drag out my feeble existence." Master Dongguo was moved to compassion and agreed to the wolf's request so that the wolf was able to hide itself from the hunters. He never expected that when the wolf came out of the bag, it bared it teeth at Dongguo and wanted to eat him. An old peasant happened to come by, and both Master Dongguo and the wolf complained to him and asked him to pass judgement. The old peasant thought for a while, then tricked the wolf into getting into the bag again and help Dongguo in killing the vicious wolf.

Story of the Wolf of Zhongshan*

*A short story by Ma Zhongxi (?-about 1512) of the Ming Dynasty.

風雨同舟

fēng   yǔ   tóng   zhōu

　　大風大雨時，同在一條船上；比喻危急時，大家同心協力，共度難關。

　　春秋時，著名軍事家孫武，在其所著《孫子兵法》中，曾說過一段有關吳越關係及如何用兵的話：善於用兵的人，應像衡山上的大蛇一樣，當蛇的頭部受擊時，必以尾部救急，尾部受襲，頭部必然前去救援，中段受到威脅時，頭尾都來救應。吳國和越國雖是仇敵，他們同乘了一條船，一旦遇上風浪，定然會如左右手那樣，互相救援。

出自《孫子兵法》*

*《孫子兵法》中國現存最早的兵書，春秋時兵家孫武作。

In the Same Boat in a Storm

Said of people assisting one another in time of trouble.

SUN Wu, the famous military strategist of the Spring and Autumn Period, wrote in his masterpiece *Sun Zi's Art of War* on the relationship between the states of Wu and Yue and on how to use military forces. The passage runs as follows: One who is good at using military forces should act as a great snake on Mount Hengshan. When its head is being attacked, its tail will come to its rescue. When its tail is under attack, its head will come to ward off the attack. When its middle section is threatened, both head and tail will come to help. The states of Wu and Yue are enemies, but they are in the same boat. When there is a storm, they will help each other like the left and right hands.

*Sun Zi's Art of War**

*China's earliest extant book on military strategy by Sun Wu who lived at the end of the Spring and Autumn Period.

侯門似海

hóu mén sì hǎi

王侯的門裏像海一樣深；形容門禁森嚴，與外面隔絕。

唐時，秀才崔郊的詩、文都很好。他姑母家有個婢女，長得端莊秀麗，能歌善舞。崔郊很愛她，她對崔郊也十分敬慕。後來，這個婢女被賣到一個大官家中。有一年，清明節時，崔郊偶然看見了她。她站在樹下，不敢招呼崔郊，崔郊也不敢走到她跟前去。兩人只是遠遠地互相望望，崔郊十分悵惘，吟詩一首：

公子王孫逐後塵，綠珠垂淚滴羅巾。

侯門一入深如海，從此蕭郎是路人。

出自《雲溪友議》*

* 《雲溪友議》唐末范攄編。

A Noble's House Is As Deep as the Sea

Describing the closely guarded residence of a noble separated from the outside world.

CUI Jiao, a scholar of the Tang Dynasty, was a good writer of both prose and poetry. He fell in love with a maid in the house of his aunt. The maid, sedate and beautiful, was a good singer and dancer. She also had a deep admiration for Cui. Later, the maid was sold into the house of a high-ranking official. During the Clear and Bright Festival one year, Cui Jiao happened to meet her. She was standing under a tree and did not dare to speak to Cui. Nor was Cui bold enough to go up and speak to her. The two could only look at each other from a distance. Cui Jiao felt very upset and wrote the following poem:

Princes and nobles are all after her,
The poor lady's scarf is wet with tears.
Deep as the sea is the noble's house where she lives,
Her lover has, from now on, become a stranger.

*Friendly Chats at Yunxi**

*Compiled by Fan Shu at the end of the Tang Dynasty.

重蹈覆轍

chóng dǎo fù zhé

重新走上翻車的老路；比喻不吸取失敗的教訓。

東漢時，竇武被桓帝封爲侯爵，他品行高尚，沒有貴族習氣。當時，朝廷中宦官勢力很大，他們把持朝政，勾結黨羽，橫行不法。朝廷的官員李膺、杜密等人反對宦官專權，猛烈抨擊宦官集團，遭到了宦官的誣告。李膺、杜密被逮入獄，受株連的人有數百。竇武對這種是非顛倒、邪正不分的現象十分氣憤。他上奏章給桓帝，痛斥宦官禍國殃民，爲忠貞志士伸寃。奏書上說：“如果不吸取過去宦官禍國的教訓，重新走上翻車的老路，恐怕秦二世覆滅的災難，很快又會重演！”竇武還把自己的印綬繳還，表示不與小人共事的決心。這樣，桓帝才把那些被株連、誣陷的忠貞之士赦免。

出自《後漢書》

Following the Track of the Overturned Cart

Said of someone who does not draw lessons from past failures.

154

DOU Wu, a man of noble conduct without the bad habits of
the aristocrats, was made a marquis by Emperor Huan of the
Eastern Han Dynasty. The eunuch officials in the court were
then very powerful. They seized government power, formed
themselves into a clique and did all kinds of evil. The court
officials Li Ying, Du Mi and others who vehemently attacked
the eunuch clique for their imperious despotism were framed
by the eunuchs. Both Li Ying and Du Mi were thrown into
prison and several hundred others were implicated. Deeply
indignant at this confounding of right and wrong, evil and
righteousness, Dou Wu wrote a memorial to the emperor
condemning the eunuchs who had brought calamity to the
country and the people and appealing for redress of the
wrong of the upright and loyal people. The memorial said,
"If the court does not draw a lesson from eunuchs bringing
calamity to the country in the past, and follow the track of
the overturned cart, the fall of the Second Emperor of Qin
may soon repeat itself." Dou Wu also handed in his official
seal to show his determination not to work with mean
persons. As a result, Emperor Huan pardoned all the upright
and loyal people who had been implicated.

History of the Later Han Dynasty

後起之秀

hòu qǐ zhī xiù

指後輩中的優秀人物。

晉朝豫章太守范寧是荆州刺史王忱的舅父。有一次，范寧誇獎
王忱說："你這樣風流俊逸，很有希望，眞是後輩中的優秀人物。"
王忱很風趣地答道："沒有您這樣的舅舅，哪有我這樣的外甥呢？"

出自《世說新語》

Up-and-Coming Young Persons

Said of outstanding persons among the younger generation.

FAN Ning, the prefect of Yuzhang in the Jin Dynasty was the uncle of Wang Chen, the governor of Jingzhou. Fan Ning once praised Wang Chen, saying, "A smart and talented man like you is full of promise. You are truly an up-and-coming young man." Wang Chen answered humourously, "Without an uncle like you, where is there the nephew like me?"

New Social Anecdotes

後顧之憂

hòu gù zhī yōu

指來自後方的憂患。

李沖在南北朝北魏孝文帝時，任尚書僕射，深得孝文帝的信任。孝文帝每次出征，朝中政事，都委託給李沖處理。

後來，李沖死去，孝文帝十分悲痛。有一次，他路過李沖的墳墓，觸景生情，更覺傷心。他說："李沖爲人，品德高尚，忠誠可靠，我交託他的國家重任，全都辦得很好，使我每次出征在外，沒有'後顧之憂'。"

出自 《魏書》*

---

*《魏書》紀傳體北魏史，北齊史學家魏收（公元506－572年）撰。

Worrying about Trouble in the Rear

Meaning having to worry about what is happening back at home.

LI Chong served as the prime minister under Emperor Xiaowen of the Northern Wei Dynasty during the Southern and Northern Dynasties and was trusted by the emperor. Every time Emperor Xiaowen went on an expedition, the affairs of the court were entrusted to Li Chong.

Later, when Li Chong died, Emperor Xiaowen was overwhelmed with grief. One day he happened to pass by the grave of Li Chong. The grave brought back past memories and he was further grieved. He said, "Li Chong was a man of integrity and lofty ideals, and a man of loyalty and reliance. Every time I entrusted him with the responsibility of the state, he did everything very well. Every time I went on an expedition, I did not have to worry about trouble in the rear."

*History of the Wei Dynasty**

*A history of the Northern Wei Dynasty in the form of annals and biographies written by Wei Shou (506-572) of the Northern Qi Dynasty.

約法三章

yuē fǎ sān zhāng

三條法律；指訂立幾條簡單明瞭的條款，大家共同遵守。

公元前206年，劉邦統帥大軍攻打秦都咸陽，秦王子嬰見大勢已去，便出城投降。劉邦進入咸陽，看到秦宮的富麗堂皇和無數如花似玉的美女，就要住進秦宮。所幸由於張良、樊噲的諫阻，才算

157

對秦宮的財寶絲毫未動，一一加上封條，立即還軍灞上。為了安定民心，嚴明法紀，劉邦把各縣豪傑都請來，說：「秦朝施行嚴刑苛法，把關中父老害苦了，現在我向你們宣佈三條法律：第一，殺人者處死；第二，傷人者治罪；第三，偷盜者懲處。」劉邦派人到各地宣傳「約法三章」，得到百姓的擁護。

出自《史記》

Agreeing on Three Articles of Law

Meaning laying down simple and clear rules so that they will be observed by all concerned.

IN 206 B.C., Liu Bang, commanding a great army, attacked the Qin capital Xianyang. When the Qin emperor Zi Ying saw that defeat was certain, he came out of the city and surrendered. Liu Bang marched into Xianyang. When he saw all the luxuries and the innumerable beautiful women in the Qin palace, he wanted to move into the palace. But Zhang Liang and Fan Kui advised him against it. As a result, the Qin palace with all the things in it was left intact and sealed up. Liu Bang immediately brought his army back to Bashang. To pacify the people and enforce strict law and discipline, Liu Bang assembled all the leading personalities from various counties and announced, "The Qin Dynasty enforced harsh laws and punishments. The people of Guanzhong suffered a great deal. I now announce only three articles of law: First, murderers will be put to death; second, those who hurt others will be penalized; third, those who steal or rob will be punished." Liu Bang then sent people to different places to make known his three articles of law and gained wide support of the people.

Records of the Historian

神工鬼斧

shén gōng guǐ fǔ

天神的工藝，鬼魂的斧頭；形容技藝精湛。

相傳，春秋時有個木匠，叫慶。他技術高明，能製造各種精巧的器具。有一次，他用木頭製成一具置放鐘鼓的架子，外形美觀精緻，凡是見到此物的人都不敢相信是人工做出來的，疑爲出自神鬼之手。

魯國的國君問慶有何秘訣。慶答道：「我做之前，先靜下心來，排除一切雜念。然後到山林中去挑選最好的木材。在製作加工過程中，專心致志，這就是所以能做出好器具的秘訣。」

出自《莊子》

By the Hand of a God and the Axe of a Spirit

Describing a superb artistic skill.

IT was said that there was a carpenter named Qing in the Spring and Autumn time. Known for his superlative skill, he was able to make all kinds of fine furniture and instruments. Once he made a wooden frame for a bell or drum. It was so exquisite and beautiful that those who saw it could hardly believe that it was made by man. They doubted if it was made by the hand of a god or the axe of a spirit.

The king of the state of Lu asked Qing what secret he had. Qing answered, "Before I begin, I let my mind rest in peace and expel all distracting thoughts. Then I will go to the forest to choose the best wood. In the course of making it, I concentrate all my mind on it. This is my secret of turning out a good piece of furniture."

The Book of Zhuang Zi

馬革裹屍

mǎ gé guǒ shī

用馬皮把屍體包起來；形容英勇作戰，死在疆場上。

　　東漢名將馬援，跟隨光武帝劉秀南征北戰，立下了汗馬功勞，被封爲侯爵。有一次，馬援凱旋回京，許多人前來歡迎慰勞。其中有個孟冀的人向馬援說了許多恭維的話，馬援說：“我總以爲你要同我說什麼大事，怎麼也這樣隨波逐流地一味誇獎我呢？你應該給以幫助和指敎才是啊！”一席話說得孟冀低頭不語。馬援接着又說：“當今匈奴、烏桓不時侵擾北方邊境，我想自告奮勇前去討平。好男兒應當戰死在疆場上，用馬皮裹着屍體而歸，怎能躺在床上，死在妻子兒女身旁?!”孟冀聽了，不勝佩服，說道：“這眞不愧爲一個大丈夫呀！”

　　馬援到了六十二歲，還馳騁疆場。後來病死軍中，實現了他“馬革裹屍”的壯志。

出自 《後漢書》

Wrapping the Body in Horsehide

To Die in One's Boots

Said of someone who died heroically on the battlefield.

MA Yuan, the famous general of the Eastern Han Dynasty, had fought north and south with Liu Xiu, who later became Emperor Guangwu. For his contributions to the dynasty, Ma was made a marquis. Once on his victorious return to the capital, many people came to congratulate him. A man named Meng Ji among them said many flattering words to Ma Yuan. Ma Yuan said to him, "I thought you had something important to say to me. Why are you following all the others

in praising me? You should have advised me and given me
instructions." His words made Meng Ji lower his head
without a word. Ma Yuan then continued, "Today, the Huns
and the Wuhuan are harassing our northern borders. I want to
volunteer to fight and defeat them. A man shoud die on the
battlefield and have his body wrapped in horsehide. How can
he die in his bed near his wife and children?" Meng Ji was
filled with admiration after hearing his words. He said, "It is
the choice of a truly great man."

Ma Yuan fought on the battlefield even when he was
sixty-two. He later died of illness while still serving in the
army and thus realized his wish to have his body wrapped in
horsehide.

History of the Later Han Dynasty

捉襟見肘

zhuō jīn jiàn zhŏu

　　一扯衣襟，就露出胳膊肘；原形容衣服破爛，生活貧困，現多
比喻顧此失彼，無法應付。

　　春秋時，魯國有一個叫曾參的人。他是孔子的一位得意弟子，
以孝著稱。曾參生活很貧困，他住在衛國的時候，沒做一件新衣，
有時一連三天灶中無火。他穿的衣服，整一下衣襟，就會露出胳膊
肘；他穿的鞋子，往上一提，就露出了腳後跟。但曾參並不以此為
苦，他穿着破衣爛鞋，整天唱着歌，自由自在地生活，天子不能召
他為臣，諸侯不能攀他為友。

出自《莊子》

Pulling the Lapels Only to Expose the Elbows

This idiom used to be said of someone in straitened circumstances and in rags and tatters, and now more often describes a situation with so many difficulties to cope with that one cannot attend to one thing without neglecting another.

ZENG Shen in the state of Lu during the Spring and Autumn Period was a favourite disciple of Confucius known for his filial piety. He was very poor. During his stay in the state of Wei, he did not make a single new coat and sometimes for three days on end there was no fire in his stove. He was so poorly dressed that when he pulled the lapels of his coat, his elbows were exposed and when he tried to pull up his shoes, his heels were exposed. But Zeng Shen did not think he was suffering any hardship. Wearing ragged clothes and broken shoes, he sang all day long and lived a carefree life. He would not accept a commission from the king for an official post, nor would he make friends with the nobles.

The Book of Zhuang Zi

胯下之辱

kuà xià zhī rǔ

褲襠下的恥辱；比喻極端的侮辱。

　　韓信是漢代軍事家、開國功臣。他年輕時家貧，被人瞧不起。有一次，一個青年人當眾侮辱韓信，說：「你雖然身高體大，喜歡佩帶刀劍，內心裏却十分膽怯。」他還說：「韓信，若你不怕死，就用劍刺我；怕死，就從我褲襠下鑽過去。」韓信注視了這個人好久，然後就低下頭從這個人叉開的雙腿中鑽了過去，又爬着走了幾步。滿街的人都嘲笑他，以爲他怯懦。後來，韓信做了楚王，他召見了當時侮辱自己讓自己從他褲襠下鑽過的那個青年人，提拔他做了楚國的中尉。韓信對各位文武官員說：「這個人是一位壯士。當初他侮辱我時，我難道不能殺了他嗎？不過殺他也沒有什麼值得稱道的，因此我就忍耐下來，而成就了今天的功業。」

出自《史記》

The Humiliation of Crawling under the Crotch

Meaning the worst kind of humiliation.

HAN Xin was a military strategist who rendered outstanding service towards the founding of the Han Dynasty. When he was young his family was poor and he was looked down upon. Once a young man humiliated him in front of a crowd of people. He said to Han Xin, "Although you are strongly built and likes to carry a sword, you are inwardly a coward. If you are not afraid to die, come and try to stab me with your sword. If you are afraid to die, then crawl under my crotch." Han Xin looked at the man for a long while and then bent down and crawled through the man's parted legs. All the people in the street laughed at him, thinking he was a coward. Later, when Han Xin became the Prince of Chu, he summoned to an interview the young man who had humiliated him, and appointed him to an official post. To all the civil and military officials, Han Xin said, "This man is a good fighter. I could have killed him when he humiliated me. But there was nothing praiseworthy in killing him. That was why I endured his humiliation and achieved what I've achieved today."

Records of the Historian

釜底游魚

fǔ　dǐ　yóu　yú

鍋底的游魚；形容在很短時間內就要死亡。

張綱是東漢順帝時的一個小官，為人忠誠，剛直不阿。他不怕專斷獨行的大將軍梁冀，上奏皇上揭露梁冀貪污腐化、殘害忠良的行為。滿朝百官為之震驚，但因梁冀勢力太大，皇帝也奈何不得。

從此，梁冀對張綱恨之入骨。

　　不久，廣陵張嬰率眾造反，事態緊迫。梁　想借刀殺人，便施陰謀，派張綱去廣陵當太守。張綱並不害怕，上任後，親自去說服張嬰歸順朝廷，並表示要懲辦貪官污吏。張嬰被說服了，哭泣着說：「我們是為了生計才相聚起事的，好像魚兒游在鍋裏，很快就會死亡，我們願意歸順朝廷。」第二天，張綱接受了他們的投降，從此廣陵太平無事。

出自《後漢書》

Fish Swimming at the Bottom of the Pot

Meaning that death is imminent.

ZHANG Gang was a junior official during the reign of Emperor Shun of the Eastern Han Dynasty. But he was honest and upright. Unafraid of the despotic Grand General Liang Ji, he wrote a memorial to the emperor exposing Liang's corruption and ruthless murder of loyal and honest people. All the officials in the court were shocked. But Liang was so powerful that even the emperor could do nothing to him. Liang Ji afterwards harboured an intense hatred for Zhang Gang.

Later, Zhang Ying staged a rebellion in Guangling and the situation was critical. Intending to kill Zhang Gang by the hand of Zhang Ying, Liang Ji hatched a plot and appointed Zhang Gang as the prefect of Guangling. But Zhang Gang was not afraid. After assuming his post, he went in persn to try to persuade Zhang Ying to come over and pledge allegiance to the court and expressed his intention of punishing corrupt officials. Zhang Ying was convinced. He said in tears, "We rose together because we want to find a livelihood. We are like fish swimming at the bottom of the pot and will soon meet our death. We're willing to come over." Zhang Gang accepted their surrender the following day and Guangling became a peaceful place ever afterwards.

History of the Later Han Dynasty

狼狽不堪

láng bèi bù kān

形容非常窘迫的樣子。

馬超是三國時一位名將。東漢末年，他與韓遂合夥，進軍潼
關。不久，曹操聚集兵馬，要渡過渭水去進攻馬、韓軍隊。馬超向
韓遂提出作戰方案：在渭水北面阻截曹兵，當河東的糧草用盡時，
曹兵必然退走。但韓遂未採納他的意見。後來，此事被曹操得知，
對馬超恨得咬牙切齒。於是曹操使出離間計，使馬、韓二人互相猜
疑，結果被曹操打得大敗。

曹操兵馬走後，馬超領着隊伍佔據了冀城，殺死涼州刺史韋
康，自稱"征西將軍"。不料韋康部將楊阜、姜叙、梁寬、趙衢集
合起來，與馬超為敵。馬超率兵出冀城攻打鹵城，楊阜、姜叙固
守，無法攻下；梁寬、趙衢乘機攻入冀城，使得馬超進退兩難，狼

狽不堪，最後，只得去四川，投奔劉備。

出自 《三國志》

In a Sorry Plight

Meaning being extremely miserable and wretched.

MA Chao was a famous general of the Three Kingdoms period. At the end of the Eastern Han Dynasty, he and Han Sui joined force and occupied Tongguan. Cao Cao soon assembled an army, crossed the Weishui River and came to attack Ma and Han. Ma Chao drew up a battle plan for Han Sui, suggesting that they should intercept the Cao army north of the Weishui River and when food and fodder were exhausted in the east of the river, the Cao army would certainly withdraw. Han Sui, however, did not adopt his idea. When Cao Cao learned about this later, he gnashed his teeth in his hatred for Ma Chao. He employed a stratagem of sowing discord between Ma and Han and making them suspect each other. As a result, both were badly defeated by Cao Cao.

After Cao Cao had withdrawn, Ma Chao led his army to Jicheng and occupied the city. He killed Wei Kang, the governor of Liangzhou and proclaimed himself to be the "General of Western Expedition". He had not expected that Wei Kang's subordinate generals Yang Fu, Jiang Shu, Liang Kuan and Zhao Qu would join hands to oppose him. Ma Chao launched an attack on Lucheng from Jicheng. But the city was stubbornly defended by Yang Fu and Jiang Shu and he could not take it. Meanwhile, Liang Kuan and Zhao Qu took the opportunity and occupied Jicheng. Ma Chao was unable either to advance or to withdraw. He found himself in a sorry plight. Eventually he had to go to Sichuan to serve under Liu Bei.

History of the Three Kingdoms

笑裏藏刀

xiào lǐ cáng dāo

形容人外表和善，内心却陰險毒辣。

唐太宗時，有個名字叫李義府的人，因善寫文章，被推薦當了監察御史。李義府還善於奉承拍馬，他曾寫文章頌揚過唐太宗，因此，博得太宗的賞識。唐高宗時，李義府又得到高宗的信任，任中書令。從此，更加飛黃騰達。李義府外表溫和謙恭，同人說話總帶微笑，但大臣們知道，他心地極其陰險，因此都說他笑裏藏刀。李義府在朝中為所欲為，培植親信，任意讓妻兒向人索取錢財，還隨意封官許願。高宗知道這些以後，曾婉轉地告誡過他，但李義府並不放在心上。有一次，李在宮中看到一份任職名單，回家後，讓兒子把即將任職的人找來，對他說：「你不是想做官嗎？幾天內詔書即可下來，你該怎樣謝我？」那人見有官做，立刻奉上厚禮。之後，高宗得知了此事，不能再容忍了，就以「洩露機密」為名，將李義府父子發配邊疆。

出自《舊唐書》*

* 《舊唐書》歷史著作，原名《唐書》，因欲與歐陽修等所撰《新唐書》相別，改現名。作者張昭遠、賈緯等。

Hiding a Dagger behind a Smiling Face

Said of someone who is outwardly friendly and kind, but inwardly treacherous and ruthless.

LI Yifu who lived during the reign of Emperor Taizong of the Tang Dynasty was recommended to serve as an imperial censor because he wrote very well. He was a man who was good at flattery. He once wrote an essay in praise of Emperor

Taizong and won the favour of the emperor. During the reign of Emperor Gaozong, Li Yifu was again trusted by the emperor. His official career was more successful and became the vice prime minister. He was kind and modest in appearance and always wore a smile when he spoke to people. But the other ministers knew that he was sinister and treacherous. They said that he hid a dagger behind his smiling face. He did what he pleased at court and built up a group of trusted followers. He allowed his wife and son to demand money and valuables from others promising them with official posts. When Emperor Gaozong heard what he was doing, the emperor mildly warned him. But the emperor's warning did not worry Li at all. Once, he happened to read an appointment document at court. When he went home, he asked his son to summon the man who was about to be appointed to an official post. He said to the man, "Don't you want to be an official? The appointment will be announced in a few days. How are you going to thank me?" Seeing that he was soon to become an official, the man immediately delivered some valuable gifts to Li. Later, when Emperor Gaozong learned about this, he could not tolerate it any more. For "divulging state secret", Li Yifu and his son were exiled to a border region.

Old History of the Tang Dynasty *

*By Zhang Zhaoyuan and Jia Wei. Originally known as the *History of the Tang Dynasty,* it was changed to the present title so as to distinguish it from the *New History of the Tang Dynasty* by Ouyang Xiu.

倒綳孩兒

dào bēng hái ér

接生婆把嬰兒包綳倒了；比喻多年老手，偶然也會把事情做錯。

宋朝時，有一個叫苗振的讀書人，赴京趕考後，以第四名考中。後來，朝廷召試館職，苗振又去應試。宰相晏殊對他說：“你做了幾年官，文學上一定荒疏了，這次赴考，應當稍微溫習一下經典。”苗振不以爲然，笑着說：“難道做了三十年接生婆的老婦，還能將嬰兒包綳倒了？”考完以後，苗振落選了。晏殊見到他，也笑着說：“苗君，你怎麼竟把嬰兒給包綳倒了！”苗振聽後，羞得面紅耳赤。

出自《事文類聚》*

* 《事文類聚》宋祝穆撰，共一百七十卷，分前、後、別、續四集。

Wrapping up a Baby Upside Down

A midwife who has wrapped up a new-born baby upside down is compared to an old hand who occasionally can also make mistakes.

MAIO Zhen was a scholar of the Song Dynasty who ranked the fourth in the civil examination held in the capital. Later, there was a court examination for vacancies at the Imperial Academy. Maio Zhen applied. Prime Minister Yan Shu said to him, "Since you've been an official for several years, you must be out of practice with your literary skill. Before you go to this examination, you should review some of the classics." But Miao Zhen thought otherwise. He smiled and said, "Could an old midwife who's been at it for thirty years ever wrap up a baby upside down?" After the examination, Miao Zhen found that he had failed. When Yan Shu saw him, he also smiled and said, "Miao, how could you have wrapped up the baby upside down?" Miao Zhen blushed with embarassment.

*Classified Narrative Writings**

*A book in four volumes and 170 chapters by Zhu Mu of the Song Dynasty.

倒屣相迎

dào xǐ xiāng yíng

倒拖着鞋去迎客；形容接待客人時的急切心情。

東漢時的大文學家、書法家蔡邕，家裏時常賓客盈門。有一天，家人報告說來了一個叫王粲的客人。蔡邕一聽此名，慌忙跑出去迎接，急得把鞋都穿倒了。

王粲進入客廳後，大家幾乎驚呆了，原來王粲是個少年，身材瘦小。大家不解，爲何蔡邕這個大官對個小孩也如此敬重。蔡邕看到大家驚愕的神色，介紹說："王粲智力超羣，才能出衆，我不如他呀。"

出自《三國志》

Wearing Shoes Back to Front to Welcome a Guest

Describing someone who is eager to welcome a guest.

CAI Yong was a great writer and calligrapher of the Eastern Han Dynasty. His house was always filled with guests. One day, his servant announced the arrival of a guest named Wang Can. As soon as Cai Yong heard the name, he was so eager to go out to welcome the visitor that he wore his shoes back to front.

When Wang Can entered the drawing room, the other guests were dumbfounded, for Wang Can was a youngster with a slight figure. They could not understand why a high-ranking official like Cai Yong should show such respect for a mere child. Cai Yong saw their surprised expression and introduced the youngster to them. "Wang Can is extra-ordinarily intelligent and unusually talented. I'm not his equal," he said.

History of the Three Kingdoms

舐犢之愛

shì　dú　zhī　ài

老牛深情地舐牛犢；比喻人愛子之情。

　　東漢末年，有一位很有才智的人叫楊修，在曹操手下當主簿。有一次，曹操領兵攻打劉備，正在左右爲難的時候，厨師給曹操送來了一碗鷄湯，裏面還有幾塊鷄肋。恰好這時，部將夏侯惇來問夜間的口令，曹操便隨口說："鷄肋，鷄肋！"楊修一聽這個口令，馬上讓隨軍準備收兵回營。夏侯惇吃驚地問楊修爲何這樣。楊修說："因爲今夜的口令是'鷄肋'，鷄肋這東西無肉，扔掉又可惜，正像我軍今日的處境。魏王下此口令，我想很快就要退兵了。"不久，曹操果然下令班師。但曹操忌恨楊修猜中自己心思，便以"惑亂軍心"爲由，將楊修殺了。

　　後來，曹操見到楊修的父親楊彪時，問他爲什麼瘦得厲害。楊彪一聽，便流着眼淚說："我仍然像老牛舐舐小犢那樣，愛着自己的孩子。"

出自《後漢書》

The Love of a Cow Licking Her Calf

Describing the warm feelings for one's child.

YANG Xiu was a man of great intelligence at the end of the Eastern Han Dynasty. He served as a secretary under Cao Cao. Once during a battle against Liu Bei, Cao Cao was in a dilemma as to what to do for his next move. A cook happened to serve Cao Cao a bowl of chicken soup with a few pieces of chicken ribs in it. While Cao Cao was drinking the chicken soup, his general Xiahou Chun came to ask what the password for that night was to be. Casually Cao Cao said, "Chicken rib. Chicken rib." When Yang Xiu heard the password, he told the army followers to pack up and get ready to withdraw. Xiahou Chun was surprised and asked him why. Yang Xiu said, "The password for tonight is 'chicken rib'. There's no meat on the chicken rib. But it's wasteful to throw it away. That's exactly the situation our army is in. From the password I can see Cao will soon order the withdrawal." Before long, Cao Cao indeed ordered the army to withdraw. But Cao Cao hated Yang Xiu for having guessed what was in his mind. He had Yang Xiu killed for his crime of "shaking the army's morale".

Later, when Cao Cao met Yang Xiu's father Yang Biao, he asked him why he had become so thin. In tears, Yang Biao said, "I still love my son like an old cow licking her calf."

History of the Later Han Dynasty

病入膏肓

bìng rù gāo huāng

心與膈膜之間的病；比喻事態嚴重，無法挽救。

春秋時，晉景公患重病，派人到秦國請醫生。秦桓公派了一位名叫緩的名醫去診治。在緩還未到之前，晉景公做了個夢，夢見兩個小孩在談話。一個說：「來人是個醫術高明的醫生，恐怕要傷害我們，我們該逃往哪裏？」另一個回答說：「我們躲在肓的上面，膏的下面，看他能把我們怎樣？」緩到了之後，給晉景公作了檢查，然後搖着頭說：「您的病已發展到肓的上面，膏的下面了，用火灸的辦法不行，用針刺也刺不到患處，服湯藥藥力達不到，實在是無法醫治了。」晉景公嘆了口氣，說：「眞是一位名不虛傳的醫生。」於是賞給了緩一筆厚禮，送他回國。不久，晉景公果然病逝。

出自《左傳》

The Disease Has Penetrated the Vitals

Beyond Cure

Literally this means the disease has reached the heart and diaphragm; figuratively it means that things have gone wrong and beyond cure.

IN the Spring and Autumn time, Duke Jing of the state of Jin was critically ill. He sent someone to fetch a doctor from the state of Qin. Duke Huan of Qin sent the famous doctor Huan to the state of Jin. Before Doctor Huan arrived, Duke Jing had a dream. In the dream he saw two children talking to each other. One of the children said, "The man coming here is a smart doctor. He probably will hurt us. Where shall we hide ourselves?" The other said, "Let's hide above the diaphragm and below the heart and see what he can do to us." When Doctor Huan arrived, he examined the duke. Shaking his head, he said afterwards, "Your illness has reached above the diaphragm and below the heart. It can't be cured by moxibustion, nor pricked by acupuncuture, nor reached by medicine. It's really beyond cure." Duke Jing sighed and said, "You deserve the reputation you enjoy." He rewarded Doctor Huan generously and sent him home. Shortly afterwards the duke indeed died of his illness.

Zuo Qiuming's Chronicles

高山流水

gāo　shān　liú　shǔi

形容音樂的美妙，也常用來比喻真摯的友情。

春秋時，晉國上大夫兪伯牙，出使楚國。某夜，月色清明，兪伯牙在船上彈起琴來。有一青年樵夫，名鍾子期，在一旁偷偷欣賞琴音。俞伯牙發現他後，就問他是什麼曲子，鍾子期說，是“孔子哭顏回”。俞伯牙和他談論樂理，他都對答如流。俞伯牙十分驚異。於是又奏起一曲，在琴音中表現山的高大之狀。鍾子期聽了，說道：“巍巍乎意在高山。”俞伯牙接着又在琴音中表現水的奔流之勢，鍾子期聽了，又說：“湯湯乎志在流水。”俞伯牙大喜，說：“你眞是我的知音啊！”兩人當即結爲兄弟，並約來年再相會。誰知第二年俞伯牙如期前來的時候，鍾子期已經病死。俞伯牙悲痛萬分，在鍾子期墓前，彈了最後一曲，就把琴摔碎，表示以後堅決不再彈琴，因爲他唯一的知音已經失去了。

出自《呂氏春秋》

Lofty Mountains and Flowing Water

Describing beautiful music. It is more often used to describe true friendship.

YU Boya was a ranking official of the state of Jin during the Spring and Autumn Period serving as an envoy in the state of Chu. One night of clear moonlight while Yu Boya was playing the lute on a boat, a young woodcutter named Zhong Ziqi listened stealthily nearby. When Yu saw him, he asked Zhong if he knew the tune he was playing. Zhong said, "It's Confucius crying over the death of Yan Hui." Yu talked about music theory with him, and Zhong answered fluently without a hitch. Yu Boya was very surprised. He played another tune, which depicted a high mountain. After hearing it, Zhong said, "This tells the loftiness of a high mountain." Yu Boya played again on the lute. The music described the swift flow of a river. Zhong Ziqi said, "Swiftly the water flows onward." Greatly pleased, Yu Boys said, "You're the one who really knows my music." The two immediately became sworn brothers and promised to meet again next year. However, when Yu Boya came to the same spot the following year, he found that Zhong Ziqi had died of illness. Overcome with grief, Yu Boya played his last tune in front of Zhong Ziqi's grave before throwing the lute to the ground and breaking it into pieces to show that he would never play the lute again because he had lost the one who really knew his music.

The Discourses of Lü Buwei

宴安酖毒

yàn ān zhèn dú

貪圖安逸，就像喝毒酒一樣能害人。

春秋時，北方的一些小諸侯國，經常遭到異族的入侵。有一次，狄人入侵邢國。邢國急向齊國求援。當時有名的政治家管仲，是齊國的宰相，他對齊桓公說：「狄人既兇殘又貪婪，我們不能讓他們得到滿足；邢國和齊國同是天子的諸侯國，親如一家，不能眼看着邢國滅亡。再說，如果齊國長期在安樂閒散中度日，那就像喝毒酒一樣，會影響君王的霸業的。我們應當出兵援救邢國。」齊桓公採納了管仲的意見，發兵救援，打敗了狄人的入侵。

出自《左傳》

Living in Comfort Is like Drinking Poisoned Wine

Meaning leading a life of ease and pleasure may ruin a man like drinking poisoned wine.

IN the Spring and Autumn time, some small vassal states in the north were often harassed by alien tribes. Once when the Di tribe invaded the state of Xing, the Xing urgently asked for help from the state of Qi. The famous statesman Guan Zhong was then the prime minister of Qi. He said to Duke Huan of Qi, "The Dis are cruel and greedy. We mustn't let them have their way. The state of Xing, like the state of Qi, is a vassal state of the king. We're as close as one family and must not sit idle and watch the state of Xing perish. Moreover, for the Qi people, living in ease and comfort for a long period of time is like drinking poisoned wine. It'll ruin the rule of the king. We must send reinforcements to Xing."

Duke Huan of Qi accepted Guan Zhong's advice, sent an army to help Xing and repulsed the invasion of the Di.

Zuo Qiuming's Chronicles

家徒四壁

jiā tú sì bì

家裏空空的，只有四面牆壁；形容十分貧窮，一無所有。

西漢時，四川成都有位大文學家叫司馬相如。他曾在漢室當過小官吏，後來閒居，因家中貧窮，生活十分艱難。

司馬相如和當時臨邛（今四川邛崍縣）的縣官王吉很要好。有一年，王吉邀請司馬相如到臨邛小住。臨邛有個大財主卓王孫，爲了顯示自己富有，宴請王吉和司馬相如。席間，王吉請司馬相如彈琴，彈後，博得滿座稱讚。卓王孫有個女兒叫卓文君，剛死了丈夫。她愛好詩文音樂，偷聽了司馬相如的彈奏後，又看他一表人才，不由得產生了愛慕之情。司馬相如知道後，也對卓文君發生好感，可是卓王孫嫌司馬相如貧窮，不同意他倆結合。他倆只得在一天晚上，偷偷離開臨邛，逃往成都司馬相如的家。卓文君到他家一看，除了四堵牆壁外，別無他物。可是卓文君願和司馬相如共度歲月。後來，漢武帝讀了司馬相如的文章，十分讚賞，並賞了他官職。從此，司馬相如遠近聞名。卓王孫也不再瞧不起他了。

出自《漢書》

A Home with Four Bare Walls

Describing extreme poverty.

SIMA Xiangru was a great literary figure in Chengdu, Sichuan, during the Western Han Dynasty. He once served as a petty official of the Han government, but later became unemployed. Reduced to poverty, he led a very hard life.

Siman Xiangru was a good friend of Wang Ji, the magistrate of Linqiong (today's Qionglai County in Sichuan Province). One year, Wang Ji invited Sima to come to Linqiong and stay for a while. There was a very wealthy man named Zhuo Wangsun in Linqiong. To display his wealth, he invited Wang Ji and Sima Xiangru to his house for dinner. At dinner, Wang Ji asked Sima to play the lute. Sima's performance won the praise of all who were present. Zhuo Wangsun had a daughter named Zhuo Wenjun whose husband had just died. She was a lover of literature and music. After listening to Sima Xiangru's performance and meeting him, she fell in love with him. When Sima learned about her love for him, he was also well disposed towards her. But Zhuo Wangsun disliked Sima because he was poor. He refused to allow his daughter to marry him. The two lovers eloped together one night and came to Sima's house in Chengdu. Zhuo Wenjun saw that Sima's house had nothing in it except the four bare walls. But she was willing to share her life with him. Later, when Emperor Wu of the Han Dynasty read Sima Xiangru's writings, he expressed deep admiration and rewarded him with an official post. From then on, Sima Xiangru's name became known far and wide and Zhuo Wangsun did not look down on him any more.

History of the Han Dynasty

家喻戶曉

jiā yù hù xiǎo

家家戶戶都知道；比喻一件事盡人皆知。

古時候，有個姓梁的女子，家中不慎失火。她哥哥的一個小孩和她自己的兩個孩子都被烈火堵在屋裏。她冒着烈火衝進屋裏，本想先把哥哥的孩子救出來，可等把孩子抱出來一看，却是自己的一個孩子。這時，火越燒越猛，再進去就有生命危險了，她急得捶胸大哭，連連說："這怎麼了得，這樣一來，家家戶戶不是都把我當成自私的人了嗎？我還有什麼臉見人啊！……"說着，不顧一切地又衝進火裏，結果被火燒死了。

出自《烈女傳》

Becoming known to Every Household

A Household Word

Said of something that is known to everybody.

THERE was a woman named Liang in ancient times. Her home one day caught fire. Her brother's child and the two children of her own were blocked in the house. Braving the fire, she rushed into the house intending to save her brother's child first. But when she carried the child out of the house, she found she had taken one of her own children. By this time, the fire had become worse and it was dangerous to enter the house again. She beat her chest with anxiety and cried, saying again and again, "How could I let this happen! It will become known to every household that I am a selfish woman. I shall be too ashamed to face anyone...." Saying so, she ran into the burning house again and was killed in the fire.

Biographies of Virtuous Women

害羣之馬

hài qún zhī mǎ

危害馬羣的壞馬；比喻危害集體的人。

傳說四、五千年以前，黃河流域有一個部落，首領叫軒轅黃帝。一天，他同幾個隨行人員乘車去具茨山見聖人大隗。途中，因路斷無法繼續前進，大家心急如焚。這時，正好碰見一個趕着馬羣的小孩。黃帝急忙上前問道："請問，你知道具茨山嗎？"小孩點了點頭。"你知道大隗住的地方嗎？"小孩笑着說："知道"。黃帝十分驚奇地說："你不僅知道具茨山，還知道大隗的住處，那麼請再對我說說怎樣治理天下吧！"小孩推辭不答。黃帝再三請求，小孩方才說："治理天下的事，並不稀奇，這如同牧馬一樣，無非是去除那些對馬羣有害的東西罷了！"這一席話，使黃帝悟出了治理天下的道理。於是連忙向小孩叩頭稱師致謝。

出自《莊子》

The Harmful Horse in the Herd

A Black Sheep

Said of someone who harms the collective.

IT was said that about four or five thousand years ago there was a tribe in the Yellow River valley headed by Xuan Yuan, the Yellow Emperor. One day, Xuan Yuan and a few of his followers went out in a cart to see the sage Da Huai who lived at Mount Cishan. On their way they found the road was damaged and they could not go any farther. As they became restless with anxiety, a child came along herding horses. The Yellow Emperor hurriedly walked up and asked, "Do you know where Mount Cishan is?" The child nodded his head. "Do you know where Da Huai lives?" The child smiled and said, "Yes." The Yellow Emperor was very much surprised. He then asked the child, "You know not only Mount Cishan but also where Da Huai lives. Then could you tell me how the country is to be ruled?" The child declined to answer. After the Yellow Emperor repeatedly begged for an answer, the child said, "There's nothing mysterious about ruling a country. It's just like herding horses. All you have to do is to get rid of the horse that is harmful to the herd." The Yellow Emperor was greatly inspired by the child's words about ruling the country. He kowtowed to the child in gratitude and honoured the child as his teacher.

The Book of Zhuang Zi

差强人意

chā　qiáng　rén　yì

還能使人滿意。

東漢開國皇帝劉秀的部將吳漢，作戰勇敢，對劉秀非常忠心。吳漢爲劉秀出生入死，打下了東漢的天下。劉秀稱帝後，吳漢被封爲大司馬。每次出征行軍，吳漢總是伴隨劉秀，不離左右。夜間宿營，劉秀未睡，他總側身侍立在旁。每當打了敗仗，將士垂頭喪氣的時候，他却激勵將士，振奮他們的精神，準備再戰。有一次，打了敗仗，一般將軍都情緒低落。劉秀見吳漢不在身旁，便派人去看大司馬在幹甚麼，回來的人報告說："大司馬正在檢查刀槍，準備進攻的武器"。劉秀聽了感嘆地說："吳公差强人意！"

出自《後漢書》

Barely Satisfactory

Meaning someone or something which is good enough to fulfil a need.

EMPEROR Liu Xiu, the founder of the Eastern Han Dynasty, had a subordinate general named Wu Han who was brave on the battlefield and extremely loyal to Liu Xiu. Wu Han braved death in helping Liu Xiu to conquer the whole country. After Liu Xiu became emperor, Wu Han was made the Minister of War. Every time Liu Xiu went on an expedition, Wu Han always accompanied him and was always close at hand. When they camped at night, before Liu Xiu went to bed, Wu Han was always at his side. When the officers and men were downhearted after a defeat, Wu Han would encourage them and arouse their spirit to fight again. Once, all the generals were low in spirits after a defeat, Liu Xiu could not find Wu Han at his side. He sent someone to see what the Minister of War was doing. The man came back and reported that he was inspecting swords and spears and preparing assaulting weapons. Liu Xiu sighed with feelings and said, "Lord Wu is just satisfactory."

History of the Later Han Dynasty

捲土重來
juǎn tǔ chóng lái

捲起塵土再回來；比喻失敗之後，力圖恢復。

秦朝滅亡之後，楚漢相爭，項羽被劉邦打敗，退到烏江。烏江亭長早已備好渡船，對項羽說：「江東雖小，但還有幾千里土地，幾十萬人口，也足以稱王，請大王趕快渡江吧！」項羽笑着回答：「我當初帶領八千江東子弟渡江西進，現在無一生還，即使江東父老不責怪我，我也沒有臉去見他們。"他又指着自己的馬對亭長說："我騎它作戰五年，戰無不勝，現敗局已定，我不忍殺死它，你帶它去吧！"說罷，即持刀與追上的敵兵斯殺。在這最後一戰中，他獨自殺死漢兵數百，自己也身負重傷，最後，自刎而死。唐代詩人杜牧遊烏江時，到項羽自刎的地方憑弔，曾寫有《題烏江亭》一詩，表示婉惜，詩內有"江東子弟多才俊，捲土重來未可知"的句子。項羽自刎烏江的故事見《史記・項羽本紀》。

出自《題烏江亭》

Kicking up the Dust and Coming Back

Meaning to make efforts to recover after a failure.

IN the struggle between Chu and Han after the fall of the Qin Dynasty, Xiang Yu of Chu was defeated by Liu Bang of Han and retreated to the bank of a river in Wujiang. The ward chief of Wujiang who had prepared ferryboats for Xiang Yu said to him, "The area east of the river is not large but covers several thousand *li* of land with several hundred thousand people. There you can be the king. Please hurry and cross the river." Xiang Yu smiled and answered, "In the beginning, I led eight thousand young men from east of the river and marched westwards. But today none of them are alive. Even if the elders in the east of the river don't blame me, I have no face to meet them." Pointing at his horse, he said to the ward chief, "I've been fighting on this mount for five years and was victorious in every battle. But now defeat is certain. I can't bear killing it. You can take it." After saying so, he picked up his sword, caught up with the enemy and threw himself into the battle. In this last battle, he alone killed several hundred Han soldiers and was badly wounded himself. In the end he killed himself by slashing his own throat. When the poet Du Mu of the Tang Dynasty toured Wujiang, he came to the spot where Xiang Yu had committed suicide to honour his memory. He wrote a poem entitled *Inscription for Wujiang Pavilion* to express his regret. In the poem are these two lines: "Among the young men east of the river are many talents; Who knows they will not kick up the dust and come back." The story of Xiang Yu committing suicide at Wujiang appears in the "Annals of Xiang Yu" in the *Records of the Historian.*

Inscription for Wujiang Pavilion

推心置腹

tuī xīn zhì fù

比喻對人信任，把心交給別人。

西漢末年，全國農民紛紛起義，反對王莽新朝。漢室劉玄、劉秀也加入了反王莽的綠林軍。公元23年，劉玄被推爲更始帝，劉秀爲蕭王。公元24年，劉秀戰勝了銅馬軍、高湖軍等，迫使他們投降，並收編他們。被收編的官兵擔心不會被劉秀信任，劉秀得知後，就讓收編的將官回自己的營寨，仍帶領他們原來的部下，而自己却只帶少數隨從到各營寨視察。被收編的人見劉秀對他們毫無戒備，於是相互議論說："蕭王待人誠懇，把赤誠的心也交給了別人，我們能不爲他赴湯蹈火嗎？"

出自《後漢書》

186

Placing Full Confidence in

Meaning to trust and bare one's mind to somebody.

AT the end of the Western Han Dynasty, peasant uprisings broke out everywhere to oppose the Xin regime set up by Wang Mang. Liu Xuan and Liu Xiu who were members of the royal family also joined the ranks of the insurgents against Wang Mang. In A.D.23, Liu Xuan was placed in the throne as Emperor Gengshi and Liu Xiu became the Prince of Xiao. In A.D.24, Liu Xiu defeated the Tongma and Gaohu armies, forced them to surrender and incorporated them into his own army. The newly incorporated officers and men were uneasy, thinking that they would not be trusted by Liu Xiu. When Liu Xiu learned how they felt, he allowed the newly incorporated generals to go back to their own camps with their own soldiers. He then inspected their camps with only a small retinue. The newly incorporated men, seeing that Liu Xiu was completely unguarded against them, began to discuss Liu Xiu among themselves. They said, "The Prince of Xiao is sincere to us and places full confidence in us. Is there reason for us not to brave dangers for him?"

History of the Later Han Dynasty

斬草除根

zhǎn cǎo chú gēn

鏟除雜草，要連根拔掉；比喻除掉禍根，以免後患。

春秋時，衛國與陳國聯合，共同討伐鄭國。鄭國國君鄭莊公，派人謁見陳國的陳桓公，希望和好。陳桓公不答應。他的弟弟公子五父勸他說：“與鄰國和睦相處，是最寶貴的東西，希望您接受鄭國的請求。"陳桓公聽後很生氣，說："鄭國是個小國，我去攻打它，它還能把我怎樣？"過了幾年，鄭國強大起來，爲雪當年陳國拒絕修好之辱，遂派大軍，進攻陳國，結果陳國吃了敗仗。對陳桓公的失敗，人們議論說："這是陳國自找苦吃，長期作惡不知悔改，終將大禍引到自己頭上。正如周朝的大夫周任講的：'作爲國君，對待壞事，就像農夫對待雜草一樣，要將它們連根拔掉，不讓它們再生長出來。'"

出自《左傳》

Digging up the Weeds by the Roots

Meaning to eliminate the roots of future trouble.

IN the Spring and Autumn Period, the states of Wei and Chen joined hands in an attack against the state of Zheng. Duke Zhuang, the sovereign of the state of Zheng, sent an envoy to Duke Huan of the state of Chen to express his wish for peace and friendship. Duke Huan, however, refused the friendly overtures. His brother, Prince Wufu tried to persuade the duke, saying, "To live in peace with neighbouring states is a thing to be treasured. I hope you'll agree to the state of Zheng's petition." But Duke Huan was angry. He said, "Zheng is a small country. I'm going to attack them and see what they can do to me." A few years later, the state of Zheng became very powerful. To wreak vengeance on the state of Chen's refusal for peace, it sent a great army against Chen. The state of Chen was defeated. For Duke Huan's defeat, people said, "The state of Chen asked for trouble. After doing evil for a long time without repenting, disaster has fallen on its own head. As what Zhou Ren, the ranking official of the Zhou Dynasty, said, 'The sovereign should deal with evil as peasants digging up weeds by the roots to prevent it from growing again'."

Zuo Qiuming's Chronicles

專橫跋扈

zhuān hèng bá hù

獨斷專行，驕橫放肆。

東漢順帝時，梁冀因姐姐是皇后，父親是大將軍，便依仗權勢，無惡不作，十分驕橫。有一次，他父親的朋友呂放對他父親講了梁冀的不良行為，他便懷恨在心，派人暗殺呂放，然後又嫁禍於人，因而殺害了一百多個無辜的人。

梁冀又極貪婪，州縣官吏必須給他進獻錢銀、珠寶，否則就橫加罪名，捉拿問罪。

後來，質帝即位，他雖年少，但很聰慧，對梁冀這種人，心中十分厭惡。一次上朝，質帝當着衆大臣的面，稱梁冀為"跋扈將軍"。梁冀懷恨在心，終於派心腹用鴆酒毒死了質帝。

出自《後漢書》

Imperious and Despotic

Said of someone who acts arrogantly and tyrannically.

LIANG Ji's sister was the empress of Emperor Shun in the Eastern Han Dynasty and his father was the Grand General. On the strength of his powerful connections, he did all kinds of evil and was extremely arrogant. Once, his father's friend Lü Fang told his father his improper behavior. Liang Ji harboured a hatred for Lü Fang and had him assassinated. He then shifted the crime on others. As a result, more than a hundred innocent people were killed.

Liang Ji was extremely greedy, too. The prefectural and county officials must deliver money and valuables to him or he would invent a crime and punish them accordingly.

Later, when Emperor Zhi, who was young and clever, succeeded to the throne, the young emperor was disgusted with people like Liang Ji. During a court sesson, he addressed Liang Ji as the "despotic general" in front of all the court officials. This kindled the hatred of Liang Ji, who eventually had Emperor *Zhi* murdered by his henchman with poisoned wine.

History of the Later Han Dynasty

眼中之釘

yǎn zhōng zhī dīng

眼中的釘子；比喻最憎恨的人或物。

五代後晉出帝時，宋州節度使趙在禮，依仗自己是皇親國戚，任意欺壓百姓，人們倍受苦害。後來，趙在禮將調任永興節度使，宋州百姓無不拍手稱快，奔走相告道："拔去了眼中之釘，眞叫人痛快啊！"不料，這話傳到趙在禮耳邊，趙請求留任宋州，也得到了出帝的批准。於是，他下令每人每年繳納一千文錢，名曰："拔釘錢"，弄得宋州百姓哭笑不得。

出自《新五代史》*

* 《新五代史》即《五代史記》北宋歐陽修（公元1007－1072年）撰。

A Nail in the Eye

A Thorn in One's Flesh

Meaning the most hateful person or thing.

IT happened during the reign of Emperor Chu of the Later Jin Dynasty in the Five Dynasties. Zhao Zaili, the Military

Governor of Songzhou, was a relative of the royal family. He bullied and oppressed the people, who suffered miserably. Later, when Zhao Zaili was about to be transferred to serve as the Military Governor of Yongxing, the people of Songzhou clapped and cheered. They ran around telling each other, "How happy we are to have the nail in the eye removed!" They never expected that the words reached the ear of Zhao. He requested to stay at Songzhou and his request was approved by Emperor Chu. He decreed that everyone was to pay a thousand coppers a year as "Nail Removing Money". The people of Songzhou did not know whether they were to laugh or to cry.

*New History of the Five Dynasties**

*Also known as *Historical Records of the Five Dynasties* by Ouyang Xiu (1007-1072) of the Northern Song Dynasty.

趾高氣揚

zhǐ gāo qì yáng

腳步抬得很高，神氣揚揚自得；形容驕傲自大，得意忘形。

公元前699年，楚國將軍屈瑕帶兵攻打羅國。出師那天，屈瑕披掛整齊，威風凜凜，向送行的官員告別後，登上華美的戰車，揚長而去。大夫鬭伯比送行回來，對他的車夫說：「屈瑕這回一定要打敗仗！你看他那樣子，走起路來，腳步抬得很高，神氣十足，防備敵人的思想早已鬆弛了。一個帶兵的人如此狂妄，肯定要失敗！」果然，由於屈瑕盲目自信和輕敵，他的軍隊一到戰場上，就遭到羅軍的猛烈反擊，楚軍慘敗。屈瑕孤身逃回，悔恨交加，感到再無臉面回都城見國君和父老，便吊在一棵樹上自盡了。

出自《左傳》

Strutting About and Putting on Airs

Holding One's Nose in the Air

Said of someone who is arrogant and complacent.

IN the year A.D.699, General Qu Xia of the state of Chu led an army to attack the state of Luo. On the day he departed for the battlefield, Qu Xia was dressed majestically in full armour. After bidding farewell to the officials who had come to see him off, he mounted a gorgeously decorated chariot and drove off. Having seen him off, the ranking official Dou Bobi said to his carriage driver, "Qu Xia will suffer defeat this time. Look at him, strutting about and putting on airs. He's completely off his guard against the enemy. An army commander who is as arrogant and complacent as he will certainly meet with defeat." Just as Bobi had expected, as a result of Qu Xia's complacence and taking the enemy lightly, his army met with a fierce counterattack as soon as it reached the battlefield and suffered a disastrous defeat. Only Qu Xia alone managed to escape. Overcome with remorse, he was too ashamed to return to the capital and face the king and his elders. He hanged himself from a tree.

Zuo Qiuming's Chronicles

殺人不眨眼

shā rén bù zhǎ yǎn

殺人時，連眼也不眨一下；形容兇惡之徒任意殺人，極其殘忍。

宋朝時，大將曹翰帶領兵馬，渡過長江，闖入廬山寺。寺裏和尚早已躲藏起來，只有德緣禪師端正地坐着不動，泰然如常。曹翰見他不行禮迎接，就怒喝道：「難道你沒有聽說過有殺人不眨眼的將軍嗎？」德緣仍然不動，不慌不忙地答道：「你哪裏知道還有我這不怕死的和尚哩！」曹翰無奈，於是改用和氣的口吻問：「老和尚，難道就你一個人在這裏，你能把別的和尚找來嗎？」德緣指着架上的大鼓說：「敲吧，一聽到鼓聲，和尚們就會到這裏。」曹翰拿起鼓槌，猛敲起來。等了一會，仍不見有和尚來，便責問道：「他們怎麼不來？」德緣說：「從鼓聲中能聽出你懷有殺人之心，所以他們不來。」說罷，慢慢起身，接過鼓槌，輕輕敲了幾下。不一會，躲藏的和尚都回到寺裏來了。

出自《五燈會元》＊

＊《五燈會元》宋代普濟和尚編。

Killing without Blinking

Said of a devilish man who kills wantonly and ruthlessly.

IN the Song Dynasty, General Cao Han crossed the Yangtze River with his army and rushed into the Temple of Lushan. All the monks in the temple had gone into hiding except Monk Deyuan who was sitting there without stirring as if nothing had happened. Cao Han was angry because the monk did not salute and welcome him. "Haven't you heard of the

general who kills without blinking his eyes?" he shouted at
the monk. Monk Deyuan still did not stir, but said
unhurriedly, "So you don't know there's a monk who is not
afraid to die!" Cao Han thereupon had no alternative but to
change his tone and asked the monk, "Old Monk, you
couldn't be the only person here. Can you call the other
monks here?" Pointing at the large drum, Deyuan said, "Beat
the drum. When the monks hear the drum, they'll come."
Cao Han picked up the drumstick and began to beat the
drum vigorously. He waited for a while, but no monk came.
"Why are they not coming?" he questioned. "They could
detect your murderous intention from the sound of the
drum. That's why they didn't come." Saying so he rose
slowly to his feet, took over the drumstick and beat the drum
lightly a few times. In a little while, the other monks who
had gone into hiding all came back to the temple.

*The Assembly of Five Lanterns**

*By Monk Puji of the Song Dynasty.

殺妻求將

shā　qī　qíu　jiàng

殺掉妻子去求得將位；比喻為了追求名利，不惜採取兇狠殘忍
的手段。

戰國初期，有位政治家和軍事家吳起。他善於用兵，在魯國服
務。有一次，齊國發兵攻打魯國，魯國想請吳起領兵抗齊，但考慮
到吳起的妻子是齊國人，恐怕在戰場上吳起念夫妻之情，心向齊
國，所以猶豫不決。吳起知道後，為了表明自己一心為了魯國，不
與齊人為伍，便將自己的妻子殺了。魯國見吳起有這樣的決心，便
命他領兵抵抗齊國，結果打了大勝仗。

出自《史記》

Killing One's Wife for the Sake of Generalship

Said of someone who resorts to ruthless means to obtain fame and wealth.

WU Qi, a statesman and military strategist of the early Warring States Period, served the state of Lu as an able commander. When Lu was attacked by the state of Qi, the Lu government wanted to place Wu Qi at the head of the troops to resist Qi. But considering that Wu's wife was from the state of Qi, the Lu government hesitated for fear that his emotional involvement with his wife should cause him to sympathize with Qi on the battlefield. Wu Qi soon learned about this. To show his wholehearted devotion to Lu and his refusal to associate himself with Qi, he killed his wife. Seeing Wu's determination, the Lu government put him in command of the Lu troops to resist Qi and won a great victory.

Records of the Historian

貪天之功

tān tiān zhī gōng

比喻把別人的功勞歸於自己。

春秋末期，晉文公重耳經過顛沛流離，終於在秦國的幫助下回到了晉國。為了報答有功之臣，他決定按功行賞。有一個跟隨晉文公出亡的功臣叫介子推，行賞時被遺漏了。介子推對重耳周圍那些居功自傲的人很不滿意，他決定不出去做官，甘守清貧。鄰人勸他去晉文公處領賞，介子推說：“到晉侯面前居功求賞，等於貪天之功以爲己有。"鄰人聽後，大爲嘆服。

　　從此，介子推與母隱居綿山不出。晉文公得知後，親往山中尋找，却不見踪迹，只得將綿山作爲介子推的掛名封田。

出自《左傳》

Arrogating Heaven's Achievement

Meaning to claim credit for what has been achieved by others.

AFTER wandering from place to place at the end of the Spring and Autumn Period, Chong Er, Prince Wen of the state of Jin, eventually returned to his own country with the help of the state of Qin. Grateful for those who had served him, he rewarded them according to their merits. One of the men who had followed him during his exile, a man named Jie Zitui, was overlooked when the rewards were dealt out. Very displeased with those around Chong Er who were arrogant on account of the service they had rendered, Jie Zitui decided not to become an official but continue to lead a humble life. His neighbours urged him to go to Prince Wen and claim his reward. Jie said, "To go to Prince Wen for reward is like claiming credit for what has been achieved by Heaven." Hearing his words, his neighbours were deeply moved.

　　From then on, Jie Zitui lived with his mother in seclusion in the Mianshan Mountains. When Prince Wen heard it, he went in person to look for him but could not find him. He eventually made Mianshan the nominal fief of Jie Zitui.

Zuo Qiuming's Chronicles

欲加之罪，何患無辭

yù jiā zhī zuì，hé huàn wú cí

想要給人加上罪名，還怕找不到藉口；形容隨心所欲地誣陷他人。

春秋時，晉國的國君晉獻公死後，大夫里克先後殺死了公子奚齊、卓子和大夫荀息。公子夷吾繼承了王位，為晉惠公。晉惠公害怕大夫里克像對待奚齊、卓子一樣對待自己，於是決定殺掉他。晉惠公派人對里克說：「你接連殺死兩位國君和一個大夫，看來，做你的國君是很困難的。」里克回答說：「我不除掉奚齊和卓子，他怎麼能當上君主？要給人加上罪名，難道還找不到藉口嗎？我已經領會他的意思了。」於是，里克便自刎而死。

出自《左傳》

One Can Always Name a Crime to Frame Somebody

Meaning that one can frame a case against somebody at will.

IT happened in the Spring and Autumn time. After the death of Duke Xian, the sovereign of the state of Jin, Li Ke, a senior official, killed Prince Xi Qi, Prince Zhuo Zi and Xun Xi, a senior official, one after another. Prince Yi Wu then succeeded to the throne and became known as Duke Hui. Fearing that Li Ke might take his life as he had killed the others, Duke Hui decided to kill Li Ke. He sent someone to say to Li, "You've successively killed two sovereigns and a senior official. It is not easy to be your sovereign." Li Ke said in answer, "If I had not got rid of Princes Xi Qi and Zhuo Zi, how could Duke Hui become the sovereign? One can always name a crime to frame somebody. I understand what his

197

intention is." Saying so, he committed suicide by cutting his own throat.

Zuo Quiming's Chronicles

既往不咎

jì wǎng bù jiù

對以往的過錯不再責備追究。

春秋時，大教育家孔子經常教育他的學生們說話要謹慎，尤其是回答國君的問話，更不能不知道强裝知道。不然，一言既出，將追悔莫及。

有一次，魯哀公問孔子的學生宰我："做社主（祭土神立的一個木牌位）應該用什麼樹木？"宰我回答說："夏代用松木，殷代用柏木，到了周代就用栗木了。用栗木的意思是，讓百姓看到就害怕，嚇得戰戰慄慄。"孔子聽到這件事後，非常生氣地說："做過的事，不要再解釋了，完成的事不便再挽救了，對已經過去的事情就不要再責備追究了。"

出自《論語》*

*《論語》儒家經典著作，是孔子的弟子關於孔子言行的記錄。

Things That Are Past, It Is Needless to Blame
Let Bygones Be Bygones

Meaning that there is no need to blame someone for his past mistakes.

CONFUCIUS, the great educator of the Spring and Autumn Period, often taught his disciples to be careful about what they said, particularly when answering the questions of a sovereign. Still less were they to pretend to know what they did not know. Otherwise, it would be too late to regret what they had said.

Duke Ai once asked Zai Wo, one of Confucius' disciples, "What wood should be used for making tablets at the altar to the god of earth?" Zai Wo said, "The Xia used pine wood; the Yin, cypress wood; the Zhou used chestnut wood, meaning to cause people to be shivering in awe." (The word chestnut also means shivering.) When Confucius heard about it, he was very angry, saying, "Things that are done, it is needless to explain; things that have been completed, it is needless to remonstrate about; things that are past, it is needless to blame."

Confucian Analects*

*A Confucian classic recording of the words and deeds of Confucius by his disciples.

從容不迫

cōng　róng　bú　pò

形容不慌不忙，非常鎮靜。

戰國時，哲學家莊子，有一次和他的好友惠子在濠水橋上觀魚。莊子說："鰷魚在水裏從容不迫地游蕩，這是魚的快樂啊！"惠子問："你不是魚，怎麼知道魚的快樂？"莊子反問道："你又不是我，怎麼知道我不知道魚的快樂呢？"惠子說："我不是你，固然不知道你所想，但你總不是魚，不可能知道魚的快樂却是無疑的。"最後，莊子解釋說："你問我怎麼知道魚的快樂，可見你已經知道我是曉得魚的快樂的。至於我爲什麼知道，那是因爲我到了濠水橋上，看見魚在水中悠游，所以覺得魚很快樂。"

出自《莊子》

Calm and Unhurried

ZHUANG Zi, a philosopher of the Warring States Period, once went to the Haoshui Bridge with his good friend Hui Zi to watch fish in the water. Zhuang Zi said, "See the silver carp swimming calmly and unhurriedly in the water. This is what happiness means to the fish!" Hui Zi questioned, "Since you are not a fish, how do you know the fish are happy?" Zhuang Zi retorted, "Since you are not me, how do you know that I don't know the fish are happy?" Hui Zi then said, "I'm not you and therefore don't know what you're thinking about. But there's no doubt that you're not a fish and it's impossible for you to know that the fish are happy." Eventually Zhuang Zi had to explain, "You asked me how I came to know the fish are happy. This shows that you already know that I know the fish are happy. As for how do I know, it's because I'm on the Haoshui Bridge and saw the fish swimming leisurely in the water and perceived that the fish are happy."

The Book of Zhuang Zi

從善如流

cóng shàn rú liú

接受好的意見，像流水一樣迅速；比喻樂於聽從別人正確的意見。

春秋時，有一次楚國派兵進攻鄭國。鄭國是個小國，抵擋不住。晉國派欒書爲元帥率領軍隊去救援鄭國。楚軍見晉軍來勢甚猛，不敢與晉軍對敵，便撤回國內。欒書想乘機繼續進軍，攻打楚國的盟國蔡國。楚國聞訊後，便立刻調動申、息兩地的駐軍開赴蔡國，準備迎戰。

這時，有兩種意見：一種是晉將趙同、趙括力促欒書佔領蔡國；另一種是欒書部下知莊子、范文子、韓獻子力勸不必出師蔡國，並對欒書說：“我們是援救鄭國來的，是正義之師，現在楚軍已撤，如我們借機攻打蔡國，就是不義的了，這種仗就不一定能夠打勝，即使打勝了，也不光彩；如果失敗了，那就更加不光彩了！”欒書覺得自己部下的話很有道理，便下令撤軍返回晉國。後來《左傳》作者在記述這段故事時，讚揚欒書“從善如流”。

出自《左傳》

Following Advice As Swiftly as a Stream Flows

Meaning readily to accept good advice.

IN the Spring and Autumn time, the state of Chu once sent an army against the state of Zheng. Being a small state, Zheng was unable to resist it. The state of Jin put Luan Shu in command of an army and came to Zheng's rescue. As the Jin army came with tremendous force, the Chu army did not dare to fight it and withdrew to its own country. Luan Shu wanted to march on to attack the state of Cai, an ally of the state of Chu. When news reached the state of Chu, it immediately sent its garrisons at Shen and Xi to the state of Cai to get ready to fight a war.

At this moment, two pieces of different advice were offered to Luan Shu: one from the Jin generals Zhao Tong and Zhao Kuo, who were for the occupation of the state of Cai; the other was from Luan Shu's subordinates Zhi Zhuangzi, Fan Wenzi and Han Xianzi, who were against attacking the state of Cai, saying, "We've come to help the state of Zheng and are an army dedicated to a just cause. Now that the Chu army has withdrawn, ours will not be an righteous army if we take the opportunity to attack Cai. We can never be sure to win. Even if we win, it gives us no glory. If we lose, we'll become more dishonoured." Believing that there was reason in what his subordinates had said, Luan Shu pulled back his army and returned to the state of Jin. Later, when Zuo Qiuming wrote about the story in his *Chronicles,* he praised Luan Shu as "following advice as swiftly as a stream flows".

Zuo Qiuming's Chronicles

鳥盡弓藏

niǎo　jìn　gōng　cáng

　　鳥打光後，彈弓就該收藏起來了；比喻事成之後，功臣被廢棄或遭殺害。

　　春秋末期，吳國和越國爭霸。公元前472年，越王勾踐在范蠡的輔佐下，終於打敗了吳國。在慶功會上，越王發現范蠡不見了。後來，有人在太湖邊找到了范蠡的外衣，衣內有一封信，信中說，他幫大王滅了吳國，是應盡的本份。眼下有兩個人留着對大王不利：一是西施，她迷惑過吳王夫差，也可能迷惑大王；另一個是他本人范蠡，手中權力大，讓人不放心。爲此，他已爲大王除掉了此二人……。過了不久，又有人給越國大夫文種送來一信，寫着："飛鳥盡，良弓藏；狡兔死，走狗烹；敵國滅，謀臣亡。越王爲人，可與共患難，不可與共安樂。子今不去，禍必不免。"至此，文種才知道范蠡沒有死，而是隱居起來了。可文種不怎麼信范蠡的話。後來，果然勾踐聽信了讒言，對文種起了疑心，並賜劍讓他自殺。范蠡卻經商致富，改名爲陶朱公，頤養天年，得以善終。

出自《史記》

When All the Birds Are Killed, the Bow Is Put Away

Said of someone who, after accomplishing success, abandons or kills those who have rendered service to him.

THE state of Wu and state of Yue were two rivals at the end of the Spring and Autumn Period. Assisted by Fan Li, Gou Jian, the king of Yue, eventually defeated the state of Wu in 472B.C. At the party celebrating the victory, the king of Yue could not find Fan Li. Later, someone found Fan Li's coat by Lake Taihu. A letter in the coat said that he had done his duty in helping the king subjugate Wu. There were at the moment two persons whose existence would harm the king. One of them was Xi Shi, who had seduced Fu Chai, the king of Wu, and probably would also try to seduce the Yue king; the other was himself, who had become too powerful to be fully trusted. For this reason he had done away with these two persons.... Shortly afterwards, someone wrote a letter to Wen Zhong, a senior Yue official. The letter said, "When all the birds are killed, the bow is put away; when the rabbits are slaughtered, the hound is cooked and eaten; when the enemy is subjugated, advisors are murdered. The king of Yue is a person with whom one can share adversities, but not happiness. Disaster will fall on you if you do not leave now." It was then that Wen Zhong learned that Fan Li was still alive but was living in seclusion. Wen Zhong himself was not fully convinced by Fan Li's words. Later, as Fan Li had expected, Gou Jian was swayed by slanderous words and became suspicious of Wen Zhong. He gave Wen a sword and ordered him to commit suicide. Fan Li on the other hand became very rich as a merchant. He changed his name into Tao Zhugong and died in peace at a ripe old age.

Records of the Historian

强弩之末

qiáng nǔ zhī mò

從强弓射出的利箭，起初勁頭很足，到最後力量就小了；比喻氣衰力竭，失去作用。

韓安國，漢初人，漢武帝時任大臣。有一次，北方的匈奴派人來漢朝要求和好，武帝就和大臣們商議對策。有一個名叫王恢的人，認爲匈奴反復無常，建議武帝發兵，把它徹底征服。韓安國極力反對，說道："人家派人來同我們和好，我們反而進攻，這是不合情理的。況且，千里遠征，路途跋涉，戰線拉得很長，人馬拖得很累，正如强弩之末，已勢衰力竭，就連極薄的細絹，也穿不過去。我們出兵，未必能獲勝！"大臣們都認爲韓安國說得有理，漢武帝也表示同意，於是接受了匈奴的求和，建立了和睦關係。

出自《漢書》

An Arrow at the End of Its Flight

Describing the weakened state of a spent force.

HAN Anguo was a minister under Emperor Wu of the early Han Dynasty. The Huns in the north once sent an envoy to the Han court to sue for peace and friendship. Emperor Wu consulted with his ministers on how to deal with it. A man named Wang Hui said that the Huns were capricious and he suggested that Emperor Wu should send an army to conquer them once and for all. Han Anguo was strongly opposed to it. He said, "They've sent an envoy to negotiate peace with us. It's unreasonable for us to attack them. Moreover, our expedition will have to travel a long distance and the battle line will be extended. Our men and horses will be exhausted by the time they reach there. It's like a powerful arrow at the end of its flight. It'll become so weak that it can't even penetrate a thin silk. Victory is not certain if we attack." The other ministers all agreed with him. Emperor Wu, who also agreed with Han, accepted the Huns' peace proposal and established friendly relations with them.

History of the Han Dynasty

異曲同工

yì qǔ tóng gōng

不同的曲子，但表演得同樣好。多形容通過不同方法，取得同樣效果。

西漢時，蜀郡成都有一位著名的辭賦家叫司馬相如。他的作品以辭藻瑰麗，氣韵非凡見稱，人們稱他為"漢賦"的代表作家。

距司馬相如七、八十年後，又出了一位著名的文學家叫揚雄，也是成都人。揚雄異常欽佩司馬相如的文才。他的作品雖受到司馬相如的影響，但却別具風格。

司馬相如和揚雄，同是西漢人，又是同鄉，兩人都以辭賦見長，文筆同樣高妙，但又各有特點，所以唐代文學家韓愈說他們是"同工異曲"，意思是說，他們兩人的作品，猶如音樂，雖然曲調不同，却同樣的美妙。

現在，人們用時則說成"異曲同工"。

出自《昌黎先生集》＊

＊《昌黎先生集》唐代韓愈（公元768－824年）作。

Different Tunes Played with Equal Skill

Meaning obtaining the same result from different approaches.

SIMA Xiangru was a famous writer of rhymed-prose from Chengdu of Shu prefecture in the Western Han Dynasty. His writings are known for their ornate diction and magnificent style. He was a representative of the rhymed-prose of the Han Dynasty.

Seventy or eighty years after Sima, another famous writer came to the fore. His name was Yang Xiong. Like Sima, he was also a native of Chengdu. An ardent admirer of Sima's literary talent, Yang Xiong was deeply influenced by Sima, but his writings are different in style from Sima's.

Sima Xiangru and Yang Xiong both lived during the Western Han Dynasty and both were from Chengdu. They both were noted for their rhymed-prose. Their writings are of equal excellence, but each has his own style. When Han Yu, a writer of the Tang Dynasty, commented on them, he said that they "played different tunes with equal skill", meaning their writings were like music with different tunes, but were equally wonderful to listen to.

*Collected Works of Changli**

*By Han Yu (768-824) of the Tang Dynasty.

欺世盜名

qī　shì　dào　míng

欺騙世人，竊取名譽。

春秋時，衛國有個叫史魚的大夫。他曾多次給衛靈公提出治國的意見，但都沒有被採納。後來史魚病重，臨終時，他囑咐兒子，在他死後不要把屍體裝進棺材，要實行“屍諫”。衛靈公聽說後，對史魚大加讚揚。

戰國時，齊國有一個叫田仲的人。他哥哥非常富有，但田仲却離開了兄長，靠編織草鞋爲生，自鳴清高不凡。

荀子認爲，史魚、田仲的行爲實際上是欺騙世人，竊取名譽。

出自《荀子》*

* 《荀子》戰國時儒家學派荀況（約公元前313－前238年）著。

Cheating the Public to Gain Fame

Meaning to fish for undeserved fame by cheating.

SHI Yu was a senior official of the state of Wei during the Spring and Autumn Period. He made many proposals to Duke Ling of Wei as to how to govern the country, but none of them were accepted. He later fell seriously ill. As he was dying, he said to his son that when he died his body was not to be coffined so that he could "offer advice by exhibiting his corpse". When Duke Ling heard of it, he praised Shi Yu highly.

A man named Tian Zhong lived in the state of Qi during the Warring States Period. His brother was a very rich man. But Tian Zhong left his brother and made his own living by making straw sandals, professing to be aloof from material comfort.

Xun Zi said that the way Shi Yu and Tian Zhong behaved was actually cheating the public to gain fame.

The Book of Xun Zi*

*By Xun Kuang (around 313-238 B.C.), a Confucian scholar of the Warring States Period.

揮汗成雨、比肩繼踵

huī hàn chéng yǔ、bǐ jiān jì zhǒng

揮灑汗水可成雨，行人肩靠肩、腳尖碰腳跟；形容人多擁擠。

春秋時代，齊國大夫晏嬰，節儉力行，忠心爲國，但身材矮小，容貌也不出衆。有一次，晏嬰出使楚國，楚靈王故意叫人在城門邊上開了一個小門，讓他從這裏入城。晏嬰冷笑道："這是狗國，出使狗國的人才從這裏進去。"楚靈王聽到報告後，只得讓人打開城門，請晏嬰進城。

第二天，晏嬰拜見楚靈王，楚靈王聳了聳肩膀說："你們齊國大概沒有人了吧，不然，怎麽派你來呢？"晏嬰答道："我們齊國都城有三萬戶人家，人多得張開衣袖就能連成一片陰影，揮灑汗水可成陣雨，走在路上，肩靠肩，腳尖碰着腳跟，怎麽會說沒有人呢？"楚靈王緊接着問："那麽，爲什麽派你來呢？"晏嬰從容地回答說：「我們齊國派使臣，歷來有個規矩：讓賢能的人出使有賢君的國家，無能的人出使君主無能的國家；我晏嬰最無能，所以只能派我出使貴國。」楚靈王聽後，瞠目結舌，無言以對。他覺得晏嬰是個出色的政治家和外交家，不得不隆重接待他。

出自《晏子春秋》

Sweat Falling like Rain, Shoulders Rubbing Shoulders and Toes Touching Heels

Describing a multitude of people, their perspiration pours down like rain as they walk shoulder to shoulder with their toes touching heels.

YAN Ying, a senior official of the state of Qi during the Spring and Autumn Period, was a hard-working man and loyal to his country. But he was short in stature and not distinguished in his features. Once he was sent as an envoy to the state of Chu. Duke Ling of Chu deliberately had a small gate dug into the city wall next to the proper city gate and asked him to enter by that gate. Yan Ying sneered and said, "So this must be the dogs' country and an envoy to the dogs' country goes through this gate." When this was made known to Duke Ling, he had no choice but to open the city gate and ask Yan Ying to enter by the city gate.

During his audience with Duke Ling the following day, the duke shrugged his shoulders and said, "The state of Qi probably has no other persons to send. Otherwise, why are you sent here?" Yan Ying retorted, "Our state of Qi has a population of thirty thousand households. There are so many people that when they unfold their sleeves, the sun is blotted out. When they perspire, their sweat falls like rain, and when they walk on the street, their shoulders rub shoulders and their toes touch heels. Why do you say there are no other people?" Duke Ling asked again, "But why of all people are you sent here?" Yan Ying answered unhurriedly, "The state of Qi has a rule in sending envoys. Worthy persons are sent as envoys to countries with worthy kings, and incompetent persons are sent to countries with incompetent kings. As I'm the most incompetent, I'm sent to your country." The duke was dumbfounded and speechless. He found that Yan Ying was an outstanding statesman and diplomat and had to treat him with proper ceremony.

Anecdotes of Yan Zi

喪家之狗

sàng　jiā　zhī　gǒu

失去了家的狗；比喻逃走時的慌張驚恐。

魯國人孔子生在動亂的春秋戰國時期。為了實現自己的政治抱負，經常奔波於各諸侯國之間。有一次，孔子來到鄭國，他和弟子們忽然走散了，弟子們趕忙分頭去找他。子貢向一位老百姓打聽，那人說：“東門口有個人，前額像堯，後頸像皋陶，肩膀像子產，下身比禹矮些（堯、皋陶、禹都是傳說中的古代聖人，子產是鄭國的令尹），看他那一副狼狽的樣子，活像喪家之狗。”子貢趕到東門，把剛才聽到的那些話，如實地告訴了孔子。孔子聽了，笑道：“他說我像這個像那個，那無所謂，他說我像喪家之狗，真是確切啊！”。

出自《史記》

A Stray Cur

Describing someone fleeing in haste and confusion.

CONFUCIUS, a native of the state of Lu, lived during the tumultuous years of the Spring and Autumn and Warring States time. To realize his political ambitions, he often travelled from one to another of the princely states. Once when Confucius was in the state of Zheng, he got lost on the way. His disciples divided themselves into several routes and began to look for him. When Zi Gong asked a man if he had seen Confucius, the man said, "There's someone at the east gate. His forehead is like that of Yao; the back of his neck, that of Gao Tao; his shoulders, those of Zi Chan, and his legs are shorter than those of Yu (Yao, Gao Tao and Yu were legendary ancient sages while Zi Chan was a governor in the state of Zheng). He was in such a sorry plight that he looked very much like a stray cur." Zi Gong rushed to the east gate and faithfully told Confucius what he had heard from the man. Confucius smiled and said, "Who the man said I looked like is unimportant. But how precise his description of me like a stray cur is!"

Records of the Historian

黃粱美夢

huáng liáng měi mèng

在黃米飯還沒有蒸熟的時間內，做了一個好夢；比喻不能實現的願望。

有一個姓盧的書生，進京趕考途中，在邯鄲一家旅店裏遇見道士呂翁，兩人一見如故，談得很投契。書生向道士訴說了家世，怨恨自己命運不好，沒有過上好日子。呂翁聽了，便取出一個青瓷枕頭，說：「你枕着它睡上一覺，就會稱心如意。」這時，店主剛煮上一鍋黃米飯。書生見離吃飯時間尚早，就高興地接過枕頭，和衣睡下，不久進入夢鄉。書生夢見自己中了進士，做了大官，後來當了宰相；還夢見自己娶了一個賢惠、美麗的妻子，生了五個兒子，十幾個孫子，兒孫個個功成名就。他享盡了人間的榮華富貴，一直活到八十多歲。當他醒來，才發現方才的一切都是一場夢。道士呂翁仍坐在身旁，店主的那鍋黃米飯還沒有熟哩！

"黃粱美夢"也作"一枕黃粱"，或稱"黃粱夢"。

出自《枕中記》*

* 《枕中記》傳奇小說，唐沈既濟（約公元780年前後在世）作。

A Golden Millet Dream

A beautiful dream that lasts no longer than the time it takes to cook a pot of millet. Meaning a wish that can never be realized.

ON his way to the capital to sit for the civil examination, a scholar named Lu met a Taoist priest named Lü Weng in a hostel in Handan. They chatted agreeably and soon became like old friends. The scholar complained to the priest about his poor family, his ill fate and that he had never lived happily. Thereupon, the priest produced a pillow of celadon porcelain and said to the scholar, "If you sleep on it, it'll answer all your wishes." At the moment the proprietor of the hostel was cooking a pot of millet. Thinking it was early to take the meal, the scholar happily placed his head on the pillow and went to sleep with his clothes on. He soon had a dream. In the dream the scholar dreamed that he had passed the civil examination and was awarded the title of Advanced Scholar, that he soon became a high official and later became the prime minister and that he married a beautiful and intelligent wife, who gave birth to five sons and the sons in turn brought him more than a dozen grandsons, who all achieved success and fame. The scholar was able to enjoy all the wealth and glory of the world and lived until he was over eighty. But when he woke up, he found it was only a dream. The Taoist priest Lü Weng was still sitting by his side and the hostel proprietor's millet was not yet cooked.

*Story of the Pillow**

*A story by Shen Jiji (fl. A.D.780) of the Tang Dynasty.

圍魏救趙

wéi　wèi　jiù　zhào

圍魏國救趙國；指在戰爭中避實就虛，迫使敵人撤兵的作戰方法。

戰國時，魏國大將龐涓領兵攻打趙國，包圍了趙國都城邯鄲。齊國接受了趙王的請求，任命田忌為大將、孫臏為軍師，發兵救趙。田忌打算直接去邯鄲，為趙國解圍，孫臏不同意。孫臏說："要想解開一團亂絲，不能強拉硬扯；要解開兩人鬥毆，不能進去同打。現在魏國主力正在圍攻邯鄲，國內一定空虛。我們不如把軍隊開往魏國的都城大梁（今河南開封），大梁受到威脅，魏軍一定從趙國撤退。這樣我們既可以援救趙國，又能打擊魏軍，比趕到邯鄲去廝殺要有利得多。"

田忌採納了孫臏的意見，直奔大梁。魏軍果然撤兵回國，解除了對邯鄲的包圍。當魏軍撤到桂陵（今河南長垣縣境內）的時候，埋伏在山中的齊軍突然衝殺出來，魏軍大敗。

出自《史記》

Besieging Wei to Rescue Zhao

A stratagem employed in war to strike at the enemy's weak point in order to force him to withdraw.

THE army under the command of General Pang Juan of the state of Wei during the Warring States Period invaded the state of Zhao and laid siege to the Zhao capital Handan. Upon receiving a request from the king of Zhao, the state of Qi dispatched an army with Tian Ji as the commanding general and Sun Bin as the advisor to come to Zhao's rescue. Tian Ji intended to march to Handan to break the siege, but Sun Bin was against it. He said, "To unravel a knotted mess of silk, one mustn't pull by force; to separate two men in a fight, one mustn't join in the skirmish. As the main force of Wei is besieging Handan, Wei must be defenceless in its own country. If we march on the Wei capital Daliang (today's Kaifeng in Henan Province), the Wei army will certainly withdraw from Zhao when Daliang is threatened. In this way we can both rescue Zhao and strike at the Wei army. It's better than joining in the battle at Handan."

Tian Ji accepted Sun Bin's advice and marched straight to Daliang. As expected, the Wei army indeed withdrew from Zhao and the siege to Handan was lifted. When the Wei army reached Guiling (in today's Changyuan County, Henan Province), it was utterly defeated by the Qi army in an ambush in the mountains.

Records of the Historian

傍人門戶

bàng rén mén hù

靠着别人的家過日子；比喻不能自立，依賴他人。

214

古時候，中國民間有一種風俗：過年時，用兩塊桃木板寫上神仙的名字掛在門旁，以便壓邪，這木板稱作“桃符”；五月初五那天，將艾蒿紮成人形懸掛門戶上方，用來驅趕毒氣，稱爲“艾人”。

有一天，桃符和艾人在一家的門上爭吵起來。桃符抬頭望着艾人罵道：“你這下賤的東西，怎麼總是在我的頭頂上！”艾人彎下身子說：“你的半截身子已經埋在土裏了，還跟我爭什麼高低呢？”桃符聽後，氣得火冒三丈，同艾人爭吵不休。這時，門神聽得實在不耐煩了，出來調解說：“別吵了，我們都是沒用的東西，正靠着別人的門戶過日子，哪裏還有閒功夫鬧這種意氣呢？”桃符和艾人聽了門神的話，羞愧地垂下了頭，不再爭辯了。

出自《東坡志林》＊

＊《東坡志林》筆記，北宋蘇軾（公元1037－1101年）撰。

Hanging on Another's Door

A Hanger-on

Said of someone who is not able to support himself but depends on others for a living.

THE Chinese people had a custom in former times of hanging peach-wood boards with the names of gods written on them on either side of the door on New Year's Day to suppress evil spirits. These boards were known as "peach tallies". Again, on the fifth day of the fifth lunar month, people tied mugwort into the shape of a human and hung it on the lintel to stop any poisonous vapour from entering the house. This was known as the "mugwort figure".

One day, the peach tally and mugwort figure on the door of a family started a quarrel. Looking up at the mugwort figure, the peach tally said abusively, "You miserable wretch! How dare you always stand above my head?" The mugwort bent down and said, "Half of you is already buried in the earth. You've no right to compare with me." The peach tally was furious and hurled more abuses at the mugwort figure. Meanwhile, the door god was annoyed by their quarrel. He came forward and said, "Stop your quarrelling. We're all useless things hanging on the door of another man for a living. We don't have the time to vent our personal feelings." After hearing what the door god said, both the peach tally and mugwort figure lowered their heads in shame and became silent.

Miscellaneous Notes of Dongpo *

*By Su Shi (1037-1101) of the Northern Song Dynasty.

程門立雪

chéng　mén　lì　xuě

　　站在程家門外的雪地裏；形容尊敬師長和對有學問的人的仰慕心情。

　　北宋時，有一位儒學家叫程頤。他有兩個學生，楊時和游酢。有一次，楊時和游酢去拜見程頤，正碰上老師在閉目養神。程頤明知有客人到來，但不理睬。楊時和游酢，不聲不響，恭立兩旁。等了半天，程頤終於睜開了眼，故作驚奇地說："你們兩位還沒有走？"那天，正是寒冬季節，學生告別出門時，外面已經積雪一尺多了。

出自《宋史》＊

＊《宋史》紀傳體宋代史，元代脫脫等（公元1314-1355年）等編寫。

Standing at Cheng's Door in the Snow

Describing the respect shown to a teacher or admiration for a learned man.

CHENG Yi, the Confucian scholar of the Northern Song Dynasty, had two disciples. They were Yang Shi and You Zuo. One day when Yang Shi and You Zuo called on their teacher at his house, they found Cheng Yi resting himself with his eyes closed. Cheng Yi knew that there were visitors, but he did not bother to open his eyes and speak to them. Yang and You stood silently and respectfully by their teacher and waited for a long while before Cheng Yi opened his eyes. He feigned surprise and said to them, "So you're still here!" It was a cold winter day. When the disciples bid farewell to their teacher, more than a foot deep of snow had accumulated on the ground.

*A history of the Song Dynasty in the form of annals and biographies compiled by Tuotuo (1314-1355) and others of the Yuan Dynasty.

衆叛親離

zhòng pàn qīn lí

衆人反對，親人離去；形容不得人心，陷於孤立。

春秋初期，衞國公子州吁，見兄長衞桓公老實可欺，便與心腹石厚密謀篡奪君位。公元前719年，恰逢周天子平王病死，各國諸侯紛紛前去弔唁。州吁得到消息後，親自爲衞桓公送行。來到西門外，州吁說：「今日兄侯遠行，薄酒奉餞。」衞桓公一飲而盡，也回敬了一杯。州吁故意失杯落地，並佯裝俯身拾杯，趁機拔出匕首將桓公刺死。州吁回宮後自立爲國君，並謊稱桓公得急病身亡。可是眞相難瞞，人們紛紛傳說州吁殺君篡位，人心不服。州吁憂心忡忡，這時石厚獻計說：「要人心歸服，得打幾次勝仗來樹立威望。」州吁於是選擇了鄭國，作爲用兵對象。鄭國莊公探聽到州吁作戰目的，就不和他爭強，佯裝戰敗。州吁「得勝」班師回衞，深以爲從此會威望大增，衆人敬佩。誰知百姓却恨他無故發動戰爭，使得人人不得安寧。後來，魯國大夫衆仲說：「州吁衆叛親離，難以濟矣。」

出自《左傳》

218

Deserted by the Masses and Followers

To Be Left in the Cold

Said of someone who has lost popular support and become isolated.

IN the early Spring and Autumn time, Prince Zhou Yu of the state of Wei found that his brother Prince Huan, the sovereign of the princely state, was an honest person and could be easily bullied. He plotted with his close follower Shi Hou to usurp the throne. When King Ping of the Zhou Dynasty died in his sickbed in 719 B.C., the princes of all the vassal states went to offer their condolences. Before Prince Huan departed, Zhou Yu accompanied him to the west gate and said, "As you're starting a long journey today, I've prepared some wine to bid you farewell." Prince Huan finished the wine and offered a cup to Zhou Yu. Zhou deliberately dropped the cup to the ground and as he bent down to pick it up, he pulled out a dagger and stabbed Prince Huan to death. Zhou Yu returned to the palace and proclaimed himself to be the sovereign and declared that Prince Huan had died suddenly of disease. But the truth could not be concealed. People began to tell one another that Zhou Yu had killed the sovereign and usurped the throne. The people were indignant. Zhou Yu was greatly worried. Shi Hou suggested, "If you want the people to support you, you must fight a few victorious battles to raise your prestige." Zhou Yu chose the state of Zheng as a target of his attack. When Prince Zhuang of the state of Zheng learned the purpose of Zhou Yu's war, he refused to fight him and pretended to be defeated. Zhou Yu thus returned "in victory" thinking that his prestige must be very high. He never expected that the people hated him for launching a war for no reason at all and disturbing their peaceful life. Zhong Zhong, a senior official of the state of Lu later said, "Zhou Yu was helpless because the masses and followers had deserted him."

Zuo Qiuming's Chronicles

衆怒難犯

zhòng nù nán fàn

衆人的憤怒難以觸犯。

春秋末期，鄭國發生了內亂。鄭國公子子孔乘機代替子駟執掌國政。為了保持自己的統治，他要官吏們立下誓約，絕對聽命於他，但遭到官吏的強烈反對。子孔很生氣，打算殺掉他們。子產前來勸阻，並建議把誓約當衆燒燬。子孔却堅持說：「立誓約，原是為了安定國家，如將它燒燬，國家就難以治理了。」子產說：「衆人的憤怒是難以觸犯的，單憑個人的願望辦事，也難以辦成，如果偏要觸犯衆人，那只能引起災禍。」後來，子孔接受了子產的意見，官吏們的情緒才逐漸安定下來。

出自《左傳》

It Won't Do to Incur the Anger of the Many

Meaning that one must not arouse the anger of many people or the public.

AN internal strife broke out in the state of Zheng at the end of the Spring and Autumn Period and Prince Zi Kong of Zheng took over the control of the government from Zi Si. To maintain his rule, he required all government officials to sign a pledge to obey him under all circumstances. But the officials were strongly opposed to it. Zi Kong was very angry and wanted to kill all of them. Zi Chan came forward and suggested that the pledge be burnt in front of everybody. Zi Kong insisted, "To sign a pledge is for maintaining peace and security of the country. If the pledge is burnt, it will be difficult to govern the country." Zi Chan said to him, "It won't do to incur the anger of the many. One can't accomplish anything simply by following one's own wish. If the anger of the public is aroused, disaster will follow." Zi Kong eventually accepted his suggestion and the anger of the officials gradually subsided.

Zuo Qiuming's Chronicles

普天同慶

pǔ　tiān　tóng　qìng

普天下共同慶祝。

晉朝元帝生了一個兒子，心中大喜，決定賞賜羣臣。一天，元帝上朝，羣臣道賀之後，元帝依次給予賞賜。當殷洪喬領賞時，殷洪喬却謙恭地說：「皇子出生，普天同慶，臣無功勞，却得如此多的賞賜，眞不敢當！」另一大臣中宗聽了向殷洪喬打趣說：「皇子出生這件事，難道能讓你有功嗎？」話音一落，文武百官都捧腹大笑起來。

出自《世說新語》

The Whole Nation Is Rejoicing

Meaning that the whole nation joins in the celebration of a happy event.

AT the birth of his son, Emperor Yuan of the Jin Dynasty was overwhelmed with joy and he decided to give rewards to all the ministers. One day after the ministers congratulated him, he began to give rewards one by one to all the ministers at the court. When it was Yin Hongqiao's turn to receive the rewards, he said modestly, "The whole nation is rejoicing over the birth of the prince. As I haven't done any service, I hardly deserve the rich rewards." At this, another minister said jokingly to Yin Hongqiao, "Do you think you're permitted to perform any service for the birth of the prince?" The civil and military officials all roared with laughter.

New Social Anecdotes

開天闢地

kāi tiān pì dì

指盤古氏開天闢地；常用來稱頌一項偉大事業的開創和完成。

相傳，世界在最古、最初的時候，天地不分，一片混沌，好像一個巨大的雞蛋，世界的開創者盤古氏就孕育其中。大約過了一萬八千年，盤古在這個原始世界的大蛋裏面，開始活動起來。他一動，大蛋破裂了。蛋裏的一部分輕而清的氣體上升爲天，另一部分重而濁的氣體下凝爲地，這樣才有天地之分。

最初，天地相距很近，盤古竭力撐持。此後，天每天升高一丈，地每天加厚一丈，盤古的身長也每天增加一丈。這樣又過了一萬八千年，盤古變成了九萬里長的巨人。他頭頂天，脚立地，使它們不再重合。

出自《藝文類聚》＊

＊《藝文類聚》唐歐陽詢（公元557－641年）等輯。

The Beginning of Heaven and Earth

Epoch-Making

This refers to Pan Gu separating heaven and earth. It is often used to eulogize the beginning or accomplishment of a great undertaking.

ACCORDING to legends, heaven and earth were not separated in the earliest times. The universe was a turbid mass like a giant egg and the creator of the world, Pan Gu, was in the middle of this mass. After about eighteen thousand years, Pan Gu began to stir in this primeval world and as he stirred the giant egg cracked. The lighter and purer gas in it rose to become heaven and the heavier and muddy part congealed to become earth. Heaven and earth were thus separated.

At first, there was only a short distance between heaven and earth. Pan Gu used all his strength to support heaven. From then on, heaven rose three metres a day and earth thickened three metres. The height of Pan Gu also increased three metres a day. After another eighteen thousand years, Pan Gu became a giant of 45,000 kilometres in height. He propped up heaven with his head while standing on earth so that heaven and earth can never come together again.

Classified Collection of Writings*

*Collected by Ouyang Xun (557-641) of the Tang Dynasty.

開門揖盜

kāi mén yī dào

打開大門，拱手迎接強盜進來；比喻引進壞人，自招禍患。

東漢末年，江東一帶是孫策的勢力範圍。吳郡太守許貢暗中派人給漢獻帝送信，建議調走孫策以免後患。不料送信人被捉獲，孫策大怒，絞死了許貢。許貢有三個門客，決心為許貢復仇。趁孫策在丹徒西山行獵的機會，向他襲擊，孫策臉上中了一箭。

回家後，孫策箭傷發作，臨死前將印綬留給弟弟孫權。孫策死後，孫權十分傷心，悲痛不止。長史張昭勸他說："現今奸邪作亂的人互相爭奪，豺狼當道，如果只顧悲哀，講究禮節，而不去考慮大事，這就像打開大門拱手迎接強盜進來一樣，豈不自招禍患！"聽了張昭的勸說，孫權止住悲傷，換上衣服，上馬視察軍隊。東吳有了新主，人心穩定。後來與蜀、魏形成三國鼎立的局面。

出自《三國志》

Opening the Door to Welcome the Bandit
Asking for Trouble

Meaning to bring disaster to oneself.

THE lower Yangtze was under the control of Sun Ce at the end of the Eastern Han Dynasty. Xu Gong, the governor of the prefecture of Wu secretly sent a messenger to Emperor Xian, proposing that Sun Ce be removed from his post to avoid trouble in the future. The messenger was, however, captured by Sun Ce, who was very angry and strangled Xu Gong to death. Three of Xu's followers were determined to avenge their master. They sprang a surprise attack on Sun when he was hunting in the West Dantu Mountains and hit Sun in the face with an arrow.

Sun Ce's wound grew worse when he returned home. Before he died he passed the seal of office to his brother Sun Quan. At the death of his brother, Sun Quan was overcome with sorrow. Zhang Zhao, a senior assistant, advised, "Bad people are stirring up trouble and fighting one another. The jackals and wolves are having their way. If you immerse yourself in sorrow and observe propriety only, instead of giving a thought to important matters, it will be like opening the door to welcome the bandit. You'll bring disaster to yourself." On Zhang Zhao's advice, Sun Quan overcame his sorrow. He changed his clothes and immediately went out to inspect the army. With a new leader, the people in the Wu area began to have confidence. Later, Wu achieved a tripartite balance of forces with the states of Shu and Wei.

History of the Three Kingdoms

畫虎類犬

huà hǔ lèi quǎn

畫出的老虎却像狗；比喻好高騖遠，沒有本領硬要去做。

馬援是東漢名將，他有兩個侄子，叫馬嚴和馬敦。這兩個人喜歡譏諷和議論朝廷上的事，並愛和俠客交往，相當浮滑。馬援在軍中聽說，便寫了一封信去教訓他們。信中說：聽到別人的過失，應該像聽到父母的名字一樣，只能聽，不能說。我最厭惡議論人家的長短，妄談國家大事。山都縣的縣官龍伯高，品行端正，謙虛節儉，廉潔奉公，我很敬重他，也希望你們仿效他。越騎司馬杜季良，豪俠好義，不論是誰，他都能交上朋友，在他父親辦喪事時，來的客人極多，我也很敬愛他，但不希望你們學他。因爲學伯高不成，還不失爲一個忠厚謙謹的人，好比把天鵝畫成鴨子，鴨子總還和天鵝接近；如你們學季良不成，就會成一個輕薄浪蕩的人了，所謂"畫虎不成反類犬"，這就差得太遠了。

出自《後漢書》

Trying to Draw a Tiger and Ending Up with the Picture of a Dog

Said of someone who is overambitious and tries to do something that is beyond his ability.

MA Yuan, the famous general of the Eastern Han Dynasty, had two nephews. They were Ma Yan and Ma Dun. The two liked to make sarcastic comments of court affairs and loved to associate themselves with chivalrous men, becoming steadily more superficial themselves. When Ma Yuan in the army heard about them, he wrote a letter advising them as to how to conduct themselves. In the letter, he wrote, "When you hear about other people's errors, you should listen as you would hear the names of your parents; you are only to listen, but not to make comments. I hate people gossiping about other people's right and wrong and talking foolishly about state affairs. Long Bogao, the magistrate of Shandu County, is a man of proper conduct, modest and thrifty, honest and devoted to public affairs. I respect him and wish you to learn from him. Du Jiliang, the Yueqi general, is a gallant and righteous man, who can make friends with anybody. When his father died, a great number of people came to his funeral. I also respect him, but I do not want you to learn from him. This is because if you follow Bogao's example but failed to become a man like him, you will still be a sincere and cautious man. It will be like drawing a swan and ending up with a duck. A duck is nevertheless still close in shape to a swan. If you failed to learn to be a man like Jiliang, you will become a frivolous and dissolute man. It will be like "trying to draw a tiger and ending up with the picture of a dog". The difference will be too great.

History of the Later Han Dynasty

畫餅充飢

huà　bǐng　chōng　jī

畫個餅來解除飢餓；比喻圖虛名而無益於實際。

三國時，魏國人盧毓，十歲時父母相繼去世，接着兩個哥哥也先後死去。在兵荒馬亂中，他辛勤努力養活着寡嫂和幼姪，人們無不讚頌他的品行。後來，盧毓做了吏部尚書，成爲魏明帝最親信的大臣。有一次，魏明帝想選拔一個適當的人做中書郎，便讓盧毓推薦，並且告訴他："選拔人才不要只看名聲，名聲好比畫在地上的餅，是不能眞正解除飢餓的。"

出自 《三國志》

Drawing a Cake to Allay One's Hunger

A Castle in the Air

Meaning something illusionary and useless in reality.

227

LU Yu was a native of the state of Wei during the Three Kingdoms period. When he was ten years old, his parents died one after the other. This was followed by the death of his two elder brothers. In the years of turmoil and war, he worked hard to support his brothers's widows and young nephews and nieces. People all praised his conduct. Lu Yu later became President of the Board of Civil Office and a trusted official of Emperor Ming of Wei. Once, Emperor Ming wanted to choose someone for the post of minister and told him, "When choosing a talent, one must not pay attention only to his reputation. Reputation is like a cake drawn on the ground; it can't really allay hunger."

History of the Three Kingdoms

結草銜環
jiē cǎo xián huán

打成草結，口銜玉環；形容感恩圖報之意。

春秋時，晉國的魏武子生病時，囑咐他兒子魏顆，在他死後，把他的妾嫁出去。後來，武子病重，又告訴魏顆，在他死後，讓他的妾陪葬。武子死後，魏顆覺得父親病危時的話可能是因爲神志不清而胡言亂語，便依照他以前的吩咐把他的妾嫁出去了。後來，秦國伐晉，魏顆領兵大戰秦軍，在戰場上，魏顆見一位老人，把遍地的草都打成結子，纏住秦軍戰馬，使秦軍大敗。當夜，魏顆做了個夢，夢見結草老人自稱是那位出嫁的妾的父親，以此來報答魏顆沒有把自己女兒做陪葬之恩。

又據說，東漢時，有個叫楊寶的九歲的小孩，有一天，在山下看見一隻受了傷的小黃雀。楊寶很可憐這隻小黃雀，便把它帶回家，每天用花蕊餵它。等黃雀傷癒後，楊寶就讓它飛走了。當天晚上，楊寶夢見一個黃衣童子，口銜四個白玉環，說是送給楊寶的禮物，並且感謝他的救命之恩，祝福他的子孫都像玉環一樣純潔清白，世代幸福。說罷，化作一隻黃雀飛去了。

前一故事出自《左傳》，後一故事出自《後漢書》。後世的人把"結草"和"銜環"合爲一句成語。

Tying Grass and Delivering Rings

Tying grass into knots and delivering rings by holding them in the mouth means paying a debt of gratitude.

IN the Spring and Autumn time, Wei Wuzi of the state of Jin fell ill. He bid his son Wei Ke that after he passed away, his concubine must be allowed to marry another man. Later, when Wuzi's illness became critical, he again told his son that after his death, his concubine must be buried alive with him. After his father died, Wei Ke felt that what his father said when he was critically ill might be just nonsense because he was not clear-headed. So he did what his father had told him the first time and married his concubine to another man. Later, there was a war between Qin and Jin and Wei Ke was in command of an army to fight the Qin. On the battlefield, Wei Ke saw an old man tying all the grass into knots so that the Qin war-horses were entangled by the grass knots. As a result, the Qin army suffered a crushing defeat. On the same night, Wei Ke had a dream and in the dream he met the grass-tying old man, who claimed to be the father of his own father's concubine. He had come to pay a debt of gratitude for not burying his daughter alive with Wei Ke's father.

It is also said that in the Eastern Han Dynasty, there lived a nine-year-old boy, whose name was Yang Bao. One day, Yang Bao saw a wounded young siskin at the foot of a mountain. Pitying it, he took it home and fed it with flower pistils until it completely recovered and flew away. On the night the bird flew away, Yang Bao dreamed of a boy in a yellow coat holding four jade rings in his mouth. The boy said to Yang Bao that the jade rings were presents for him and thanked Yang for having saved his life and wished Yang's future generations would be as pure as jade and live happily generation after generation. After saying so, the boy turned into a siskin and flew away.

Zuo Qiuming's Chronicles and
History of the Later Han Dynasty

勢如破竹

shì rú pò zhú

破竹子，只要破頭幾節，以後就能順刀劈開；形容作戰或工作節節勝利。

西晉時，晉武帝司馬炎企圖吞併吳國，但大臣們却各有不同看法，只有杜預的意見和晉武帝暗合。於是晉武帝派杜預爲鎭南大將軍，率領大軍，南下攻打吳國。戰事進展順利，出兵十天，就佔領了長江下游各城鎮。可是這時，有人說，吳國立國久，又是大國，恐難一下子打垮它。又說，天氣太熱，行軍不便，不如暫停進軍，等到冬天再說。杜預聽後，却不以爲然。他說：“今天我們的兵威

正盛，就像破竹子一樣，數節之後，必然迎刄而解”。於是晉軍繼
續攻打吳國，果然節節勝利，滅了吳國。

出自《晉書》

Like Splitting a Bamboo

Meaning achieving successes one after another in war or in work.

SIMA Yan, Emperor Wu of the Western Jin Dynasty, wanted to conquer the state of Wu, but his ministers held different views. Only Du Yu's view coincided with that of Emperor Wu. So Du Yu was appointed as Great General for Suppressing the South to lead an army against the state of Wu. The war progressed smoothly for Western Jin and within ten days the Western Jin army occupied all the cities and towns in the lower Yangtze. At this point, some people said that Wu had existed for a long time, was a big country and could not be vanquished so easily. Others said that the weather was hot, which was not good for the army on the march. It would be better to hold the attack and wait until winter time. Du Yu, however, thought otherwise. He said, "Our army is at the height of its morale. It's like splitting a bamboo. After the first few sections, the rest could be easily split." The Jin army thus continued the attack. Indeed, victory was won one after another and the state of Wu was subjugated.

History of the Jin Dynasty

解衣推食

jiě yī tuī shí

脱下衣服給別人穿，分出食物給別人吃；比喻對人體貼照顧，甘苦與共。

楚漢相爭時，韓信奉漢王劉邦之命率兵進攻齊國，項羽派大將龍且前去救援。結果被韓信打得大敗，龍且戰死。

項羽見韓信很有本事，於是就派武陟去勸說韓信脱離漢王劉邦，自己獨自稱王。韓信拒絕了武陟的勸誘，對他說：“我以前在項王部下，職位低下，說話沒有人聽，計謀沒有人用，所以我改投漢王劉邦。現在漢王授我大將軍印，讓我統率數萬軍隊。他脱下衣

服給我穿，分出食物給我吃。我說的話，他能聽從，我的計謀他能
採納。漢王這樣信任我、尊重我，我怎能背離他呢！" 武陟見勸說
不成，只好失望地回去了。

出自《史記》

Doffing Garments and Sharing Food

Doffing one's garments for someone to wear and sharing food
with him. Meaning to treat someone with great kindness and
sharing weal and woe with him.

WHEN the states of Chu and Han rivalled for supremacy, Han
Xin was ordered by Liu Bang, the king of Han, to march on
the state of Qi. Xiang Yu sent General Long Qie to come to
Qi's rescue. Long Qie's army was utterly defeated and Long
himself was killed in battle.

Seeing that Han Xin was a competent general, Xiang Yu
sent Wu She to try to persuade Han Xin into leaving Liu Bang
and to proclaim himself a king. Refusing Wu She's advice,
Han Xin said to him, "I served under Xiang Yu in the past.
My position was low. Nobody listened to what I said and my
ideas were not used. That was why I came over to Liu Bang.
Liu has given me the seal of a general and placed me in
command of tens of thousands of troops. He doffed his
garments for me to wear and shared food with me. He listens
to what I say and applies my ideas. He trusts me and respects
me. How can I betray him?" Having failed in his attempt, Wu
She went back disappointed.

Records of the Historian

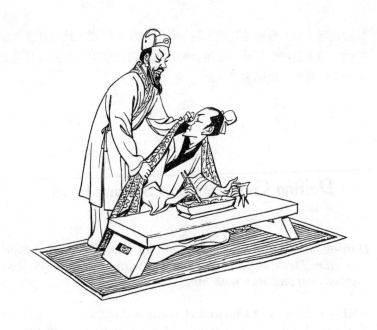

傾城傾國

qīng chéng qīng guó

使全城全國為之傾倒；用來形容絕色女子。

漢武帝時，有一位音樂家叫李延年，他很受漢武帝的喜愛。

有一次，李延年給漢武帝跳舞時唱了一首歌。歌中唱道："北方有一位佳人，舉世無雙，獨立不羣。她看一眼，能叫整座城池的人傾倒；她再看一眼，能叫一個國家的人傾倒。"漢武帝聽完問道："難道世上真有這樣的佳人嗎？"平陽公主乘機說："李延年的妹妹就是這樣一位美人。"於是，漢武帝召見了李延年的妹妹。一看，果然是位絕代佳人，便選進宮中當了夫人。

出自《漢書》

Overwhelming a City and a Country

Said of a woman of extraordinary beauty by whom the people of a whole city or country were overwhelmed.

THERE was a musician named Li Yannian at the time of Emperor Wu of the Han Dynasty. He was a favourite of the emperor.

Once Li Yannian sang a song while performing a dance for Emperor Wu. The song said, "There is a great beauty in the north. Being unrivalled in the world, she stands above all others. A glance from her may overwhelm a whole city and another glance from her may overwhelm a whole country." Emperor Wu asked after the performance, "Is there really such a beauty in this world?" Princess Pingyang said, "Li Yannian's sister is such a beauty." The emperor immediately sent for Li's sister. When she came, the emperor found that she was really an extraordinary beauty. The emperor eventually chose her as his wife.

History of the Han Dynasty

道聽途說

dào tīng tú shuō

在路上聽來的話；一般泛指沒有根據的傳聞。

從前，有叫艾子和毛空的兩個人。有一次，毛空告訴艾子說："有一隻鴨子一次生了一百個蛋。"艾子不信，毛空說："可能是兩隻鴨子生的。"艾子還是不信，毛空又說："大概是三隻鴨子生的。"就這樣，最後一直增加到十隻鴨子，艾子還是不信。

過了一會兒，毛空又告訴艾子說："上個月天上掉下一塊肉，長三十丈，寬二十丈。"艾子不信，毛空說："是二十丈長。"艾子還是不信，毛空又說："是十丈長。"最後艾子問毛空："你剛才說的鴨子是誰家的？肉掉到什麼地方？”毛空回答說：“我都是在路上聽別人這麼講的。”艾子轉身對着同行的學生說：“你們可不能像他這樣‘道聽途說’啊！”

出自《艾子外語》＊

＊《艾子外語》明代屠本畯輯。

Roadside Gossip

Hearsay

What is heard on the road. Usually meaning groundless rumour.

ONCE upon a time there were two men, one named Ai Zi and the other Mao Kong. One day, Mao Kong told Ai Zi, "There's a duck that has laid a hundred eggs in a day." Ai Zi did not believe him and Mao Kong said, "There're probably two ducks." Ai Zi still did not believe him. So Mao Kong said, "The eggs were probably laid by three ducks." He went on until he increased the number of ducks to ten. But Ai Zi still would not believe him.

Some time later, Mao Kong told Ai Zi, "A big slab of meat dropped down from the sky last month. It's three hundred feet long and two hundred feet wide." Ai Zi did not believe him and Mao Kong said, "It's two hundred feet long." When Ai Zi still did not believe him, Mao Kong said, "Maybe it's a hundred feet long." Finally Ai Zi asked Mao Kong, "Whose duck is it that laid the eggs? Where did the meat fall?" Mao Kong told him, "I heard them on the road from others." Ai Zi turned to his disciples who were accompanying him, and said to them, "You mustn't listen to the roadside gossips like him."

Other Sayings of Ai Zi*

*Collected by Tu Benjun of the Ming Dynasty.

運籌帷幄

yùn chóu wéi wò

在軍帳中籌謀策劃；比喻善於分析敵我形勢，決定正確的作戰方針。

劉邦做了漢朝開國皇帝後，曾在洛陽南宮舉行盛大宴會，他對眾將領說："請你們說實話，不要隱瞞我，為什麼我能統一天下，而項羽却丟失了天下呢？"高起、王陵回答說："陛下能夠同大家共享利益，打了勝仗論功行賞；而項羽則妒賢嫉能，有功績的人遭陷害，有才能的人被懷疑，打了勝仗也不獎賞，這就是他失敗的原因啊！"劉邦說："你們只知其一，不知其二。在軍帳中籌謀策劃，決定勝負，我不如張良；治理國家，安撫百姓，我不如蕭何；統帥百萬大軍，戰必勝，攻必取，我不如韓信。我能重用這三位人，這就是我能統一天下的原因。項羽手下只有一位范增，還得不到重用，這就是他失敗的原因。"

出自《史記》

Planning Strategies in a Tent

Meaning to be good at analyzing a battle situation and laying down correct principles of operation.

WHEN Liu Bang became the first emperor of the Han Dynasty, he gave a magnificent banquet at the South Palace in Luoyang. He said to his generals at the banquet, "All of you please speak the truth and not to hide anything from me. Why is it that I've been able to gain control of the country while Xiang Yu lost that control?" Gao Qi and Wang Ling said in answer, "It's because Your Majesty can share the gains with us and give rewards according to each one's merits after winning a victory. But Xiang Yu was jealous of people who were able and virtuous persons, persecuted those who had rendered meritorious service, suspected those with talents and gave no rewards even when victories were won. These are the reasons of his defeat." Liu Bang said, "You know only one side of it but not the other side. In planning strategies in a tent to decide victory or defeat, I'm not as good as Zhang Liang; in governing the country and pacifying the people, I'm not as good as Xiao He; in commanding an army a million strong, winning victory in every battle and taking every place we attack, I'm not as good as Han Xin. I entrust important responsibilities to these three persons. That's the reason why I've been able to unify the country. Xiang Yu had only Fan Zeng, and even Fan Zeng was not given any important responsibility. That's the reason of his failure."

Records of the Historian

嫉惡如仇

jí è rú chóu

恨壞人壞事，像恨仇人一樣。

西晉時，朝廷腐敗。晉武帝司馬炎在位時有宮女近萬人，整日飲酒作樂。到了晉惠帝司馬衷時，各地發生飢荒，他竟問老百姓為什麼不吃肉粥。

當時，任尚書右丞、司徒左長史的傅咸多次上書給晉武帝和晉惠帝，對朝政的寬弛、世俗的奢侈進行了勸諫和批評，並奏免了一些官吏，使京都肅然，貴戚懾伏。對於他這種"勁直忠果"，"勁按警人"的行動，不少人深為敬佩。後來房玄齡為他作傳時說他"識性明悟，嫉惡如仇。""嫉"一作"疾"。

出自《晉書》

Hating Evil as an Enemy

Meaning hating evil persons and things as they would be enemies.

THE court was corrupted during the Western Jin Dynasty. When Sima Yan, Emperor Wu, reigned, there were nearly ten thousand palace maids with whom the emperor caroused all day long. By the time of Emperor Hui, famine struck in many places and the emperor actually asked why the people were not eating meat porridge.

Fu Xian, a minister's assistant, petitioned to Emperors Wu and Hui many times, offering advice and criticizing the laxity of the government and the extravagance of the snobs. As a result of his memorials to the emperor, some officials were removed from office. The capital was put in better order and the nobles and royal relatives were cowed into behaving properly. Many people were filled with deep admiration for Fu Xian's "honesty and loyalty in giving warning". Later, when Fang Xuanling wrote Fu's biography, he said that Fu "knew thoroughly about human nature and hated evil as an enemy".

History of the Jin Dynasty

爾虞我詐

ěr yú wǒ zhà

你欺騙我，我欺騙你；比喻互相猜疑，互相欺詐。

春秋時，楚莊王率兵攻打宋國，把宋國都城睢陽（今河南商丘縣南）團團圍住。幾個月後，被圍困的宋軍吃光了糧食。但是，由於將士們在大臣華元的率領下，同仇敵愾，堅守不懈，宋國都城一直未被楚軍攻下。這時，楚軍將士也已疲勞不堪，口糧中斷，準備退兵。替楚莊王駕車的申叔時建議，如果在城的周圍修建房屋，種田屯糧，做出長期圍困的樣子，宋國就會因害怕而投降。楚莊王採納了他的意見。這樣一來，宋軍果然驚慌起來。一天夜裏，華元隻身潛入楚營，把楚軍統帥子反從床上拉起來，喝道："我們國君叫我告訴你，城裏雖然處境困難，我們寧願死去，也決不會屈膝投降！如果你們退兵三十里，我們願意談判。"子反見自己落入華元手中，只好答應，並及時報告了楚莊王。莊王見宋國人決心抵抗，只好答應楚軍後撤三十里，楚宋兩國講和，簽定了盟約，盟約上寫了："我無爾詐，爾無我虞。"意思是我不欺騙你，你不要欺騙我。後來演變爲相反的意思爲"爾虞我詐"。

出自《左傳》

240

Cheating and Deceiving Each Other

Said of people who suspect and try to deceive each other.

DURING the Spring and Autumn time, Duke Zhuang of the state of Chu attacked the state of Song and placed a tight cordon about Suiyang, the capital of Song (south of today's Shangqiu in Henan). The encirclement lasted for several months until the Song army in the city had exhausted its food supply. But under the command of Minister Hua Yuan, the Song generals and soldiers fought with one heart and put up a stubborn defence, and the Chu army was never able to take the capital. In the meantime, the Chu soldiers were also tired out. As their food supply was also interrupted, they were ready to withdraw. Shen Shushi, who was driving the carriage of Duke Zhuang of Chu, suggested that if the Chu soldiers began to build houses around the city, plant the fields for food grain and appear to be ready to stay for a long time, the Song side would be scared into surrendering. Duke Zhuang approved Shen's idea and the Song army was indeed alarmed. One night, Hua Yuan stole his way alone into the Chu camp. He pulled the Chu commander Zi Fan from his bed and shouted at him, "My sovereign wants me to tell you. Although we were in a difficult situation in the city, we'll rather die than surrender. If you withdraw fifteen kilometres, we're willing to negotiate." Being a prisoner of Hua Yuan, Zi Fan had no choice but to agree. When he told Duke Zhuang what had happened, the duke agreed to withdraw fifteen kilometres as he saw that the Song people were determined to resist. The states of Chu and Song eventually reached agreement for peace and signed a pact. In the pact it was written "I shall not cheat you, nor will you deceive me." Later, the phrase was used in a negative sense to mean "cheating and deceiving each other".

Zuo Qiuming's Chronicles

管中窺豹
guǎn zhōng kuī bào

從竹管裏看豹；比喻所見到的只是一部分，而不是全部。

晉代著名書法家王羲之的兒子王獻之，少年時就有很大名聲。有一次，他觀看家中門生玩擲骰子遊戲，發現有個人要輸，便說："南邊的風力不強。"門生們笑道："這個小孩像從竹管裏看豹子，居然也能看出一斑一點來。"王獻之生氣地說："你們不要小看人！遠的，我慚愧不如荀奉倩（即荀粲，三國時魏人，為人清高，很有才學）；近的，我慚愧不如劉眞長（即劉惔，王羲之的朋友）。"說完，便拂袖而去。後來，王獻之成了著名書法家，與其父王羲之齊名，被後世並稱"二王"。

出自《晉書》

Viewing the Leopard through a Tube

Meaning what one sees is only a part of the picture of things instead of the whole.

WANG Xianzhi, the son of Wang Xizhi, a famous calligrapher of the Jin Dynasty, became quite well known even when he was still a youngster. Once, while watching some of the family's retainers playing a game of dice, he found that one of them was about to lose. So he said, "The southern wind is not strong." The retainer laughed and said, "Even a child looking at the leopard through a bamboo tube is able to see some of the black spots." Wang Xianzhi was annoyed and he said, "Don't think I'm too young. Among those who lived long ago, I'm ashamed that I'm not as good as Xun Fengqian (also known as Xun Can, a native of Wei of the Three Kingdoms period, noted for his uprightness and learning); among those who are near, I'm ashamed that I'm not as good as Liu Zhenchang (also known as Liu Tan, a friend of Wang Xizhi's)." After saying so he went off in a huff. Wang Xianzhi later became a famous calligrapher in the same calibre as his father. The two of them became known to later generations as the "two Wangs".

History of the Jin Dynasty

齊人攫金

qí rén zhuó jīn

齊國人搶奪金子；形容利令智昏。

齊國有一個人，利慾熏心，整天想發財。一天早晨，他穿好衣服，到市場上去閒逛，忽然看到有人賣金子，忙奔過去，伸手抓了一把，轉身便走。後來被人抓回扭送官衙。在審問他為什麼偷金子時，他回答說：「我拿金子的時候，只看見了黃燦燦的金子，並沒有看見有人在呀！」

出自《列子》

The Gold Grabber from Qi

Meaning someone who is blinded by lust for gain.

A man in the state of Qi was obsessed by his lust for gain. All day long he thought nothing but how to get rich. One morning he put on his clothes and went to the marketplace for a stroll. There he saw someone selling gold. He rushed over, seized the gold, turned and ran. He was captured later and taken to court. When he was questioned why he robbed the man of his gold, he said, "When I grabbed the gold, I saw only the glittering metal and didn't see the man."

The Book of Lie Zi

賓至如歸

bīn zhì rú guī

客人像回到自己的家一樣；形容客人受到很好的招待。

春秋時，鄭國子產奉鄭簡公之命，出訪晉國。晉平公擺出大國架子，沒有迎接他。子產就命隨行人員把晉國的賓館圍牆拆掉，把車馬開進去。晉國大夫士文伯責備子產說："我國爲保證諸侯來賓的安全，所以修了賓館，築了高牆。現在你把牆拆了，來賓的安全由誰負責？"子產回答說："我們鄭國小，所以要按時前來進獻。這次貴國國君沒有空閒接見我們。我們帶來的禮物既不敢冒昧獻上，又不敢讓這些禮物日曬夜露。我聽說從前晉文公做盟主時，接待諸侯來賓並不這樣。那時賓館寬敞漂亮，諸侯來了，像到家裏一樣。而今，你們的離宮寬廣數里，賓館却像奴隸住的小屋，門口窄小，連車子都進不去；客人來了不知什麼時候才能被接見。這不是有意叫我們爲難嗎！……"

士文伯回去向晉平公報告。晉平公自知理虧，便向子產認錯道
歉，並立即下令興工，重修賓館。

出自《左傳》

When Guests Arrive, They Feel at Home
Feeling at Home

Said of guests who have been warmly received.

ZI Chan of the state of Zheng during the Spring and Autumn
Period visited the state of Jin as an envoy of Duke Jian of
Zheng. Duke Ping of Jin, however, put on airs of a big
country and did not come to welcome him. Zi Chan thus
ordered his followers to pull down the walls surrounding the
guest house of the state of Jin so that his carriages could
drive in. The Jin official Shi Wenbo rebuked him, saying,
"We've built the guest house and the high walls to protect the
safety of visiting princes and guests. Now you've pulled down
the walls, who is going to take care of the safety of the
guests?" Zi Chan answered, "Our state of Zheng is a small
country. But we always deliver our tributes in time. Your
sovereign has no time to receive us. We daren't take the
liberty to present the gifts we've brought with us, nor do we
dare to expose them to the sun and dew. I heard that during
the days when Duke Wen of Jin was head of the alliance, he
didn't treat his guests like this. The guest house was bright
and beautiful and when guests arrived they felt at home. But
today, your Li Palace extends for several kilometres, but the
guest house is like a small hut for slaves. The gate is narrow
and carriages can't drive in. When guests arrives, they don't
know when they will be received. Isn't this deliberately
making things difficult for us?"

When Shi Wenbo relayed to Duke Ping what Zi Chan had
said, the duke realized that he was in the wrong. He
apologized to Zi Chan and immediately ordered the guest

house to be rebuilt.

裹足不前
guǒ zú bù qián

停住腳步，不往前走；形容顧慮重重。

戰國末期，楚國有個叫李斯的人。他看到楚國國勢日衰，便投奔秦國，並做了秦國丞相。

當時，秦國統一六國，已是大勢所趨。所以六國中一些有才能的人紛紛投奔了秦國。這些人來到秦國後影響了秦國貴族的權勢。恰巧這時一個叫鄭國的韓國人在秦國進行間諜活動被發覺，秦國貴族便借此煽動秦王驅逐一切客卿。李斯也在被驅逐之列。於是李斯就給秦王寫了《諫逐客書》。書中說，帝王不排斥人才，才能使他的德業發揚光大，如今秦國卻讓人才去輔助敵國；拒絕客卿，讓他們去幫助別國立功業，使天下有才能的人都停住腳步不入秦國，這種做法，就等於把武器和糧食送給敵人！秦王看了李斯的諫書後，覺得很有道理，就下令撤銷了逐客令。

出自《諫逐客書》＊

＊《諫逐客書》散文集，秦李斯（？－前208年）作。

Hesitating to Move Forward

Holding Back

Meaning having misgivings and shrinking from doing something.

247

LI Si was a native of Chu at the end of the Warring States Period. Seeing that the state of Chu was steadily declining, he went over to the state of Qin and became the Prime Minister.

At that time, the unification of the six states by Qin was already a foregone conclusion. Some talented people from the six states came one after another to the state of Qin. The arrival of these people, however, encroached upon the power and rights of the Qin aristocrats. It happened that a man named Zheng Gou from the state of Han was found out to be carrying out espionage activities. The Qin aristocrats took this opportunity to urge the Qin king to drive out all the guest officials. As Li Si was also among those to be expelled, he wrote the "Letter Advising Against the Expulsion of Guests", in which he said, "Only a king who does not discriminate against talented people can develop his virtuous cause. But today the state of Qin is allowing people of talent to assist the enemy countries and closing the door against guest officials so that they can help the cause of other countries. People of talent in the whole world hesitate to move forward and come to the state of Qin. This is tantamount to delivering weapons and grain to the enemy." After reading Li Si's letter, the Qin king found that what Li Si said was right. So he annulled the order to expel the guest officials.

Letter Advising Against the Expulsion of Guests*

*A collection of essays by Li Si (?-208 B.C.) of the Qin Dynasty.

養虎遺患

yǎng hǔ yí huàn

養了一隻虎，給自己留下禍患；比喻縱容壞人壞事，自己反受其害。一作"養虎貽患"。

楚王項羽和漢王劉邦，在秦國滅亡以後，互相爭奪天下，形成"楚漢相爭"的混戰局面。雙方輾轉互攻，各有勝負。後來戰事呈膠着狀態，在廣武山（今河南境內）隔澗對壘，長時期相持不下。雙方達成協議，以鴻溝為界，西邊歸漢，東邊歸楚。項羽放回了拘押在楚軍中的劉邦的父母妻子，宣告戰事結束。楚軍開始向東撤退。漢軍也準備撤回關中去。這時，劉邦的謀士張良和陳平勸說道："我們已經佔據了半個天下，而且諸侯都歸順了我們。現在楚軍兵疲糧絕，這正是滅楚的大好時機！我們應當趁此機會徹底消滅它，否則，像養好一隻老虎，會給我們自己留下大禍害呀！"劉邦認為有理，便下令追擊項羽。結果漢軍大敗楚軍，項羽被圍困在垓下。

出自《史記》

Rearing a Tiger Is to Invite Future Trouble

Meaning to connive at bad persons or things will bring disaster to oneself.

AFTER the fall of the Qin Dynasty, Xiang Yu, the king of Chu, and Liu Bang, the king of Han, rivalled with each other for control of the country. The two sides fought each other in a tangle warfare, with victories and defeats breaking even. Later, the war gradually came to a stalemate across a gully of the Guangwu Mountains (in today's Henan Province). The two sides then came to an agreement, making the gully their borderline, to the west of which belonged to Han and to the east of which, Chu. Xiang Yu set free Liu Bang's parents and wife, who had been detained by the Chu army, and declared the end of the war. As the Chu army began to pulled back towards the east, the Han army was also getting ready to withdraw to the Central Shaanxi Plain. Liu Bang's advisors Zhang Liang and Chen Ping then advised, "We've occupied half of the country and the vassal princes have declared

allegiance to us. The Chu army is exhausted and short of
grain. This is an excellent opportunity to destroy Chu. We
should take this opportunity to destroy them once and for all.
Otherwise, it will be like rearing a tiger to invite future
trouble for ourselves." Liu Bang thought that they were
right. He ordered his army to pursue and attack Xiang Yu.
The Chu army was eventually utterly defeated by the Han
army and Xiang Yu was surrounded at Haixia.

Records of the Historian

寧爲玉碎，不爲瓦全

nìng wéi yù suì，bù wéi wǎ quán

　　寧願作爲玉器被打碎，也不願作泥瓦而保全；比喻寧爲正義事
業而死，也不願苟且偷生。

　　公元550年，獨攬東魏朝廷大權的丞相高洋，廢掉孝靜帝元善
見，自稱文宣帝，建立了北齊。高洋爲了培植自己的勢力，對舊臣
大加剿伐，元氏宗室很多近親都被殺戮。這時，定襄縣縣令元景安
貪生怕死，想向高洋請求將自己的姓氏改爲高姓，以討文宣帝的歡
心。元景安的堂兄元景皓知道後，說：“怎麼能拋棄自己的宗祖而
隨人家的姓呢？大丈夫寧做玉器被打碎，也不做泥瓦求保全！”第
二天，元景安把堂兄這番話告訴了高洋，高洋立即將元景皓斬首。
元景安却因此受到高洋的賞識，受賜改姓高氏，不但保住了性命，
而且還升了官。

出自《北齊書》*

*《北齊書》歷史著作，唐李百藥撰。

Rather Be a Broken Jade than a Whole Tile

Meaning rather to die for a just cause than live in humiliation.

IT happened in A.D.550. Prime Minister Gao Yang of the Eastern Wei Dynasty, who had seized all powers in his own hand, dethroned Yuan Shanjian, Emperor Xiaojing, and declared himself Emperor Wenxuan and founded the Northern Qi Dynasty. In order to cultivate his own forces, Gao Yang did all he could to eliminate the former ministers and officials. Many close relatives of the Yuan royal house were killed. The magistrate of Dingxiang County, Yuan Jingan, who was afraid to die, requested to change his name into Gao so as to please Emperor Wenxuan. When Yuan Jinghao, Yuan Jingan's cousin, heard about it, he said to him, "How could you abandon the name of your ancestors and adopt the name of another man? A hero would rather be a broken jade than a whole tile." The following day, Yuan Jingan reported what his cousin had said to Gao Yang, who promptly put Yuan Jinghao to death. Yuan Jingan was accordingly rewarded and given the name of Gao. He not only preserved his life, but also was promoted.

History of the Northern Qi Dynasty *

*By Li Baiyao of the Tang Dynasty.

厲兵秣馬

lì bīng mò mǎ

磨快兵器，餵飽戰馬；形容作好打仗的準備。

春秋時，秦國和晉國聯合攻打鄭國。在危急中，鄭國起用老臣燭之武來到秦軍營中，對秦軍說，如果鄭國滅亡了，晉國更強大，而秦國力量反而會削弱。秦國答應退兵，派大將杞子駐在鄭國幫助防守。晉國見秦軍撤走，也只好退兵回國。

　　有一天，杞子暗中派人報告秦穆公：「我掌握着鄭都北門的鑰匙，如果秘密派兵來攻，我作內應，可以順利佔領。」秦穆公滿心歡喜，不顧大夫蹇叔的勸阻，派孟明視、西乞术、白乙丙統率大軍前去偷襲。當秦軍來到離鄭國不遠的滑國時，恰巧鄭國商人弦高來此販貨，看到秦軍來襲，他急中生智，一面派人火速回國報信，一面假冒鄭國使者，拿着禮物，代表鄭國國君慰勞秦軍。孟明視以為鄭國早有準備，不敢冒然進兵。這時，杞子已收拾好行裝，備好車輛，磨快了兵器，餵飽了戰馬，隨時準備出戰。他哪裏知道，鄭穆公此時已得到弦高的密報，已派人對他下了逐客令。杞子知道預謀已敗露，慌忙逃走了。秦軍眼看成功無望，敗興而歸。當路過殽地時，又遭晉軍伏擊，全軍覆沒。

出自《左傳》

Sharpening the Weapons and Feeding the Horses

Meaning to get ready for battle.

THE state of Qin and the state of Jin in the Spring and Autumn Period launched a joint attack against the state of Zheng. In the crisis, the state of Zheng recommissioned the veteran official Zhu Zhiwu, who then brought himself to the camp of the Qin army. He said to the Qin army that if Zheng perished, Jin will become more powerful and the Qin forces will be weakened. The Qin army agreed to withdraw and sent its general Ji Zi to help Zheng in its defence. When Jin saw that the Qin army had withdrawn, it had no choice but to return to its own country.

One day, Ji Zi secretly sent a messenger to Duke Mu of

Qin with a report, which said, "I now have the key to the north gate of the Zheng capital. If an army can be sent secretly to attack the Zheng capital, I can help from the inside. We can then easily occupy the city." Duke Mu was highly pleased and, despite senior official Jian Shu's advice against it, sent Meng Mingshi, Xi Qishu and Bai Yibing with an army to start a surprise attack. When the Qin army reached the state of Hua, not far from Zheng, a Zheng merchant named Xuan Gao happened to be there on business. When he saw that the Qin army was about to attack his country, he hit upon an idea in the emergency. He immediately sent someone back to report while he himself masqueraded as a Zheng envoy with gifts to present to the Qin army on behalf of the Zheng sovereign. Meng Mingshi thought this to be an indication that the state of Zheng was prepared, and hesitated about launching a rash attack. Meanwhile, Ji Zi had already packed and readied his carriage, sharpened his weapons and fed his horses, and was ready to throw into battle. Little did he know that Duke Mu of Zheng had by now received the urgent report from Xuan Gao and sent someone to drive him out. Seeing his plot was exposed, Ji Zi hurriedly fled. When the Qin army saw that there was no hope of success, it became disheartened and withdrew. When it reached the place named Xiao, it was ambushed and completely destroyed by the Jin army.

Zuo Qiuming's Chronicles

模棱兩可

mó léng liǎng kě

摸棱角，而不肯定摸哪一面；比喻意見或語言含糊，不肯定。

唐朝，有個叫蘇味道的人，很有才學，二十歲時就考中了進士。可是，他爲官多年，辦起事來總是缺乏決斷，下官向他請示，往往既不表示同意，也不表示反對。到了非要他作出決斷時，他也總是含含糊糊。蘇味道對自己這種處事態度非常得意，誇耀說：「決定事情不能說得太明白，否則，出了錯就會遭到別人指責，那時後悔可來不及了。但是如果摸着棱角而不肯定摸哪一面，就可以避免其禍了。」其實，當時許多人對他並不滿意，人們叫他「摸棱手」，或者干脆叫「蘇摸棱」。

「摸棱」亦作「模棱」。

出自《舊唐書》

Ambiguous

Meaning what is said or written is uncertain or vague.

THERE was a learned man named Su Weidao in the Tang Dynasty. He passed the second-degree civil examination and became an Advanced Scholar when he was twenty. He served as an official for many years, but when he did things he never made clear decisions. When his subordinates asked for instructions, he was often neither for nor against what was to be done. When it was he who had to make the decision, he was always uncertain and vague. Su Weidao was very pleased with his way of handling affairs. He even bragged about it, saying, "Decisions cannot be too clear. Otherwise, if there is anything that goes wrong, you'll be censured and it will be too late to regret. If you're ambiguous, you can avoid such disaster." As a matter of fact, many people at the time were dissatisfied with him. They called him "the ambiguous man" or "the ambiguous Su".

Old History of the Tang Dynasty

數典忘祖

shǔ diǎn wàng zǔ

列舉典章的時候，竟忘記了它們的本源；一般比喻忘本，有時候也比喻對自己國家的歷史毫無所知。

春秋時，晉國有一個大夫，叫籍談。他的祖先曾經作過司典，掌管典章制度。有一次，他出使周朝。周景王問他，晉國爲什麼沒有貢物。籍談回答說：“因爲晉國從來沒有受過周王室的賞賜，所以也沒有器物可獻。”周景王責備他說：“從晉國的始祖唐叔開始，就不斷受到周王室的賞賜，你身爲晉國司典的後裔，應該知道這些史實。”說得籍談無言可對。

籍談走後，周王說：“籍談眞是數典而忘其祖啊！”

出自《左傳》

Looking After Historical Records but Forgetting One's Own Ancestors

Meaning forgetting one's own origin or being completely ignorant about the history of one's own country.

JI Tan was a senior official of the state of Jin in the Spring and Autumn Period. His ancestors had served as officials in charge of historical records. Once, he was sent to the Zhou court as an envoy. King Jing of Zhou asked him why the state of Jin had not brought any tributes. Ji Tan said, "Since the state of Jin has never received any rewards from the Zhou royal house, we haven't brought any tributes." The Zhou king rebuked him, "Beginning from its founder, Tang Shu, the state of Jin has continually received the rewards of the Zhou house. As a descendant of officials of Jin in charge of historical records, you should know this historical fact." Ji

Tan could say nothing in answer.

After Ji Tan had left, the Zhou king said, "Ji Tan is really one who looks after historical records but forgets his own ancestors."

Zuo Qiuming's Chronicles

箭在弦上，不得不發

jiàn zài xián shàng，bù dé bù fa

比喻情況十分緊急，形勢所迫，不能中止。

三國時，陳琳是著名文學家、"建安七子"之一。他原在袁紹手下掌管文書工作。有一次，袁紹吩咐他起草一份聲討曹操的檄文，陳琳按袁紹的意思，很快就寫成了。文章寫得淋漓酣暢，把曹操罵得一無是處，連曹操的祖宗三代也被狠狠地奚落了一番。

曹操有個頭痛病。這天，曹操正犯病時，收到了陳琳寫的這篇檄文。由於文章寫得好，曹操越看越興奮，並高興地說："文章寫得太好了。它把我的病也醫好了。"曹操雖然在看到痛罵自己的地方很生氣，但他仍然很喜歡陳琳的才氣。後來，當曹操擊敗袁紹後，就設法把陳琳爭取過來，還讓他掌管有關軍國大事的重要文件的起草工作。有一次，曹操問陳琳："當初你為袁紹寫文章罵我，為什麼還要罵到我的父親和祖父頭上呢？"陳琳回答說："當初我在袁紹手下，他要我寫，我就寫了，這好比'箭在弦上，不得不發'，也是沒有法子的事啊！"聽了陳琳的解釋，曹操哈哈大笑起來。

出自《太平御覽》＊

＊《太平御覽》共一千卷。北宋李昉（公元925－996年）等輯。

Like an Arrow on the Bowstring

Meaning that forced by urgent circumstances, one has to go ahead.

CHEN Lin was a famous writer of the Three Kingdoms period and known as one of the "Seven Talents of Jianan". He served at first as a secretary of Yuan Shao. Once, Yuan Shao asked him to draft an official denunciation against Cao Cao. According to Yuan Shao's ideas, he quickly finished it. The denunciation was so forcefully and vividly written that Cao Cao was condemned until nothing appeared to be right about him. Even Cao Cao's ancestors of three generations before him were thoroughly ridiculed.

Cao Cao was a sufferer of migraine. The day when Cao Cao received the denunciation he was suffering from the periodic headache. The essay was so well written that the more Cao Cao read it the more he became interested. He said happily, "The essay is so well written that it has cured my headache." Although Cao Cao was very angry when read the sentences that condemned him, he still liked Chen Lin's talent. When Cao Cao defeated Yuan Shao, he managed to win over Chen Lin to his side and asked him to draft documents concerning important military operations and state affairs. Once, Cao Cao asked Chen Lin, "When you wrote the essay for Yuan Shao to condemn me, why did you have to curse my father and grandfathers?" Chen Lin told him, "I was serving under Yuan Shao. I wrote what he told me to write. It was 'like an arrow on the bowstring'. I had to go ahead. I was helpless about it." After hearing Chen Lin's explanation, Cao Cao roared with laughter.

Taiping Imperial Encyclopaedia*

**Collated by Li Fang (925-996) and others of the Northern Song Dynasty in 1,000 volumes.

餘勇可賈

yú yǒng kě gǔ

勇氣還有剩餘，可以出賣；比喻精神旺盛有餘。

　　春秋時，有一次齊國派兵進攻魯國和衞國。晉國爲了援救魯國
和衞國，派出大軍，會合魯衞兩國的軍隊，進入齊國境內。齊國軍
隊也前來迎戰。齊將高固，非常勇猛。兩軍交鋒後，高固單獨駕了
一輛戰車，衝入晉軍，用大石頭逢人就砸，打死打傷不少晉軍。最
後乘着從晉軍繳獲的戰車返回齊營。他耀武揚威，神氣十足，在戰
車上高聲喊叫：“誰需要勇氣，快來買啊！我還剩下不少的勇氣，
可以出賣呢！”

出自《左傳》

With Leftover Courage for Sale

Meaning with more energy to spare.

IT happened during the Spring and Autumn Period. The state
of Qi sent an army against the states of Lu and Wei. To help
Lu and Wei, the state of Jin joined force with the armies of
Lu and Wei and marched into the territory of the state of Qi.
The Qi army thus engaged the combined forces. Gao Gu was
a ferocious general of Qi. In the battle, Gao all alone steered a
chariot and rushed into the Jin army. He threw large pieces
of stone at whomever he saw, killing and wounding a great
number of the Jin soldiers. He eventually returned to the Qi
camp, riding in a chariot he had captured from the Jin army.
He made a great show of his victory, shouting from the
chariot, "Whoever wants courage, come and buy it from me.
I've leftover courage for sale."

Zuo Qiuming's Chronicles

258

膠柱鼓瑟

jiāo zhù gǔ sè

把瑟的弦柱用膠黏住去彈奏；比喻拘泥成規而不知道變通。

戰國時，秦國攻打趙國。趙孝成王任命趙括為主將，指揮趙軍，抵抗秦兵。當時相國藺相如勸阻趙王說：「趙王如果派趙括做主將，就好像把瑟的弦柱黏住了再彈奏一樣。因為趙括是個空有虛名的人，他只知道死讀兵書，而不懂得靈活運用。」但是，趙王不聽，還是任命趙括為趙軍主將。結果趙國大吃敗仗，趙括也送了命。

出自《史記》

Gluing the Tuning Pegs of a Zither

Stiff as a Poker

Meaning to be rigid and inflexible.

WHEN the state of Qin attacked the state of Zhao during the Warring States time, King Xiaocheng appointed Zhao Kuo as the chief general in command of the Zhao army fighting against the Qin force. Lin Xiangru, the Prime Minister, tried to stop the Zhao king from sending Zhao Kuo. He siad, "Sending Zhao Kuo as the chief general is like gluing the tuning pegs of a zither before playing on it. Zhao Kuo has only an empty reputation. All he knows is slavishly reading military textbooks instead of applying them flexibly." But the Zhao king refused to listen to him and Zhao Kuo was appointed as the chief general. As a result, the Zhao army suffered a heavy defeat and Zhao Kuo lost his life on the battlefield.

Records of the Historian

膠漆相投

jiāo qī xiāng tóu

膠和漆黏在一起；形容朋友之間的牢固友情。

東漢時，有個叫雷義的書生，他和同郡人陳重非常要好，在仕途上也相互謙讓。起初，太守張雲推舉孝廉時，陳重覺得自己不如雷義，便想把孝廉讓給雷義，太守沒有答應。後來，他倆同時被皇帝選爲尚書郎。雷義曾爲一犯人辯護並願代其服罪而被黜。陳重也借病退職。

不久，雷義又被刺史推舉做官。雷義覺得自己不如陳重，便提出把官位讓給陳重。刺史不同意，雷義便披頭散髮地裝瘋，不去上任。

當時，鄉里人感慨地說：“膠和漆黏在一起是很堅固了，但却比不上雷義和陳重兩人的友情牢固。”

出自《後漢書》

As Close as Glue and Paint

Said of a steadfast friendship.

A scholar named Lei Yi during the Eastern Han Dynasty was a devoted friend of Chen Zhong, who was a native of the same prefecture. They were such good friends that they even offered their opportunity for promotion to each other when they served as officials. At first, Chen Zhong was recommended by Prefect Zhang Yun to be a candidate for an official post. Chen thought he was not as good as Lei Yi and wanted to give the candidacy to Lei. But the prefect did not agree. Later, both of them were chosen by the emperor as imperial assistants. When Lei Yi argued in defence of a prisoner and volunteered to serve the sentence for him, he was removed from his post. Chen Zhong then also resigned on the pretext that he was ill.

Shortly after Lei Yi's removal from his post, he was recommended by the local governor to serve as an official. Lei thought that Chen Zhong could do better at that post and proposed that the post be give to Chen. When the governor disagreed, Lei Yi pretended that he was mad and refused to go to the post.

People of their town at the time were moved to say, "Glue and paint can become very firm when they stick together. But they are not as firm as the friendship between Lei Yi and Chen Zhong."

History of the Later Han Dynasty

樂此不疲

lè cǐ bù pí

做喜歡做的事情，就不覺得疲勞。

東漢光武帝劉秀，自幼辦事勤快。他當了皇帝以後，主持朝政仍然很勤勉，處理問題十分用心。他經常與大臣、公卿、將軍們一起談論治國的辦法，直到半夜才去休息。太子看到父親這樣操勞，就勸他說："您雖然有大禹、湯武那樣的賢明，但沒有黃帝、老子那樣的養性之福，希望您愛惜自己的身體，保養好精神。"劉秀說："我喜歡做這些事，並不覺得疲勞。"

由於劉秀兢兢業業處理朝政，國事太平，百姓安樂。

出自《後漢書》

Pleasure Takes Away the Fatigue

Meaning when a person takes pleasure in doing something, he does not feel the fatigue resulting from doing it.

LIU Xiu, Emperor Guangwu of the Eastern Han Dynasty, was diligent even when he was a child. When he became emperor, he was also very diligent in supervising court affairs and was attentive in handling various problems. He often discussed ways of ruling the country with the ministers, nobles and generals and did not rest until after midnight. When the crown prince saw that his father was tiring himself out, he tried to talk him around. He said, "You're wise and able as Yu the Great and Tang Wu, but you don't have the fortune of the Yellow Emperor and Lao Zi to attain mental tranquility. I hope you'll treasure your health and preserve your energy." Liu Xiu said, "As I'm interested in these things, I don't feel the fatigue."

As a result of Liu Xiu's conscientious work and careful handling of state affairs, the country prospered in peace and the people lived happily.

History of the Later Han Dynasty

樂極生悲

lè jí shēng bēi

快樂到極點反而生出悲傷；形容歡樂過度。

戰國時，齊威王經常通宵飲酒作樂，不理朝政。楚國乘機出兵進攻齊國。齊王派淳于髡去趙國請來救兵，才解了齊國之圍。

在慶賀淳于髡搬兵有功的宴會上，齊王問淳于髡喝多少酒才會醉？淳于髡回答說："我喝一斗也醉，喝一石也醉。"齊威王不解其意，又問道：“先生喝一斗酒就醉了，怎麼能喝得了一石呢？”

淳于髡想借此機會規勸齊威王不要通宵飲酒，於是就委婉地說：“道理是這樣的：如果大王賞給我酒，在喝酒的時候，大王坐在我面前，法官站在我旁邊，御史站在我後邊，我就感到恐懼，喝上一斗也就醉了；若是在民間，不分男女坐在一起，一邊飲酒，一邊遊戲，喝上八斗也不會醉；假如到了夜裏，主人把我留下，無拘無束地坐在一起，這時喝上一石，也不會醉。所以古人說，酒喝到了極點，就不能遵守禮節，人快樂到了極點，就會發生悲哀的事情。”

齊威王聽出淳于髡是在諷諫自己，從那以後就不再通宵飲酒了。

出自《史記》

Extreme Joy Begets Sorrow

Meaning that it is not good to indulge in excessive pleasure.

KING Wei of the state of Qi during the Warring States Period often indulged in carousing and pleasure-seeking throughout the night and left government affairs unattended. The state of Chu took the opportunity to launch an attack against Qi. The king of Qi had to send Chunyu Kun to the state of Zhao for reinforcements before the seige was relieved.

At the banquet celebrating Chunyu's service in securing help, the Qi king asked Chunyu how much wine he could drink before he got drunk. Chunyu Kun answered, "Drinking one measure can make me drunk; drinking ten measures can also make me drunk." The king did not understand him and questioned, "Since one measure can make you drunk, how can you drink ten measures?"

Chunyu Kun wanted to take the opportunity to try to persuade King Wei into giving up carousing throughout the night. In a roundabout way he said, "The reason is this. When

Your Majesty gives me wine to drink, one measure can make me drunk because with Your Majesty sitting in front of me, high judges standing by my side and imperial censors behind me, I feel frightened. But when I'm among the ordinary people, with men and women sitting together and drinking while playing games, eight measures won't make me drunk. If the host asks me to stay overnight and sitting in an extremely unrestrained atmosphere, even ten measures cannot make me drunk. This is why the ancients said that excessive wine makes one forget about propriety, and extreme joy begets sorrow."

King Wei of Qi realized that Chunyu Kun was exhorting him by innuendo and stopped the all-night drinking party from then on.

Records of the Historian

談虎色變

tán hǔ sè biàn

一說到老虎，臉色就變了；比喻一談到恐怖的事就非常害怕。

北宋時，有一位著名教育家叫程頤。他認為凡事必須親身經歷，才能眞知。爲了說明這個道理，程頤對他的弟子講了一個故事：有一個人曾被老虎咬傷，當人們再次提到老虎傷人的時候，旁邊聽到的人雖然也感到害怕，但這個被老虎傷過的人却更加緊張，臉色大變，和大家害怕程度大不相同。原因就是他親身感受過老虎的厲害。

出自《二程全書》*

*《二程全書》後人對程顥、程頤兄弟著作的合編。程顥（公元1032－1085年）、程頤（公元1033－1107年）同爲北宋理學奠基者，故稱"二程"。

Turning Pale at the Mention of a Tiger

Said of someone who becomes frightened at the mere mention of something terrifying.

CHENG Yi was a famous educator of the Northern Song Dynasty. He maintained that true knowledge comes only from personal experience. To illustrate this, he told a story to his disciples: A man was once wounded by a tiger. When people talk about a tiger hurting people, listeners are frightened. But they are not as frightened as the man who has been wounded by a tiger. He becomes tense and turns pale. The reason is that he has personally experienced the ferocity of the tiger.

Collected Works of the Cheng Brothers *

*A book compiled by later people of the works of Cheng Hao (1032-1085) and his brother Cheng Yi (1033-1107), founders of Neo-Confucianism and known as the Cheng brothers.

緣木求魚

yuán　mù　qiú　yú

爬到樹上去捉魚；比喻方法不對，達不到目的。

戰國時，齊宣王想稱霸天下。孟子勸他放棄武力，用仁政征服天下。

孟子說：“大王動員全國軍隊攻打別國，這是爲什麼？”齊宣王回答說：“爲了滿足我最大的慾望。”孟子問：“您最大的慾望是什麼？”齊宣王却笑了笑，不答。孟子接着問：“是因爲好東西不夠吃嗎？是因爲好東西不夠穿嗎？是因爲沒有好藝術品看嗎？還是因爲侍候您的人太少？”齊宣王連忙說：“不，不，我不是爲了這些。”孟子說：“那麼，我明白了。您是想征服天下，是不是？如果是，我看好比爬樹捉魚，是不能達到您的目的的。”齊宣王說：“會有這樣嚴重嗎？”孟子說：“恐怕比這還嚴重。爬樹捉魚，最多是捉不到，不至於有什麼禍害。如果以武力滿足自己獨霸天下的慾望，不但達不到目的，其後果就不堪設想啊！”

出自《孟子》

Climbing a Tree to Seek for Fish

Meaning one cannot achieve the intended purpose by a wrong method.

KING Xuan of the state of Qi in the Warring States Period wanted to dominate the world. Mencius advised him not to use military force, but to win supremacy by benevolent government.

Mencius asked, "Why is it that Your Majesty has mobilized the army of the whole country to attack a neighbouring country?" King Xuan of Qi answered, "My object is to seek for what I greatly desire." Mencius then asked, "What is it that you greatly desire?" King Xuan smiled, but did not answer. Mencius asked again, "Is it because you don't have enough good things to eat, or because you don't have enough good clothes to wear, or because you don't have good works of art to please your eyes, or because you don't have enough attendants to serve you?" King Xuan then said, "No. These are not my desires." Mencius said, "Now I understand. So you want to dominate the world. If that is the case, I think it is like climbing a tree to seek for fish. You cannot achieve your purpose." King Xuan said, "Is it so bad as that?" Mencius replied, "It is even worse. If you climb a tree to seek for fish, even though you may not get fish, you will not suffer any subsequent calamity. But if you try to satisfy your desire of dominating the world by using military force, the result will be too dreadful to think of if you cannot achieve your purpose."

The Book of Mencius

彈冠相慶

tán guān xiāng qìng

揮去帽子上的灰塵，為即將做官而互相慶賀，多為貶意。

西漢時，有叫王吉和貢禹的兩個人，他們是同鄉，又是很要好的朋友。王吉在漢宣帝時曾被任命為大夫，後來罷免了他。貢禹做了幾年官也被罷免了。漢元帝即位後，王吉又出來做了大官。貢禹聽到這個消息，認為自己又將有機會向上爬，於是把自己帽子上的灰塵揮去，準備出去做官。當時有人諷刺他們說："王吉在位，貢公彈冠。"

出自《漢書》

Flicking Dust from the Hat and Congratulating Each Other

Used in most cases derogatorily to mean congratulating each other on the prospect of getting good appointments.

WANG Ji and Gong Yu of the Western Han Dynasty were two good friends from the same hometown. Wang Ji was appointed a senior official during the reign of Emperor Xuan of the Han Dynasty before he was removed from office. Gong Yu also served as an official before he was removed from office. When Emperor Yuan of the Han Dynasty ascended the throne, Wang Ji again became a high-ranking official. When Gong Yu heard the news, he thought that he now also had a chance to become a high official. So he brought out his hat and began to flick the dust on it and was ready to assume his post as an official. People of that time said sarcastically of them, "When Wang Ji assumes office, Gong Yu flicks dust from his hat."

History of the Han Dynasty

輸攻墨守

shū gōng mò shǒu

公輸班進攻，墨翟防守；比喻攻守雙方勢均力敵。

　　春秋時期，聰明的木匠公輸班（世稱魯班）為楚王製作了攻城的雲梯，準備攻打宋國。這個消息被墨翟（亦稱墨子）知道了。墨翟是反對戰爭的。他走了十天十夜，來到楚國，勸說公輸班不要幫助楚王攻擊宋國。公輸班不肯。墨子說：“讓咱們來演習一下進攻和防守吧！”說罷，墨翟解下腰帶圍成一個四方形，當做城牆；又拿一塊木板，當做防禦武器，讓公輸班攻城。公輸班使用他的雲梯，先後發動九次進攻，都被墨翟擋回去了。這時，公輸班已感到技窮力竭，但墨翟的防守本領還沒有用完。在一旁觀戰的楚王對墨翟的防禦才能表示欽佩，於是打消了進攻宋國的念頭。

出自《墨子》＊

* 《墨子》戰國墨翟（約公元前468－前376年）著，墨翟是墨家學派的創始人。

Shu on the Attack and Mo in the Defence

Meaning that the two sides match each other in strength.

DURING the Spring and Autumn Period, the clever master carpenter Gongshu Ban (also known as Lu Ban) designed a "cloud-climbing" ladder for the king of Chu in preparation for attacking the cities of the state of Song. When this became known to Mo Di (also known as Mo Zi), who was against war, he travelled for ten days and nights to the state of Chu and tried to persuade Gongshu Ban not to help the king of Chu to attack the state of Song. But Gongshu Ban would not listen to him. So Mo Di said, "Let us play a game of attack and defence." As he said so, he untied his waist band and formed a square with it as a city wall. He used a wooden board as a weapon of defence. Gongshu Ban was to attack the city with his "cloud-climbing" ladder. Gongshu made nine attacks, but each time he was repulsed by Mo Di. By this time Gongshu was at the end of this tether, but Mo Di's defence tactics were far from exhausted. The king of Chu, who was watching by their side, expressed admiration for Mo Di's defence skills and gave up the idea of attacking the state of Song.

The Book of Mo Zi*

*By Mo Di (about 468-376 B.C.) of the Warring States Period who was the founder of the Moist school of philosophy.

樹欲靜而風不止

shù yù jìng ér fēng bù zhǐ

樹要靜而風不停；比喻事物的客觀存在和發展不以主觀的意志為轉移。

有一天，孔子正在趕路，忽然聽到悲切的哭聲，便對車夫說："快點！前面有品德高尚的人。"到跟前一看，原來是皋魚。只見他身披粗布衣裳，手拿一把鐮刀，站在路邊痛哭流涕。孔子下車問道："你家又沒有喪事，為何哭得這樣傷心呢？"皋魚回答說："我有三個過失：年輕時好學，周遊了諸侯各國，等我回來時，父母已經去世，沒有盡到奉養雙親的責任，這是過失之一；只是為了自己高潔的志向，拒絕侍奉國君，這是過失之二；年少時擇人交往，所以親友少，而到了老年時無所依靠，這是過失之三。樹欲靜而風不止，兒子想奉養老人而高齡的老人却沒有多少時間等晚輩去盡孝心了。"

皋魚講的正是孔子所宣揚的，因此，孔子聽後連聲稱讚。

出自《韓詩外傳》*

*《韓詩外傳》本書雜述古事古語，西漢韓嬰（約公元前157年前後在世）撰。

The Tree May Prefer Calm, but the Wind Will Not Stop

Meaning things take their own course regardless of one's will.

ONE day when Confucius was on the road, he heard someone weeping mournfully. He said to the carter, "Hurry up. There's someone of noble character ahead." When he reached the spot, he saw that it was Gao Yu, who was in coarse clothes with a sickle in his hand weeping bitterly. Confucius got off the cart and asked, "You're not mourning somebody. But why are you weeping so bitterly?" Gao Yu said in answer, "I've made three mistakes: When I was young, I was eager to learn and I travelled to all the princely states. But when I returned home, both my parents were dead. I did not fulfil my duty of looking after my parents. That's my first mistake. I claimed to be lofty and honest and refused to serve the sovereign. That's my second mistake. When I was young, I was so choosy about making friends. As I have few friends and relatives, I have no one to rely on now that I'm old. This is my third mistake. The tree may prefer calm, but the wind will not subside. When the son wishes to serve his old parents, his parents don't have much time to wait for their son's filial piety."

What Gao Yu said was exactly what Confucius advocated. This was why Confucius was full of praise for Gao Yu.

Miscellaneous Notes on the Poetry of Han Ying*

*A collection of anecdotes and old sayings compiled by Han Ying (who lived around 157 B.C.) of the Western Han Dynasty.

噤若寒蟬

jìn　ruò　hán　chán

像冷天的蟬一樣，一聲不鳴；形容不敢作聲。

東漢時，有個叫杜密的人，爲人穩重質樸，少年時就顯示出了少有的才華，後爲司徒胡廣所賞識，任代郡太守。

後來，杜密棄官還鄉，但他對政事依然十分關心，經常向當地太守王昱舉薦好人好事，揭發壞人壞事。當時，同郡劉勝也自蜀郡告老還鄉，他同杜密相反，只知明哲保身，閉門謝客，不問政事，對好事壞事一概不管。有一次，王昱對杜密說：“劉勝是個清高之士，很多人都稱讚他呢！”杜密知道王昱名爲讚揚劉勝，實則責備自己，便說：“劉勝地位很高，受到上賓的禮遇，但他看到好人不推薦，聽到壞事也不作聲，像冷天的蟬一樣。他只求自己平安無事，對國家不負責任，其實是個罪人，有什麼可稱讚的呢？”杜密接着又說：“我發現了賢人向你推薦，對違法失節的壞人敢向你揭發，使你能賞罰分明，不也是爲國家盡了一點力嗎？”王昱聽了，十分欽佩，便愈加厚待杜密了。

出自《後漢書》

As Quiet as a Cicada in Cold Weather

Shutting Up One's Mouth Like a Clam

Said of someone who keeps quiet out of fear.

DU Mi of the Eastern Han Dynasty was a steady and unpretentious person. Even when he was young, he displayed unusual talent. He was later recognised by Grand Councillor Hu Guang and appointed an acting prefect.

Some years later, Du Mi resigned from his post and returned home. But he still closely concerned himself with government affairs and often recommended to the local prefect Wang Yu what was good and exposed what was bad. At that time, there was another person named Liu Sheng, who had retired from the post of prefect from Sichuan. Contrary to Du Mi, he cared only of keeping trouble out of his door, refused to see visitors, kept himself away from political affairs and closed his eyes to whatever was good or bad. Once Wang Yu said to Du Mi, "Liu Sheng is a man of lofty personality. Many people speak highly of him." Du Mi knew that he himself was actually being blamed though Wang Yu was praising Liu Sheng. So he said, "Liu Sheng is high in social position and is being treated as an honoured guest. But he never recommends a good person when he sees one and when he hears about bad things, he keeps quiet as a cicada in cold weather. He cares only to keep trouble from himself and is irresponsible to the country. He is in fact a guilty person. What is there worthy of praising about him?" Du Mi then continued, "I recommend to you talented people whenever I see them and inform you of bad persons who act in violation of propriety so that you can make a clear distinction between what is to be rewarded and what is to be punished. Am I not doing my share for the benefit of the country?" After listening to him, Wang Yu admired him all the more and treated him with greater respect.

History of the Later Han Dynasty

舉足輕重

jǔ   zú   qīng   zhòng

一抬腳就影響兩端的輕重；比喻所處地位重要。

公元25年，漢光武帝劉秀雖已建立了東漢政權，但全國尚未統一。當時，天水的隗囂和蜀地的公孫述也都在稱王稱帝，爭奪天下。擁有河西五郡的大將軍竇融看到劉秀在政治、軍事上佔優勢，有意順附，便召集各郡太守和本地名流商討，決定派使者帶着書信和禮物前往洛陽。劉秀大喜，隆重接待了使者，並給竇融寫了一封書信，信中說：「蜀地有公孫述，天水有隗將軍，現蜀漢相攻，你的地位極為重要，一抬腳就會影響兩端的輕重，無論你站在哪一方，都可以決定一方的成敗。」從此，竇融一心一意盡忠於劉秀。劉秀得到竇融的支持，實力大增，最後終於消滅了隗囂和公孫述，統一了天下。

出自《後漢書》

A Step Taken Decides the Balance

Holding the Balance

Said of someone who plays a decisive role.

WHEN Liu Xiu, Emperor Guangwu, set up the national government of the Eastern Han Dynasty in A.D.25, the country was not yet unified. Kui Xiao in Tianshui and Gongsun Shu in Sichuan both claimed to be emperors and rivalled Liu Xiu for control of the country. Grand General Dou Rong who was in control of the five prefectures west of the river saw that Liu Xiu was politically and militarily in a superior position, and intended to yield his allegiance to Liu Xiu. He called a meeting of the governors of the prefectures and local notables to discuss it. They decided to send an emissary with a letter and gifts to Luoyang. Liu Xiu was highly pleased. He received the emissary with great ceremony and wrote a letter to Dou Rong, in which he said. "There are Gongsun Shu in Sichuan and General Kui in Tianshui. They are launching a combined attack. Your position is highly critical. A step taken by you will decide the balance. Victory and defeat will be decided by which side you stands." From then on, Dou Rong became wholeheartedly loyal to Liu Xiu. With Dou Rong's support, Liu Xiu's strength increased greatly and unified the whole country after destroying Kui Xiao and Gongsun Shu.

History of the Later Han Dynasty

舉案齊眉

jǔ àn qí méi

把盛飯的盤子舉得和眉毛一樣高；表示對丈夫的愛慕和夫妻互

敬互愛。

東漢時，有個叫梁鴻的讀書人，年輕時家裏很窮，後來因刻苦讀書成了一個學問家。於是很多有錢人家都爭着前來攀親。梁鴻生性剛直，藐視權貴，對這些求親的一概拒絕了，唯獨看中了相貌雖不漂亮，但與自己志同道合的鄰家女子孟光，並娶她為妻。

孟光剛到梁鴻家時，穿戴得不免漂亮些，梁鴻一直七天都不理睬她。到了第八天，孟光挽起髮髻，拔去首飾，換上布衣布裙，開始勤勞操作。梁鴻高興地說：“好啊！這才是我的妻子哩！”

梁鴻和孟光婚後互助互愛，彼此又極有禮貌，真是相敬如賓。梁鴻每天勞作歸來，孟光總是把飯菜都準備好，擺在托盤裏，雙手捧着，舉得和自己的眉毛一樣高，恭敬地送到梁鴻面前，梁鴻高興地接過來，兩人愉快地進餐。

出自《後漢書》

Holding the Tray to the Height of the Brows

To hold the tray containing a meal to the height of the eyebrows symbolizes love and mutual respect between husband and wife.

LIANG Hong was a scholar of the Eastern Han Dynasty. His family was very poor when he was young. But he studied hard and eventually became a very learned man. Many rich families wanted to marry their daughters to him. But Liang was an upright man and regarded with disdain those who were rich and powerful. He refused all their offers and decided to marry Meng Guang, the daughter of his neighbour, who was not beautiful, but cherished the same ideals as his own.

When Meng Guang first came to Liang Hong's house, she was rather gorgeously dressed. Liang Hong refused to speak to her for seven days. On the eighth day, when Meng Guang coiled up her hair, removed her ornaments, changed into common cotton clothes and began to work in the house, Liang was pleased. "Good. You're now my wife," he said.

After their marriage, Liang Hong and Meng Guang loved and helped each other and treated each other with extreme courtesy as if they were each other's guest. Every day, when Liang came home from work, Meng would have supper ready. She would put the meal in a tray, raised it to the height of her brows and delivered it to Liang. Liang would happily took it from her and the two of them would then enjoy their supper together.

History of the Later Han Dynasty

錦囊妙計

jǐn　náng　miào　jì

封在錦囊中的神機妙算；常比喻能及時解決緊迫問題的巧妙方法。

三國時，東吳大將周瑜為了索還荊州，趁蜀主劉備喪妻續娶之機，假意將吳侯孫權的妹妹許配給劉備，想把劉備騙到東吳，作為人質來換取荊州。蜀軍師諸葛亮看穿了周瑜的計謀，建議主公劉備將計就計，前往東吳，並派將軍趙雲隨行。臨行前，諸葛亮對趙雲說：「你這次保主公到東吳去，我這裏有三條妙計裝在三個錦囊中，你隨身帶上，依計行事。」

到了東吳，劉備和趙雲依照諸葛亮定下的計策行事，不但沒有讓東吳把劉備作為人質，反而很順利地與孫權的妹妹成親，使周瑜的計策落空，東吳賠了夫人又折兵。

出自《三國演義》

Wonderful Stratagem in a Brocade Bag

Meaning a clever way of dealing with an emergency

IT happened during the period of the Three Kingdoms. General Zhou Yu of the state of Wu wanted the state of Shu to return the city of Jingzhou to Wu. As Liu Bei, the master of Shu, had just lost his wife and wanted to remarry, Zhou Yu falsely promised that Sun Quan was going to marry his younger sister to Liu Bei. His intention was that once Liu Bei was in Wu, he would be detained as a hostage to be exchanged for the return of Jingzhou. Zhuge Liang, the Shu military advisor, saw through Zhou Yu's scheme and suggested to Liu Bei that he was to go to Wu accompanied by General Zhao Yun and beat Zhou Yu at his own game. Before their departure, Zhuge said to Zhao Yun, "For your escorting of our master Liu Bei to Wu, I have three stratagems concealed in three brocade bags. You should carry them on your person and act accordingly."

Once in Wu, Liu Bei and Zhao Yun acted according to Zhuge Liang's stratagems. Instead of allowing himself to be detained by Zhou Yu as a hostage, Liu Bei married Sun Quan's sister. Zhou Yu's scheme fell through, and the state of Wu lost a lady and suffered defeat on the battlefield.

Tales of the Three Kingdoms

罄竹難書

qìng zhú nán shū

用盡全部竹子也寫不完（紙張未發明前，一切記事都寫在竹子上）；形容罪惡很多。

隋朝末年，李密和翟讓等反對隋煬帝，組織瓦崗軍佔據洛口（洛陽附近），攻下了河南、河北的不少地方。李密曾寫了一篇聲討隋煬帝的檄文，發送各郡、縣傳佈。檄文列舉了隋煬帝十大罪狀，並且說：“罄南山之竹，書罪無窮；決東海之波，流惡難盡！”

出自《舊唐書》

Even All the Bamboo Cannot Record

Before paper was invented, all records were put down on bamboo slips. That even all the bamboo cannot record means that there are too many crimes to be recorded.

AT the end of the Sui Dynasty, Li Mi and Zhai Rang organized the Wagang Army to fight against Emperor Yang of the Sui Dynasty. They occupied Luokou (near today's Luoyang) and many places in Henan and Hebei. Li Mi once wrote a call to arms in which he listed ten major atrocities of Emperor Yang, saying, "Even all the bamboo on the South Mountain cannot record his crimes; all the water of the East Sea cannot wash away his evils."

Old History of the Tang Dynasty

279

擢髮難數

zhuó fà nán shǔ

把頭髮拔下來作籌碼，也難以計數；比喻罪行多到無法計算。

　　戰國時期，魏國有個叫范雎的人，很有才能。有一次，魏國派大夫須賈出使齊國，范雎隨同他前往。他們到了齊國，齊襄王因仰慕范雎的盛名，派人給他送去許多黃金和禮物，范雎沒有接受。須賈知道後，就認爲范雎把機密泄漏給齊國了。回國後，宰相魏齊信以爲眞，叫人毒打范雎，眼看他快要死去，就用蓆子把他捲着扔了。後來范雎甦醒過來，改名張祿，逃到秦國，做了宰相。

　　有一次，秦國要發兵進魏國。魏國十分恐慌，就派須賈去秦國求和。當須賈到秦國得知秦國宰相張祿就是范雎後，嚇得渾身發抖，連忙爬到秦相府向范雎請罪。范雎責問須賈道：“你知道你的罪狀有多少嗎？”須賈叩頭說：“我的罪狀太多，拔下頭髮來作籌碼，也數不完啊！”范雎心胸開闊，不記舊仇，放了須賈，讓他回魏國去了。

出自《史記》

As Countless as the Hairs on the Head

Meaning too numerous to count.

FAN Sui of the state of Wei during the Warring States Period was a man of talent. The state of Wei once sent Xu Gu as an envoy to the state of Qi accompanied by Fan Sui. When they arrived in Qi, King Xiang of Qi, who was an admirer of Fan Sui, gave him a great quantity of gold and gifts. Although Fan Sui refused to take them, Xu Gu thought that Fan Sui must have sold state secrets to Qi. After they returned to their own country, Prime Minister Wei Qi believed Xu Gu and had Fan Sui beaten almost to death. He was rolled up in a mat and thrown in the wilderness. It was a long time before he recovered from his coma. He changed his name into Zhang Lu and fled to the state of Qin, where he later became the prime minister.

One day, the state of Qin wanted to attack the state of Wei. The state of Wei was greatly alarmed and Xu Gu was sent to Qin to sue for peace. When he reached Qin, he learned that the prime minister was none other than Fan Sui, now named Zhang Lu. Shivering with fear, he prostrated on the ground and begged Fan Sui to forgive him. Fan Sui asked Xu Gu, "Do you know how many crimes you've committed?" Xu Gu kowtowed and said, "My crimes are as countless as the hairs on the head." Being a broad-minded man, Fan Sui forgave the old wrongs, set Xu Gu free and let him return to the state of Wei.

Records of the Historian

點石成金

diǎn　shí　chéng　jīn

把石頭點化成黃金；比喻將不高明的詩文修改成佳作的能力。

晉代，有個叫許遜的人，曾當過旌陽縣令，時常裝鬼弄神，施符作法，如同仙人一般，老百姓稱他爲“許眞君”。

有一次，他看到許多百姓繳不上租稅，就動了惻隱之心，用法術把石頭點化成金子，替百姓上繳了拖欠的租稅。

出自《神仙傳》

Touching a Stone and Turning It into Gold

Usually meaning to turn a crude essay or poem into a literary gem.

XU Xun of the Jin Dynasty once served as the magistrate of Jingyang County. He often moved about as an immortal and played magic tricks. People therefore called him Xu the True Priest.

One day, when he saw that the people were too poor to pay taxes, he was moved by compassion. He applied magic and turned stones into gold, with which he paid the taxes for the people.

Tales of Immortals

膽大如斗

dǎn dà rú dǒu

膽像斗一樣大；比喻做事大膽。

三國時期，蜀國的姜維膽量很大，也有才幹，得到軍師諸葛亮的器重，委任他為征西將軍，並且竭力培植他。諸葛亮死後，蜀國的兵馬就由他統率，任蜀國的大將軍。他繼承諸葛亮的遺志，多次領兵攻打魏國，都沒有取勝。後來魏國征伐蜀國，蜀國寡不敵衆，遭到慘敗，後主劉禪投降。

不久，魏國的鍾會陰謀叛變魏王，姜維認為時機已到，便假意與鍾會勾結，企圖趁機恢復蜀國。不料事機敗露，姜維被魏兵所殺。魏兵剖開他的肚子，發現姜維的膽像斗一般大。

出自《三國志》

With a Gall As Big as the Peck

Said of someone who is bold and courageous.

JIANG Wei of the state of Shu during the Three Kingdoms period was not only courageous, but also talented. Zhuge Liang, the military advisor of Shu, thought highly of him, appointed him as General of Western Expedition and did all he could to support and train him. When Zhuge Liang died, Jiang Wei became the Grand General of Shu in command of all the armed forces. He carried out Zhuge's behest and launched repeated attacks against the state of Wei, but failed to gain victory. Later when Wei attacked Shu, Shu was hopelessly outnumbered and suffered disastrous defeats. Liu Chan, the last king of Shu, surrendered himself.

Shortly afterwards, Zhong Hui of the state of Wei plotted a mutiny against the Wei king. Jiang Wei, who thought that his chance had come, pretended to side with Zhong Hui and intended to take the opportunity to re-establish the state of Shu. But his plan was exposed and he was killed by the Wei soldiers. When the Wei soldiers disemboweled him, they found that his gall was as big as the peck.

History of the Three Kingdoms

糟糠之妻

zāo kāng zhī qī

吃糟糠時娶的妻子；指曾經共過患難的妻子。

東漢時，有一個叫宋弘的人。他學識淵博，爲人正直，很得漢光武帝劉秀的賞識，被封爲太中大夫。

劉秀的姐姐湖陽公主死了丈夫。劉秀和她談論了滿朝的大臣，想看看她愛慕哪一位，以便給她改嫁。湖陽公主說："滿朝大臣，只有宋弘才貌雙全。"為此,劉秀召見了宋弘,對他說:"俗話說,一個人地位高了,就要改交一批富朋友;發了財就要停妻另娶,這可是人之常情啊!"宋弘回答說:"我聽說,一個人在貧賤時交的朋友是不能忘記的;和自己共患難的結髮之妻是不能拋棄的。"劉秀見此情形,對湖陽公主說:"看來沒有什麼希望使宋弘停妻另娶了。"

後人根據宋弘對劉秀說的話引伸出了"糟糠之妻"這句話。

出自《後漢書》

A Wife of Chaff-Eating Days

Meaning a wife who has shared the husband's hardships.

SONG Hong of the Eastern Han Dynasty was an upright man of profound learning. Liu Xiu, Emperor Guangwu, spoke highly of him and made him a senior official.

When Liu Xiu's sister, Princess Huyang's husband died, Liu Xiu discussed all the court officials with her and wanted to know which one she liked so that she could remarry. Princess Huyang said, "Of all the court officials, only Song Hong has both looks and talents." Liu Xiu then summoned Song Hong and said to him. "As the saying goes, 'When a man rises in position, he makes new and rich friends; when a man becomes rich, he divorces his wife and remarries.' This is human nature." Song Hong said in reply, "I heard people say that one mustn't forget his friends of difficult days, and one mustn't abandon his wife who has shared his hardships." When Liu Xiu learned how Song Hong felt, he said to Princess Huyang, "It seems there is no hope of making Song Hong divorce his wife and remarry."

The idiom "a wife of chaff-eating days" is an extension of what Song Hong said to Liu Xiu.

History of the Later Han Dynasty

鴻鵠之志
hóng hú zhī zhì

鴻鵠的志向；比喻胸懷遠大志向。

秦末，有一位叫陳涉的農民，因家境貧寒，給人耕田。有一次，陳涉把鋤頭往田梗上一扔，憤憤不平地在那裏發呆。忽然，他對另一個耕田人說：“我們當中的人，如果日後誰富貴了，可不要忘記了咱們這些窮苦人啊！”聽到陳涉這番話，有的人就笑着說：“我們這些窮光蛋，何來富貴。”陳涉嘆氣地說：“唉，小小的燕雀怎麼能瞭解鴻鵠的遠大志向呢！”

後來，陳涉和吳廣率九百人起義，並在陳縣（今河南淮陽）建立了張楚政權，陳涉被推為王。

出自《史記》

The Aspirations of a Swan Goose

Meaning lofty aspirations.

CHEN She was a peasant who lived at the end of the Qin Dynasty. As his family was poor, he had to plough the fields for others. One day, he threw his hoe on the ridge of the field indignantly and stood there in a daze. Suddenly he said to another ploughman, "If anyone of us prospers in the future, he mustn't forget the others of us poor sufferers." Hearing what Chen She had said, someone laughed and said, "How can we poor paupers prosper?" Chen She said with a sigh, "Oh, how can a bramble finch understand the lofty aspirations of a swan goose?"

Years later, Chen She and Wu Guang led a group of nine hundred people in an uprising and established the Zhangchu regime in Chenxian (today's Huaiyang in Henan Province). Chen She was chosen by his followers as the king.

Records of the Historian

鞭長莫及

bian cháng mò jí

鞭子再長，也打不到（馬肚子上）；比喻力量所不能及的事。

公元前594年，楚國攻打宋國。宋文公派大夫樂嬰齊到晉國求援。晉景公召集大臣商議，準備出兵援救，大夫伯宗勸阻說："我們不能出兵。古話說：'雖鞭之長，不及馬腹'，我們哪裏管得着楚國的事呢？不如暫不出兵，且等楚國國勢衰退以後再說吧。"

晉景公聽了伯宗的話就另派了一位大夫到宋國去安慰一番，並沒有援助宋國。

出自《左傳》

Beyond the Reach of the Whip

Beyond One's Control

Said of something that is beyond one's ability to do.

THE state of Chu attacked the state of Song in A.D.594.
Duke Wen of Song sent Senior Official Yue Yingqi to the
state of Jin to ask for help. After discussing it with the court
officials, Duke Jing of Jin decided to dispatch an army to
help Song. A senior official named Bo Zong advised against
it. He said, "We must not send our army. As the ancients
said, 'Although the whip is long, it cannot reach the belly of
the horse.' What right do we have to interfere with the affairs
of the state of Chu? It is advisable not to send our army and
wait till the power of the state of Chu begins to decline."

Duke Jing of Jin took Bo Zong's advice and sent an official
to the state of Song to express concern instead of dispatching
an army.

Zuo Qiuming's Chronicles

騎虎難下

qí hǔ nán xià

騎在猛虎身上，難以下來；形容處於進退兩難的境地。

公元328年，東晉大將蘇峻起兵反叛朝廷，逼攻京師建康（今
南京），大臣溫嶠組織聯軍討伐叛軍。由於叛軍力量強，聯軍不能
一時取勝，主師陶侃的情緒有些消沉。溫嶠對陶侃說："在當前的
形勢下，不能回轉方向，正像騎在猛虎身上難以下來一樣，只有把
它打死才是唯一出路。"陶侃聽了溫嶠的話，覺得很有道理，就振
作精神，最後終於打敗了叛軍。

出自《晉書》

Unable to Dismount from a Tiger

Holding a Wolf by the Ears

Meaning to be caught in an awkward dilemma.

IN A.D.328, General Su Jun of the Eastern Jin Dynasty staged a revolt against the court and threatened to take the capital Jiankang (today's Nanjing). Minister Wen Qiao organized an allied army to fight against him. Because the army in revolt was powerful, the allied army could not win immediate victory. Tao Kan, the commander of the allied army, looked depressed. Wen Qiao then said to him, "With the situation as it is now, we cannot turn back. It's as difficult as trying to dismount from a tiger. The only way out is to kill the tiger." Wen Qiao's words sounded reasonable to Tao Kan, who plucked up his courage and eventually defeated the revolting army.

History of the Jin Dynasty

騎驢覓驢

qí lü mì lü

騎着驢找驢；比喻東西本在自己手中，却偏到別處尋找。

"騎驢覓驢"一語，最早見於宋代道原所著的《景德傳燈錄》一書。後來，人們據此編出一個笑話：有個農夫趕着五頭驢子去趕集。走到半路他想數一數驢子，數了好幾次，總是四頭，他埋怨自己過於粗心大意，竟把驢子丟失了一頭。等他趕到集上，又重新數了數，恰好是五頭。他這才恍然大悟，原來是他在路上數的時候，把自己騎的那一頭給忘記了。

出自《景德傳燈錄》*

*《景德傳燈錄》佛教書，內容叙述禪宗師徒相承的語錄和事迹。宋道原編。

Looking for the Donkey While Sitting on It

Meaning to look for something that is already in one's hand.

THE idiom "Looking for a donkey while sitting on it" first appeared in the *Jingde Records of Handing Down the Lamp* written by Dao Yuan of the Song Dynasty. Someone later invented a joke based on it: A peasant was taking five donkeys to the market. He counted his donkeys on the way. Although he counted them several times, he found there were only four. He blamed his own carelessness for having lost a donkey. When he reached the market, he counted his donkeys again. There were five. It was then that he realized that while counting his donkeys on the road, he forgot to count the one that he was sitting on.

Jingde Records of Handing Down the Lamp*

*A Buddhist classic compiled by Dao Yuan of the Song Dynasty, recording the words and deeds of Zen Buddhists.

289

曠日持久

kuàng rì chí jiǔ

荒廢時間，拖延很久；比喻做事拖延時間很長，又沒有結果。

戰國時，燕國攻打趙國。趙惠文王打算割讓三座城池給齊國，要求齊國派名將田單統帥趙軍，抵禦燕軍。趙國大將趙奢不同意，他說：「難道趙國就沒有人能領兵了嗎？仗還沒打，先失三城，那怎麼行！」趙奢又說：「田單即使肯來，也可能敵不過燕軍，那就白請他來了；倘若田單眞有本領，也未必肯爲趙國出力，因爲如果趙國强大起來，對齊國的霸業不是很不利嗎？」趙奢最後說：「田單要是來了，他必定要把趙國拴在戰場上，荒廢時間，拖延不決，幾年之後，會把趙國的人力、物力、財力消耗殆盡，後果不堪設想！」

但是，趙惠文王不聽趙奢的勸告，還是請了齊國的田單做趙軍的統帥。結果，不出所料，拖了很長時間，付出了很大代價，却沒有取得勝利。

出自《戰國策》

Dragging On Fruitlessly for a Long Time

Meaning that though much time has been wasted, no results have been achieved.

WHEN the state of Yan attacked the state of Zhao during the Warring States Period, Duke Huiwen of Zhao intended to cede three cities to the state of Qi and ask the state of Qi to send their general Tian Dan to take command of the Zhao troops to resist the Yan army. Zhao She, the Grand General of the state of Zhao, disagreed. He said, "Is there no one who can take command of the troops in the state of Zhao? How can we allow three cities to be taken by others before fighting starts?" He then continued, "Even if Tian Dan comes, we are not sure that he can beat the Song army. If he can't, it would be in vain to ask him to come. If Tian Dan is really a capable general, we're not sure he will serve the state of Zhao. If the state of Zhao becomes strong, it will threaten the domination of the state of Qi." Finally Zhao She said, "When Tian Dan comes, he will surely tie the state of Zhao on the battlefield and waste our time. A few years later, when the manpower, resources and financial reserves are exhausted, the results would be too dreadful to contemplate."

But the duke of Zhao did not heed Zhao She's advice. Tian Dan was invited to take command of the Zhao army. As it was expected, the war dragged on fruitlessly for a long time and a great price was paid for it without winning victory.

Anecdotes of the Warring States

難兄難弟

nàn xiōng nàn dì

用來稱讚同樣有才有德的兄弟；也形容落在同樣困境的兄弟。

東漢人陳寔有兩個兒子，大的叫元方，小的叫季方。父子三人都是當時的名士，人稱三君子。有一次，元方的兒子長文和季方的兒子孝先，由於各論自己父親的功德而爭了起來，相持不下，就去問祖父陳寔。陳寔笑道："元方難爲兄，季方難爲弟。"意思是說，他們兄弟倆的德才都很好，難以分出高低。

出自 《世說新語》

Two of a Kind

Said of two brothers with the same merits and talents. It also means fellow sufferers in a difficult situation.

CHEN Shi of the Eastern Han Dynasty had two sons. The elder son was called Yuanfang and the younger one, Jifang. Father and sons were all noted literary figures of the time, known as the Three Gentlemen. One day, Yuanfang's son Changwen quarrelled with Jifang's son Xiaoxian over the virtues and merits of each other's father. As neither of them would give way, they came to their grandfather. Chen Shi smiled and said, "Yuanfang and Jifang are two of a kind. It's difficult to say who is superior."

New Social Anecdotes

鵬程萬里

péng chéng wàn lǐ

大鵬鳥飛一萬里；比喻志向遠大，前途無限。

傳說遠古時候，北海裏有一條名叫鯤的大魚，它能變成鳥。這隻鳥叫鵬，身體特別大，光說它的背，就不知有幾千里，飛起來，翅膀就像烏雲遮天蓋日。有一次，大鵬鳥從北海飛往南海，翅膀一撲，就擊起三千里的巨浪；乘着一陣暴風，直上雲霄，一衝就是九萬里。目光短淺的小鷃雀對大鵬鳥飛得這麼高，這麼遠，很不理解地說：「它要飛那麼遠幹什麼啊？像我這樣跳上躍下，也有幾丈的活動範圍，要飛，在草叢中穿來轉去，也夠逍遙了。」

出自《莊子》

A Roc Can Fly Ten Thousand Miles

Meaning having a bright future or a future full of promise.

IT is said that in the remote past there was an enormous fish known as *kun* in the North Sea. It could transform itself into a roc, a giant bird. The roc was so big that its back alone was several thousand miles long. When it took to flight, its wings obliterated the sun like dark clouds. Once, the roc flew from the North Sea to the South Sea. As it flapped its wings, it stirred up waves of three thousand miles. With the help of a hurricane, it soared to top of the clouds and covered ninety thousand miles with one flap of its wings. The short-sighted finch was puzzled as to why the roc had to fly to such heights. It said, "Why does it fly to such heights? Hopping up and down like me, I need only a few dozen metres of area to move about. If I want to fly, I can amuse myself by hovering over the bushes."

The Book of Zhuang Zi

鷄犬升天

jī quǎn shēng tiān

鷄和狗都升天成仙；比喻一人做了高官，同他關係好的人也跟着得勢。

漢朝時，淮南王劉安信奉道教。他相信得道之後能變成神仙於是，就出外修煉。八位仙翁向他傳授煉丹術。煉成的仙丹吃下後，果然升天而去。剩下的幾顆仙丹，被鷄狗當成食物爭着吃了。結果，這些鷄狗也一隻隻升了天，成了神鷄神狗。

出自《神仙傳》

Even Chickens and Dogs Ascend to Heaven

Meaning that when a man becomes a ranking official, those close to him will rise with him.

LIU An, the Prince of Huainan, of the Han Dynasty was a believer of Taoism. He believed that once he had mastered the Tao, he would become an immortal. So he left home to study the Taoist doctrine. Eight immorals taught him how to prepare elixirs. When he succeeded in making elixirs, he swallowed some and indeed ascended to heaven. The few leftover elixirs were, however, eaten by chickens and dogs as food. As a result, the chickens and dogs also ascended to heaven and became immortal chickens and dogs.

Tales of Immortals

294

鑿壁偷光
zuò bì tōu guāng

鑿開牆壁，偷點亮光；形容刻苦好學。

西漢時，有個叫匡衡的人，非常勤奮好學，但家境貧困，買不起蠟燭。匡衡的鄰居，家境富裕，夜間燭火通明。匡衡請求晚上去他家讀書，但鄰居不允許。不得已，匡衡想了一個辦法，偷偷地在牆壁上鑿了一個小洞，讓鄰居的亮光透過來，借着這點亮光讀書。

用這種方法，匡衡讀完了一些書，但他買不起新書。有一天，他發現一個財主家裏藏着許多書，於是他向財主提出：願意幫助幹活，不要工錢。財主很奇怪，問其原因，匡衡說：「我給你幹活，不要工錢，只是想借你家裏的書看看。」財主聽說只借書看而不要工錢，很是高興。匡衡就這樣讀了很多書，因而成爲一個很有學問的人。

出自《西京雜記》*

---

*《西京雜記》古小說集，東晉葛洪（公元284－364年）作。

Borrowing Light through a Hole in the Wall

Said of someone who is diligent in his studies.

Kuang Heng of the Western Han Dynasty was extremely diligent in his studies. Because his family was poor, he had no money to buy candles. His neighbour was rich and his house was illuminated brightly throughout the night. Kuang Heng asked him if he could come to his house to study, but was met with refusal. Helpless as he was, Kuang Heng thought of a way. He secretly dug a hole in the wall so that his neighbour's light could shine into his room, and by this light he could read.

In this way, Kuang Heng finished reading a number of books. But he could not afford to buy new books. One day, he found that there were many books in a rich man's house. He proposed to the rich man that he would work for him without pay. The rich man was puzzled and asked him why. Kuang Heng said, "I want to work for you without pay because I want to borrow your books." The rich man gladly agreed, and Kuang Heng was able to read a great number of books and became a learned man.

Miscellaneous Notes of the Western Capital*

*A collection of ancient stories by Ge Hong (284-364) of the Eastern Jin Dynasty.

附錄
Appendices

英文索引
English Index

I

K

L

M

N

U

V

W

漢語拼音索引
Chinese Phonetic
Alphabet Index

309

311

引用書目
Bibliography

Anecdotes of the States   by Zuo Qiuming

Anecdotes of the Warring States   by Liu Xiang (77-6 B.C.)

Anecdotes of Yan Zi   by Yan Ying (?-500 B.C.)

Anecdotes Past and Present   by Feng Menglong (1574-1646)

Annals of Wu and Yue   by Zhao Ye (fl.A.D.40)

Assembly of Five Lanterns, The   by Monk Puji

Biographies of Virtuous Women   by Liu Xiang (77-6 B.C.)

Book of History, The   by Confucius (551-479 B.C.)

Book of Lie Zi, The   by Lie Yukou (fl.314 B.C.)

Book of Mencius, The   by Men Ke (Mencius, 372-289 B.C.)

Book of Mo Zi, The   by Mo Di (c.468-376 B.C.)

Book of the Song Dynasty, The   by Shen Yue (441-513)

Book of Xun Zi, The   by Xun Kuang (c.313-238 B.C.)

Book of Zhuang Zi, The   by Zhuang Zhou (369-286 B.C.)

Classified Collection of Writings   by Ouyang Xun (557-641)

Classified Narrative Writings   by Zhu Mu

Collected Works of Changli   by Han Yu (768-824)

Collected Works of Emperor Wu of Wei   by Cao Cao (155-220)

Collected Works of the Cheng Brothers   by Cheng Hao(1032-1085) and Cheng Yi (1033-1107)

Collection of Lost Stories   by Wang Jia (?-c.390)

Confucian Analects

Discourses of Lü Buwei, The (*also* Lü's Spring and Autumn Annals)   by Lü Buwei (?-235 B.C.)

Explanations of Classics   by Lu Deming

Explanations of Customs   by Ying Shao (fl.178)

Forest of Cranes and Dews of Jade   by Luo Dajing (fl.1224)

Friendly Chats at Yunxi   by Fan Shu

History of the Eastern Jin Dynasty

History of the Han Dynasty   by Ban Gu (A.D.32-92)

History of the Jin Dynasty   by Fang Xuanling (579-648)

History of the Later Han Dynasty   by Fan Ye (398-445)
History of the Northern Dynasties   by Li Yanshou
History of the Northern Qi Dynasty   by Li Baiyao
History of the Southern Dynasties   by Li Yanshou
History of the Three Kingdoms (*also* Annals of the
    Three Kingdoms)   by Chen Shou (233-297)
History of the Wei Dynasty
Inscription for Wujiang Pavilion
Jingde Records of Handing Down the Lamp
Letter Advising Against the Expulsion of Guests   by Li Si
    (?-208 B.C.)
Letter to Han Jingzhou   by Li Bai (701-762)
Letter to Wei Duan   by Kong Rong (153-208)
Miscellaneous Notes of Dongpo   by Su Shi (1037-1101)
Miscellaneous Notes of Qingbo   by Zhou Hui (1126-?)
Miscellaneous Notes of the Western Capital   by Ge Hong (284-
    364)
Miscellaneous Notes on the Poetry of Han Ying   by Han Ying
    (fl.157 B.C.)
More Notes from Rong Studio   by Hong Mai (1123-1202)
More Strange Tales   by Li Fuyan (fl.831)
Narrative Poems   by Meng Qi
New Anecdotes of the Great Tang   by Liu Su (fl. 820)
New History of the Five Dynasties   by Ouyang Xiu (1007-1072)
New Prologue   by Liu Xiang (77-6 B.C.)
New Social Anecdotes   by Liu Yiqing (403-444)
Notes from the Old Scholar Hamlet   by Lu You (1125-1210)
Notes of Guoting   by Fan Gongchang (fl.1147)
Notes on a Tour of the West Lake   by Tian Rucheng (fl.1540)
Notes on Tang Poetry   by Ji Yougong (fl.1126)
Old History of the Tang Dynasty   by Zhang Zhaoyuan and Jia
    Wei
Other Sayings of Ai Zi   by Tu Benjun
Records of Strange Happenings   by Hong Mai (1123-1202)
Records of the Historian   by Sima Qian (145-? B.C.)
Song of the Gentleman

Story of the Pillow   by Shen Jiji (fl.780)
Story of the Wolf of Zhongshan   by Ma Zhongxi (?-1512)
Sun Zi's Art of War   by Sun Wu
Taiping Imperial Encyclopaedia   by Li Fang (925-996)
Tales of Immortals   by Ge Hong (284-364)
Tales of the Three Kingdoms   by Luo Guanzhong (c.1330-1400)
Third Collection of Notes from Rong Studio
Words and Deeds of Famous Officials of the Five Dynasties
Zuo Qiuming's Chronicles   by Zuo Qiuming

中國歷史年代簡表
A Chronology of
Chinese Dynasties

夏	約公元前21世紀——公元前16世紀
商	約公元前16世紀——公元前11世紀
周	約公元前11世紀——公元前221年
西周	約公元前11世紀——公元前770年
東周	公元前770年——公元前221年
春秋	公元前770年——公元前476年
戰國	公元前475年——公元前221年
秦	公元前221年——公元前207年
漢	公元前206年——公元220年
西漢	公元前206年——公元24年
東漢	公元25年——公元220年
三國	公元220年——公元280年
魏	公元220年——公元265年
蜀	公元221年——公元263年
吳	公元222年——公元280年
晉	公元265年——公元420年
西晉	公元265年——公元316年
東晉	公元317年——公元420年
南北朝	公元420年——公元589年
南朝	公元420年——公元589年
宋	公元420年——公元479年
齊	公元479年——公元502年

梁	公元502年——公元557年
陳	公元557年——公元589年
北朝	公元386年——公元581年
北魏	公元386年——公元533年
東魏	公元534年——公元550年
西魏	公元535年——公元557年
北齊	公元550年——公元577年
北周	公元557年——公元581年
隋	公元581年——公元618年
唐	公元618年——公元907年
五代十國	公元907年——公元979年
宋	公元960年——公元1279年
北宋	公元960年——公元1127年
南宋	公元1127年——公元1279年
遼	公元916年——公元1125年
金	公元1115年——公元1234年
元	公元1271年——公元1368年
明	公元1368年——公元1644年
清	公元1644年——公元1911年

Xia	c. 21st century — 16th century B.C.
Shang	c. 16th century — 11th century B.C.
Zhou	c. 11th century — 221 B.C.
Western Zhou	c. 11th century — 770 B.C.
Eastern Zhou	770-221 B.C.
Spring and Autumn Period	770-476 B.C.
Warring States Period	475-221 B.C.
Qin	221-207 B.C.
Han	206 B.C. — A.D. 220
Western Han	206 B.C. — A.D. 24
Eastern Han	25-220
Three Kingdoms	220-280
Wei	220-265
Shu	221-263
Wu	222-280
Jin	265-420
Western Jin	265-316
Eastern Jin	317-420
Southern and Northern Dynasties	420-589
Southern Dynasties	420-589
Song	420-479
Qi	479-502
Liang	502-557
Chen	557-589
Northern Dynasties	386-581
Northern Wei	386-534
Eastern Wei	534-550

Western Wei	535-557
Northern Qi	550-577
Northern Zhou	557-581
Sui	581-618
Tang	618-907
Five Dynasties and Ten Kingdoms	907-979
Song	960-1279
Northern Song	960-1127
Southern Song	1127-1179
Liao	916-1125
Kin	1115-1234
Yuan	1271-1368
Ming	1368-1644
Qing	1644-1911

漢語拼音發音指南
Guide to Chinese
Phonetic Alphabet

請注意以下幾點：

q 發英文中ch的聲音，如cheer, chimney, chin。

x 發英文中sh的聲音，如she, ehell, shoe。 shell

z 發英文中ds的聲音，如reads, récords, seeds。

c 發英文中ts的聲音，如dots, products, students。

* * * *

中國普通話裏有四種聲調，每個字都有一種聲調，即音調的升降。如：

> 第一聲（一），高而平；
> 第二聲（╱），升；
> 第三聲（╱），由降而升；
> 第四聲（╲），降。

聲調符號標在主要母音上邊，如這個主要母音是 i ，則不標。

聲調在漢語中很重要，同音的字由於聲調不同，字義也就不同。如：

mā	má	mǎ	mà
媽	麻	馬	罵
yī	yí	yǐ	yì
一	移	椅	譯

Watch out for these letters:

q sounds like *ch* in "*ch*eer", "*ch*imney", "*ch*in".

x sounds like *sh* in "*sh*e", "*sh*ell", "*sh*oe".

z sounds like the final *ds* in "rea*ds*", "recor*ds*", "see*ds*".

c sounds like the final *ts* in "do*ts*", "produc*ts*", "studen*ts*".

***   ***   ***

Every Chinese character has a tone which is actually the contour of the rise or fall in pitch during pronunciation. There are four tones in *putonghua* (common speech), shown by the following marks:

  — 1st tone, high and level;

  ∕ 2nd tone, rising;

  ∨ 3rd tone, falling-rising; and

  ＼ 4th tone, falling.

The tone mark is placed above the main vowel; when the main vowel is "i", the dot is omitted.

The tones are extremely important. Characters which have the same sound (that is, are spelled the same way in the phonetic alphabet) may have different meanings, and this is indicated by the tone. For example:

ma	ma	ma	ma
mother	hemp	horse	scold

yi	yi	yi	yi
one	move	chair	translate

Chinese Phonetic Alphabet	International Phonetic Alphabet	Chinese Phonetic Alphabet	International Phonetic Alphabet	Chinese Phonetic Alphabet	International Phonetic Alphabet	Chinese Phonetic Alphabet	International phonetic Alphabet
b	[p]	s	[s]	ê	[ɛ]	ian	[ian]
p	[p']	zh	[tʂ]	er	[ər]	in	[in]
m	[m]	ch	[tʂ']			iang	[iaŋ]
f	[f]	sh	[ʂ]	ai	[ai]	ing	[iŋ]
d	[t]	r	[ʐ]	ei	[ei]	iong	[yŋ]
t	[t']			ao	[au]	ua	[ua]
n	[n]	y	[i]	ou	[ou]	uo	[uɔ]
l	[l]	w	[w]	an	[an]	uai	[uai]
g	[k]			en	[ən]	ui, uei	[uei]
k	[k']	a	[a]	ang	[aŋ]	uan	[uan]
h	[x]	o	[o]	eng	[əŋ]	un, uen	[uən]
j	[tɕ]	e	[ɤ]	ong	[uŋ]	uang	[uaŋ]
q	[tɕ']	i	[i]	ia	[ia]	ue	[yɛ]
x	[ɕ]	u	[u]	ie	[iɛ]	uan	[yan]
z	[ts]	u	[y]	iao	[iau]	un	[yn]
c	[ts']	-i	[ɿ] [ʅ]*	iu, iou	[iəu]		

[ɿ] used after z, c, s; [ʅ] used after zh, ch, sh, r.